Conspicuous and Inconspicuous Discriminations in Everyday Life

In everyday life, people negotiate on issues, entertain offers and coun-teroffers, and gain or lose in terms of economic capital, political power, communal status, and social influence. Although life goes on in the form of compromise, feelings of discrimination or misfortune haunt consciously or unconsciously in the minds of living individuals. History continues in the spirit of forgiveness, but residues of exploitation or injustice remain conspicuously or inconspicuously on the records of progressing civilizations.

This study follows an average everyday life to compare individuals with individuals, individuals with organizations, and organizations with organizations in their everyday interactions. Through the eyes of the person, conspicuous and inconspicuous discriminations by one against another, whether individual or organizational, are identified in different occasions, on a typical day, at home, in the workplace, in the community, within the country, around the world, and throughout the course of life.

In the style of Socrates, Plato, Wittgenstein, and other classical schol-arship, this study uses ordinary, typical situations to demonstrate critical points, reveal subtle connections, and present important arguments. It offers vivid examples for what social scientists strive to find: the extraordinary from the ordinary, the unfamiliar from the familiar, the different from the similar, and the significant from the trivial. This study offers an opportunity for readers to reflect upon their social experiences, and rethink and reshape their everyday acts and actions.

Victor N. Shaw is a professor of sociology at California State University-Northridge.

Routledge Studies in Social and Political Thought

For a full list of titles in this series, please visit www.routledge.com.

Conspicuous and Inconspicuous Discriminations in Everyday Life

Victor N. Shaw

Routledge
Taylor & Francis Group

LONDON AND NEW YORK

First published 2013
by Routledge
711 Third Avenue, New York, NY 10017

Simultaneously published in the UK
by Routledge
2 Park Square, Milton Park, Abingdon, Oxfordshire OX14 4RN

*Routledge is an imprint of the Taylor and Francis Group,
an informa business*

First issued in paperback 2015

Library of Congress Cataloging-in-Publication Data
Shaw, Victor N.
   Conspicuous and inconspicuous discriminations in everyday life / by
Victor N. Shaw.
      pages cm. — (Routledge studies in social and political thought ; 80)
   Includes bibliographical references and index.
   1.   Discrimination.   2.   Interpersonal relations.   I. Title.
   HM821.S538 2013
   305—dc23
   2013001629

ISBN 978-0-415-84084-2 (hbk)
ISBN 978-1-138-95263-8 (pbk)
ISBN 978-0-203-76689-7 (ebk)

Typeset in Sabon
by IBT Global.

Contents

Introduction

Life is a journey. In time, it divides into years, months, weeks, days, and even hours. Throughout the course of a lifetime, there are stages, such as infancy, childhood, adolescence, adulthood, and senior age. Over space, life revolves around home, builds on work, touches upon a profession, expands in a community, traverses within a nation, and reaches out to the world. Along various extensions of a whole life, there are roles played, deeds made, identities acquired, and statuses achieved, from the head of a family to the position holder of a workplace to membership in a professional association to citizenship of a country and, for a few, to certain reputations around the world.

As people live their lives at every moment and in different settings, they negotiate on issues and make offers concerning each other's fundamental interests. By contrast and comparison, some gain while others lose in terms of economic capital, political power, communal status, and social influence. Although life goes on in the form of compromise, feelings of discrimination, mistreatment, or misfortune haunt consciously or unconsciously in the minds of living individual beings. Although history continues in the spirit of forgiveness, residues of prejudice, exploitation, or injustice remain explicit or implicit on the records of progressing human civilizations.

This study follows an average member of society, Alibaba, to compare and contrast individuals with individuals, individuals with organizations, and organizations with organizations in their everyday dealings and interactions. Through his eyes, conspicuous and inconspicuous discriminations by one against another, whether it be individual or organization, are identified and presented from different occasions and settings, on a typical day, at home, over the workplace, across the profession, in the community, within the nation, around the world, and throughout the course of life.

Each case or situation of discrimination is described and analyzed uniformly in five standard sections. "The Particular" presents the case from the observation and experience of Alibaba. "The Discriminator" focuses on discriminators and their acts of discrimination, whereas "The Victim" draws attention to victimizations suffered by individuals or organizations under the situation. "The Compromise" presents both sides and their respective perspectives to see how the situation, though problematic, sustains itself as part of social equilibrium or as an episode of the everyday life continuum. Finally, "The Universal" attempts to uncover and learn from the case or situation something general and significant, sociologically or otherwise.

1 Methodological Approach

This is a study of everyday life. It is sociological in particular and social science in general.

What is everyday life? Everyday life is the life lived day to day by all individuals in society. It involves physical maintenance, such as eating, bathing, and dressing. It includes mental exercises, such as reading, speaking, and writing. It encompasses social engagements, from verbal communication, material exchange, and cooperative activity to productive labor. Everyday life is repetitive: people do the same things every day. It is also afresh: each day is a different day in life. Everyday life is routine: people follow similar schedules or sequences from day to day. It is exciting as well: challenges may arise unexpectedly, whereas breakthroughs can come by huge surprise. Everyday life is trivial: people fill most of their day with unimportant activities. It is critical, too: one may say words, make decisions, or perform acts on any particular day that impact not only the life of various individuals, but also the fate of an organization, a community, or a country. Most important, everyday life is all about how each and every individual lives, how society sustains, how the world exists, how history unfolds, and how human civilizations progress.

Is there any sociology or sociological significance in everyday life? Sociology is the study of society. Specifically, it inquires what makes society, what sustains society, and what changes society. Everyday life entails acts and activities by individuals in all different settings. It hence affords an abundance of sociological knowledge as how individuals congregate, creating social forces, forming social institutions, and maintaining social momentums, or how society dictates, molding individual minds, moderating individual acts, and cultivating individual roles (Goffman 1959; Rogers 1984; Adler, Adler, and Fontana 1987; Bourdieu 1987, 1990; Larkin 1988; Bourdieu and Wacquant 1992; Moore 1992; Green 2000; Sutherland 2000; Certeau 2002; Highmore 2002a, 2011; Droit 2003; Freud 2003; Caproni 2004; Meyer 2006; Sheringham 2006; Hardie 2008; Lefebvre 2008; Mauk and Metz 2009; Douglas 2010; Sue 2010; Myers 2011; Sommers 2011; Brinkmann 2012; Inglis and Thorpe 2012).

From a methodological point of view, the question is then this: what approach, scheme, or tool is appropriate and necessary to fetch sociological knowledge from everyday life?

OBSERVATION AND EXPERIENCE

Observation is both a natural way to view and an indispensable tool to study everyday life. Experience, in comparison, is broader, larger, and more general. It not only provides a background against which everyday life unfolds under observation or without notice, but also serves as a storage where information about everyday life accumulates from observation and other sources (Rauhut and Winter 2010; Bakeman and Quera 2011; Callan and Reed 2011; Hanzel 2011; Isaacowitz and Stanley 2011; Bold 2012; Brinkmann 2012).

The Subject

The subject of everyday life observation and experience is a person who possesses specific demographic characteristics, lives in particular social settings, and owns certain levels of observing and experiencing skills or proficiencies.

In terms of demographics, younger people may adventure into extraordinary activities for intense observation, while older people can benefit from a greater variety of perspectives for a balanced experience. Men take notice of things that women tend to miss in their observation. Over the history of the United States of America, whites enjoy social dominance as blacks struggle to cope with slavery, segregation, marginalization, and various other forms of discrimination. In the melting pot of any cosmopolitan city, different ethnic groups may still seek to keep their respectively cultured ways of life. Most important, people divide and differentiate by levels of education, categories of employment, amounts of income, and standards of living or lifestyles. A well-trained individual is likely to work in an air-conditioned office, while people with no or little education tend to labor in an environment with exposure to various natural and unnatural hazards. Farmers in the countryside may to a large extent live on the crops they grow, while skilled workers in the city can relatively freely participate in the consumer market with the cash income they earn from industrial employment. A homeless person can relate stories of living in poverty, whereas perhaps only a millionaire may have lived experiences to boast about flying in first-class cabins, staying at luxury resorts, dining in upscale restaurants, playing over the best golf courses, and visiting significant tourist sites around the world.

With respect to social settings, there are comparisons between mansions and apartments, affluent communities and poor neighborhoods, private schools and public educational institutions, comfortable offices and harsh working conditions, high-paying professions and labor-intensive occupations, upscale lifestyles and low standards of living, or in more summary terms, among upper, middle, and lower social classes. Observation is limited to a situation just as experience remains lodged in social settings. Individuals living in one social setting may never have the opportunity to observe and experience things typical of another social setting. For example, only people who have flown private jets, attended public schools, stayed in hostels, or lived a luxury lifestyle can recollect real and valid observations about each of those particular social settings in their experience. There are, however, people who are able to cross-observe different settings by way of work or a change in life. For example, a lower-class woman works as a maid in an upper-class family, a university professor studies homeless drug addicts, and a person breaks through different social class barriers to become a wealthy and powerful member of his or her society.

Regarding observing skills and experiencing proficiencies, age, maturity, training, and occupation can all make a difference. Older people may see more out of the ordinary simply because they have observed more events and experienced a greater variety of things in their life. A trained social scientist can generalize something from the extraordinary in academic research just as a physician or psychiatrist can make a diagnosis on the basis of a patient's symptoms in medicine. Overall, as one progresses in one's profession, lifestyle, and social environment, one is likely to attain certain levels of skills or proficiencies to observe and experience various nuances of everyday life, from the matter of quality, justice, or meaningfulness to the issue of quantity, insufficiency, or significance.

This study follows Alibaba as an everyday life regular or representative. Cases are identified in his commonsensical eyes or through his normal observation and experience. By measure of personal characteristics, Alibaba is a middle-age nonwhite man living in the United States with his wife, daughter, and son. He was born and raised in a foreign country, where he received his bachelor's degree. He came to the United States to pursue advanced study in his early twenties and has been living in America with professional employment since graduation. Alibaba visits the country of his birth regularly and has traveled to different parts of the world because of work as well as for leisure. In terms of mobility through social strata, Alibaba worked on odd low-paying jobs while in school. He and his family shared a small apartment with another family, lived in a side unit when his wife worked as a live-in housekeeper for a wealthy family, and even stayed in a low-income housing compound for a period of time. Now, the Alibabas live in their own two-story house in a well-off suburb, just like many other middle-class families throughout the suburban community.

Alibaba's attention to discrimination relates directly to his experience in various everyday life settings, especially at work, as a member of a racial-ethnic minority in the United States. He knows too well from his own experience that he does not receive the same level of recognition, compensation, and respect for the things he does the same as members of the majority and that to enjoy an amount of attention, benefit, or reward the same as members of the majority, he usually has to do a lot more. Also, it ought to be pointed out that in observation of specific situations of discrimination, Alibaba as a well-educated individual is often sharper, more to the point, and more transcendental from his own circumstance than any regular everyday life actor or role-player.

The Object

The object of observation and experience can be people, things, and their interconnections at particular times and in specific settings. A member of an ethnic minority, a resident making trouble in a local community, a developed country taking advantage of an undeveloped nation in the world, and a particular case of discrimination or victimization are all objects under observation and in experience by individuals from society to society.

An object is by definition in itself and by itself. In other words, it exists in independence from any subject of observation and experience. For example, a white person remains white whether he or she is being observed. Employees not treated equally in an organization, customers ripped off by businesses in the marketplace, or poor countries shortchanged by wealthy nations over international trade can be measured, compared, and documented with data, whether those things are being experienced.

In effect, however, an object is often inseparable from the subject it involves. A person is white with social significance because he or she is perceived, treated, and experienced as white in a society where race matters. People, groups, or organizations faring differently in social exchanges are normally or abnormally let go without notice. A situation of discriminations is questioned, investigated, and substantiated with numbers or evidence only when the subjects concerned feel strong about it, present it somewhere, and insist that it be handled one way or the other.

In this study, all the cases described are general. Each can happen anytime when similar people and things converge. Each may stay as a typical, representative, and universal occurrence above and beyond the original circumstance in which it takes place or is experienced by a particular individual. On the other hand, all the cases presented are specific. Some might have appeared trivial if it had not invoked a strong feeling in Alibaba's experience. Some could have never surfaced if it had not become clearly noticeable under Alibaba's observation. Of course, Alibaba observes and experiences as a unique person with all his personal and social peculiarities.

The Process

Observation and experience in everyday life are participant-centered. They begin, stay, and end up with everyday life participants. When nonparticipant observation is designed, it still has to be implemented with individual participants through their specific activities in different everyday life settings.

Observation and experience in everyday life are natural occurrences in either structured or nonstructured formats. Structurally, everyday life observation takes place in institutional settings such as family, workplace, and community, while everyday life experience accumulates through stages of life from childhood to adolescence to adulthood and by categories such as personal life, professional career, and social relationship. In the meantime, life is essentially spontaneous. Individuals can say and do things without planning and preparation. People may have to deal with issues in shock and surprise. Observation must therefore follow the pulse or the rhythm of life as it flows naturally from day to day. Structure for the purpose of research is to be seen only after life crystallizes into shapes and residues.

In this study, observer Alibaba is not a trained social scientist. He observes life as he lives it. There is no special design, planning, or effort made for purposes other than life. Sometimes, Alibaba attempts to replicate times and settings in order to observe something again. He talks to people in similar situations in order to confirm something he has observed. He makes generalizations when he observes something consistently from time to time or from place to place. However, all these acts are natural, either out of personal curiosity or for the sake of social adaptation in his everyday life. In terms of adaptive survival, for example, he can remain calm, prepared, and effective when he knows something is likely to happen under certain circumstance.

The Outcome

For most people, observation and experience from everyday life remain in everyday life. The effect of previous experiences feeding on future observations is natural, becoming automatically part of individual development, growth, and maturation. In content, certain experiences may orient one to certain situations for observation of similar things or accumulation of similar experiences. In other words, observation tends to expand and extend itself in the same line, whereas experience is likely to enrich and fulfill itself on the same track. More generally, one is a product of one's own social experience. By measure of skills, attention to something may cause one's interest to observe and experience it. Repeated observations can sharpen one's skills to see greater details from phenomenal occurrences, while years of experience may afford one to discern more subtleties using common cues and clues. As expressed succinctly in the old saying, experience matters.

Beyond individuals, some may write diaries, some may tell stories, and a few may publish autobiographies about their personal observations and experiences. When all these records and recollections are shared and spread, individual acts and deeds will then translate into social consequences. People learn from each other to become better everyday life observers, experiencing organisms, and living subjects within a community, from generation to generation, across society, and around the world.

The General

Observation is part of everyday life. Individuals live their everyday life by observing what they do, how individuals congregate to form social groupings, how individual actions translate into social effects, how they learn from tradition, and what they contribute to society. Studying everyday life depends upon observation. Participant observation exposes the details of everyday life as the subject lives it, whereas nonparticipant observation reveals the nuances of everyday life as it is led by the object. Even a secondary analysis of dairies, stories, and biographies owes to observation which lies behind all written and uttered recollections of everyday life scenes and actions.

Experience emerges from as well as feeds on everyday life. People experience life as it unfolds through day-to-day routines and rituals. Life accumulates in experience when people engage in different everyday life actions and activities. While no experience exists without life, life becomes richer and more meaningful only through experience. Studying everyday life is to apply experience to describe, explain, and record experience. Experienced versus inexperienced researchers studying people with more or less experience in everyday life can obviously generate different findings and analyses as research outcomes.

Finally, between observation and experience, the former expands and extends the latter, while the latter builds upon and encompasses the former. For example, observations of various incidents and situations add to one's experience, making oneself not only a higher skilled observer, but also a more experienced living organism in everyday life. Similarly, experiences with different activities and scenarios involve one in a multitude of trainings and exercises for seeing, recording, and adapting to social reality, pushing up one's skills of observation as well as one's capabilities of experience to higher levels.

REFERENCING AND REFLECTION

Observation is literally to watch things as they are, exist or change. To see what a thing means and how it connects to other things, especially how two or more things are related to one another over time or across space, one needs to engage in referencing and reflection (Luhmann 1985; Bourdieu 1987; Bourdieu and Wacquant 1992; Highmore 2002b; Alvesson and Skoldberg 2009; McIntosh 2010; Chang 2011; Chesters 2012; Peterson 2012).

The Subject

Anyone who lives can qualify as a subject of referencing and reflection. There is certainly a process of development involved. One must have an experience before one can reflect upon any particular incident, referencing one thing to another in the general background of experience. And one builds one's experience as soon as one applies one's growing senses to observe things in the environment.

In everyday life, people differ in their abilities for referencing and reflection. Age matters as a longer living experience may present a larger inventory of known things for association, comparison, and reflection. Education makes a difference when it teaches students analyzing, reasoning, and generalizing skills. Professional practice and individual lifestyle may show considerable effects because some types of work as well as some ways of life may prompt people to actively search for or to habitually come across certain connections among things in the world.

As the subject of referencing and reflection in this study, Alibaba takes notice of various conspicuous and inconspicuous discriminations in everyday life to a large degree due to his unique personal characteristics and social experiences. Moreover, he seems to act upon some of his general assumptions and beliefs about individuals, groups, society, human civilizations, and the world as well. For instance, individuals are supposed to be self-sufficient in Alibaba's mind. One discriminates against someone else, one's group or society, and even the world or human civilizations if one takes more than one contributes over one's lifetime.

The Object

Referencing and reflection may center on acts, events, and settings, as well as people concerned and issues involved. When a thing is under the radar as an object, referencing and reflection are to define its meaning, calculate its value, and determine its significance in comparison to other things. For instance, a recently completed trip is compared to all other trips made in one's experience or to someone else's travel to the same destination or for the same purpose to see if it is cost-effective, worthwhile, or meaningful.

When a person is on focus as an object, referencing and reflection are to assess one's acts and actions, evaluate one's position and status, and compare one's goals with means, performance with ability, or gain with loss. Especially when the object becomes the same as the subject or when one reflects upon oneself, referencing and reflection can usually serve as essential strategies to find better ways to do one's job or live one's life on the basis of one's past and existing experiences.

Compared to observation, reflection aims more at connections among people and things. In fact, it is only through referencing and reflection that sequencing, linkage, and structuring can be identified and verified to find relative importance or significance of each and every act, actor, and situation within and outside individual experience.

In this study, Alibaba seems to draw heavily upon referencing and reflection in noting and validating various deficits and differentials in social exchanges. As a result, discrimination and victimization become a common theme or object when Alibaba reflects upon people and things in his everyday life.

The Process

Referencing and reflection can take place when observation is under way. They may occur before or after observation. However, in order to conduct any meaningful referencing and reflection, one must have a sufficient inventory of observations in one's experience.

Referencing and reflection involve a series of mental operations on the part of the subject toward the object. First, the object has to be identified, defined, and categorized. Is it a person, an event, or a situation? Second, an objective needs to be set or highlighted. What is the purpose of reflection, for self-assurance, learning, or future improvement? Third, a principle of relevance and a standard of quality must be established or delineated. By what logic or on what ground is the object to be referenced? What criterion is used to evaluate the object? Fourth, connections are to be found between the object and its various referents. Where does the object stand? How similar or different is it to or from other objects? What lessons can be learned? Finally, a record is to be cataloged in memory or in the universe of experience. When does a particular episode of referencing and reflection take place? What does it add to self-experience?

In this study, Alibaba discerns meaningful connections, such as discrimination and victimization, among people and things as an ordinary person. It is obvious that people in everyday life hold standards, set goals, assume attitudes, take positions, and can therefore find unique chains of act and action in social relational dynamics. While Alibaba can entertain his commonsense curiosity with self-discoveries from referencing and reflection, sociologists may add to human knowledge by scientific findings they make from standard research, which may involve anchoring, framing, contrasting, comparing, and other qualitatively inquisitive procedures.

The Outcome

The general outcome of referencing is connection. Specifically, connection may turn out to be strong or weak, direct or indirect, associational or correlational, and phenomenal or structural. For example, correlation can be either a matter of coincidence or a result of structural interdependence. With connection in sight, there can be a clear identification of an individual subject, object, or situation, a meaningful comparison between one thing and another, and a logical sequence of developments or a natural chain of events over time and across space.

Reflection moves beyond connection, generating inferential knowledge in different forms. Inductively, rules, patterns, and trends can be generalized from frequent, repetitive, or common occurrences or connections to provide direction and guidance for future acts and actions. On the other hand, specific incidences or situations can be particularized to feature light shed by general laws or to showcase learning deduced from universal principles. Most important, reflection sharpens observation, expands the horizon of referencing, exercises thinking, deepens understanding, and enriches overall experience in everyday life.

The variety of cases, especially in terms of subtlety and sophistication, noted by Alibaba in this study, demonstrates vividly what ordinary people may learn from referencing and reflection in everyday life.

The General

Referencing and reflection are part of the thinking process for people in everyday life. Through referencing, people place things in different categories or levels in terms of meaning or significance. By way of reflection, people make comparisons and contrasts, find patterns and rules, and fine-tune strategies and tactics. With both, people own a system of organized, informing, and inspiring experiences as their assets and resources for future challenges and undertakings. In other words, referencing and reflection are essential means and methods people use to adapt to the environment, to stay fit in social competition, and to survive everyday life or attain a better life in the real world.

In social research, referencing and reflection can be applied as important methodological approaches or instruments separately or in combination. By itself, referencing generates definitions or identifications and classifications or typologies, whereas reflection results in inductions or generalizations and deductions or inferences. In combination, referencing and reflection inform observation, inspire analysis, feed imagination, stimulate comparison, and overall enlighten thinking for critical ideas and theories. As a matter of fact, referencing and reflection are key elements in both sociological imagination and critical thinking.

For this study, Alibaba engages in referencing and reflection primarily as an average everyday life person. On the other hand, he is an educated individual with an interest to find things general and special for other people to learn, follow, criticize, or reject. This double-dipping clearly illustrates how referencing and reflection may play out with tangible social and scientific benefits when social scientists who live an everyday life themselves apply referencing and reflection as research methods or tools to study everyday life.

CASE SELECTION AND ANALYSIS

Everyday life offers an abundance of people, things, and connections for research. This study follows an everyday life individual, Alibaba, through different things he does, different people he deals with, different groupings he belongs to, and different arenas he reaches, to see how one person, group, or even thing may consciously or inadvertently take advantage of another in their mutual interactions.

Case

Cases presented in this study are labeled situations. Each case involves a setting or context, a criterion or assumption, a comparison or contrast, and an analysis or treatment.

Individual cases, as noted by Alibaba, are not necessarily obvious, representative, serious, or significant. Depending upon people and their respective mindsets, interests, or experiences, some situations can be more conspicuous, common, meaningful, or important than others. However, one thing obvious and for sure is that many more similar situations can be identified to illustrate that imbalance may occur instantly and constantly in social exchange, making one an unjust gainer and another a pitiable loser. For example, on any typical day, one could run into various situations where one gains as a shameless discriminator or loses as a miserable victim. Or around the world, there can be many more instances of nation-to-nation exploitation, manipulation, or discrimination, besides the five situations documented in this study.

Setting

Setting refers to the physical space in which or the time frame by which a case occurs. Generally, spatial settings include home, workplace, profession, community, country, and the world where people are likely to frequent or stay when they go about their everyday life. Time settings can be days, weeks, months, and years, as well as stages of human development individuals have to pass by or move through as they take their everyday life journey from birth to death.

Specifically, each case or situation selected in this study takes place at a particular time, in a particular space, involving identifiable people and things. For example, rush hours and lunch breaks are specific time periods; traffics, restaurants, universities are peculiar places; and Alibaba, a colleague, a supervisor, and the United States of America are definable persons, entities, or things.

Criterion

As discrimination or victimization is alleged on each case or situation, some kind of claim, evaluation, or judgment is obviously made on the basis of some assumptions, criteria, or standards.

Common assumptions used in this study are these: individuals are supposed to be self-sufficient; gain on something by one is normally balanced by loss on the part of another; human civilizations progress upon individual, societal, and generational contributions. With one or two of these assumptions in mind, anyone who takes or consumes more than what he or she creates, earns, or deserves as a fair share can be legitimately labeled as a discriminator against others, society, or even mankind.

Criteria or standards of evaluation against which discrimination is determined in this research include both tangible and intangible interests, such as money, power, fame, influence, pleasure, pain, and status. For example, an old husband deprives a young wife of sexual pleasure she is entitled to from marriage; a poor-performing employee dragging a highly productive coworker from accelerated promotions causes the latter to lose money and status; and the United States of America steals wealth and talents from many other countries when it welcomes the rich, the young, the pretty, the educated, and the trained around the world.

Comparison

Just as gain or loss is an issue of contrast, discrimination or victimization is a matter of comparison. One gains in contrast to what one invests or because someone else loses. One discriminates or becomes a victim in comparison with what one deserves by one's fair share or entitlement in a given role, status, or situation.

Comparison and contrast can legitimately and meaningfully take place between and among individual, group, institutional, and societal entities. Individual to individual comparisons may involve persons who are closely related by birth, marriage, employment, or profession as well as people who are literally unrelated yet can be collectively lumped together in a crowd, a community, a nation, or just the human species. A working wife may noticeably suffer from an unemployed husband, while taxpayers obviously have to foot the bills for fellow citizens who are welfare dependent. Basis of comparison can be ideologically assumptive or commonsense adaptive. For example, if one believes that every individual ought to be self-sufficient, one would consider a disabled or addicted person who depends upon his or her family for day-to-day support a discriminator. On the other hand, one can always find reasons in the commonsense world or the mundane life as to why parents, spouses, or siblings have responsibilities to take care of their forever-dependent family members.

Individual to group comparisons look into the contribute-and-take relationship an individual has with the group he or she belongs to. The concept of a fair share assumed in group and grouping norms serves as an essential yardstick by which judgment about whether a member is a discriminator or a victim can be convincingly made. Groups may include specific groups, such as a cohort, a club, a family, a school, or an employment organization, that individuals participate in closely and routinely during everyday life. They may also refer to general groupings, from a generation, a profession, and a nation to the human species, that individuals belong de facto as they are. As such, individual to group comparisons encompass all of the following: individual to organization, individual to profession, individual to community, individual to nation, individual to civilization, and individual to the world or to mankind. For instance, an employee causing troubles to rather than making profits for an employer falls under this category. So does an individual who contributes more than he or she takes in a lifetime in relation to a country, the world, and social progress.

Group to group comparisons explore the relationships different organizational entities have with one another in social exchange. Included first are original group to group comparisons, when a group literally means a collection of people or a small group, such as a workshop and a department, within a large organization. There are also group to institution, institution to institution, institution to nation, and nation to nation comparisons, when groups refer generally to all types of institutions, from business corporations, professional organizations, and unions to governments. Comparing groups necessitates objective examinations of organizational boundaries, inputs, outputs, and rules. It also calls for subjective reflections upon common sense, custom, and tradition as the latter often weighs heavily on what and how judgment is made over whether one unit of an organization makes its due contribution to the whole organizational system or whether organizations deal fairly with one another. For example, in a state of dictatorship, ordinary civil units may not necessarily feel they are exploited in fundamental interests. Or only a scholar who firmly believes in sovereign equity, integrity, and sanctity can sense how small, poor, or weak nations are constantly taken advantage of by large, rich, or strong countries in the world.

Analysis

Description and analysis of all cases are uniformly handled in five sections: "The Particular," "The Discriminator," "The Victim," "The Compromise," and "The Universal." "The Particular" presents the case in its original settings as Alibaba notes it in his everyday life. "The Discriminator" identifies discriminators, elucidating how they discriminate. "The Victim" focuses on victims, explaining what discriminations they have to deal with. "The Compromise" follows both discriminators and victims, exploring reasons as to what holds both sides together in social interactions. "The Universal" reflects upon the case for general learning about human dynamics.

To keep the spirit of everyday life, description is immersed in the flow of worldly reality, while analysis is fine-tuned with the rhythm of common-sense wisdom. There ought to be no surprise if some cases are not considered necessarily clean, clear, and pure in accordance with an academician's standards or if some analyses are not deemed sufficiently abstract, critical, or general from a scholar's points of view.

2 On a Typical Day

The day is the most basic unit of time that people see and experience in their life. Every day is a common day as people follow a habituated routine from one day to another. Every day is a unique day when people realize that there is only one of that particular day in the course of their individual lives.

Between commonality and particularity, there is then typicality. Indeed, when every day is neither so common nor so unique, it is definitely typical. On a typical day, people enter different arenas or exit different networks, join in different interactions or get off different groupings, tackle different issues or dodge different matters, and face different contrasts or experience different comparisons as they go about their everyday life (Dixit and Nalebuff 1991; Friberg 1993; Walker and Rogan 2007; Edwards 2008; DeBell 2009; Felson and Santos 2010; Cornwell 2011; Dalai Lama 2011; Anderson 2012; Sommers and Sommers 2012).

SITUATION 1

The United States is an automobile society. Whether you drive, walk, or take a ride, you become part of the traffic flow. Operating a vehicle in the network of transportation, a driver turns into an active player in the arena of automobile versus automobile, automobile versus pedestrian, and pedestrian versus pedestrian interactions.

The Particular

Alibaba drives his daughter to school every morning. In order to drop off her at the school gate ten minutes before the bell rings at 8:00 a.m., he has to leave home no later than 7:15 a.m.

It was a regular weekday. Alibaba pulled out of his private driveway at 7:13 a.m. First, at a three-way stop intersection, Alibaba was forced to yield to a delivery truck that entered the intersection a few moments after he did, costing him about half a minute delay in movement. Second, when he entered the freeway from the carpool lane, Alibaba was unexpectedly overtaken by a car that was supposed to stop behind the metered red light in the non-carpool lane of the entry ramp. He slammed the brakes instinctually, feeling an immediate increase of his heartbeats. Third, when he was about to move into the first lane on the freeway, Alibaba was warded off by three large trucks traveling one after another. Since he was not able to move into the first lane in time, Alibaba missed the entry into the carpool lane in which he could have moved five to seven minutes faster until its next entry/exit at this time of the day on the multilane freeway. Fourth, Alibaba just missed a green light and was the first to stop behind the stop line on the exit ramp. Although three lanes are provided on the ramp for motorists to turn right or left into the same number of lanes in each direction on the main road, traffic signals seem ill-designed or maladjusted at this intersection with an obvious discrimination against vehicles coming out of the freeway. In fact, Alibaba waited more than two minutes before the light turned green for him.

Fifth, Alibaba was pushed behind a car whose driver suddenly changed her direction from the left turn lane to the center lane at an intersection on the main road. By the time he got his turn to cross the intersection, the light turned red instantly. He waited nearly two minutes before the traffic signal granted him right of way. Sixth, Alibaba was helplessly idling behind a courteous driver who graciously stopped behind a green light to allow the left-turning vehicles from the opposite direction to enter the ramp into a freeway. Although the lane was long clear for the courteous driver to move forward, the left-turning motorists from the opposite direction followed closely one after another as if they wished to exhaustively enjoy every bit of the courtesy granted to them. In the meantime, the courteous driver might also take the moment to fully appreciate his own perceived generosity, grace, or nobleness in front of the stream of moving vehicles. Obviously, nobody knew if he was aware of or cared enough to heed to Alibaba and other drivers behind, who were anxiously waiting to exercise their priorities of way to reach where they must be by a certain time. Unfortunately for Alibaba, he had to wait for the next round of signals after the courteous driver sped through the yellow light. Seventh, Alibaba drove behind a string of slowly moving vehicles on the roadside lane when he changed into another main road. By the time he was close enough, he found that it was an illegally parked car that had caused the slowdown. Finally, on the road of his child's school, Alibaba had to stop twice, once for a car backing from a private driveway to move ahead of him, and again for a car blocking one-third of his way to turn left into the other side of the road.

With all these hassles or little mishaps along the way, Alibaba reached his daughter's school by 8:20 a.m., about thirty minutes later than the time he had planned for. Being late, Alibaba's daughter first had to report to the school's attendance office. The incidence would eventually show up as one count of tardiness on her report card. She already missed her homeroom meeting, where important news and announcements were made for the day. She now could only run to catch part of the class in the first period, depending upon what was scheduled for the period. If the period was arranged for a major exam, the child would have to wait in the school library for the following period.

Upon dropping his daughter at school, Alibaba rushed to his appointment for an annual physical examination. However, since he was more than thirty minutes late, he had to reschedule it for three months later.

The Discriminator

The traffic is a public arena where moving subjects and objects negotiate and compromise on their rights of way for passage. Normally, drivers, motorists, bicyclists, pedestrians, and other participants know what they do, follow traffic rules, observe codes of movement, exercise caution, courtesy, and patience, and assume all necessary responsibilities. There are times when one moving object unfairly gains advantage over another. There are occasions where some participants unwillingly lose their rights of way to others. Overall, however, people and vehicles remain even with each other in terms of gain and loss. And the traffic flows.

In the time frame of his navigation through the traffic on that regular weekday, Alibaba ran into a row of discriminators whose randomly released forces happened to accumulate systematically at him in a convergent pool of effects. Individually, Alibaba's first discriminator was an aggressor who stole his right of way at the three-way stop intersection. The truck driver might feel embarrassed, shameless, or nothing at the moment when he sped through the intersection ahead of Alibaba. Perhaps, the truck driver feels that he has a justifiable cause for public accommodation, assuming that everyone knows in the community that he has to rush-deliver many items before a certain time in the morning pledged or promised by his company to its customers. Alibaba's second discriminator was a rule-violator who rushed against a metered red signal for the single-person vehicle and failed to yield to the moving automobiles from the car pool lane as both lanes merged in a one-lane ramp into the freeway. The rule-breaking driver might feel lucky that she was not followed by the police, that she raced ahead as she desired in the rush-hour traffic, and that she avoided a near collision with Alibaba. With that sense of luck in her mind, she probably did not have any idea as how she made Alibaba's heartbeat crazy for a while. The third discrimination against Alibaba came from a group of three inconsiderate truckers. Truckers are not supposed to drive their large, fully loaded trucks on the first lane while traveling through a multilane freeway. They followed each other on the first lane; perhaps they were fearful of losing sight of each other, perceived the area they were passing through at the moment as confusing or treacherous, had a bad experience of missing each other over part of their journey, or just happened to have one of their fellow truckers take a wayward lead in a short period of time. Whatever reasons they might have, they interfered with the normal traffic flow on the freeway, and for Alibaba in particular, prevented him from entering the car pool lane as he so intended. The fourth discrimination faced by Alibaba stemmed from the invisible army of traffic designers, engineers, or planners who determine how roads are divided, how intersections are regulated, and how signals are set. While they plan, design, and maintain the traffic arena in professional competency most of the time, a few of them can sometimes make a lot of people suffer everyday with ill-designed roads, badly partitioned intersections, irrationally metered signals, or misguided traffic controls.

Alibaba's fifth discriminator was a change-of-mind driver who already moved into the left turn lane but somehow wanted to reverse to the center lane to go forward on the main road. The driver might show an honest plea for accommodation, assistance, or mercy on her face or have a similar feeling in her mind. However, when she inched her car into the center lane, she held the traffic flow on both left turn and center lanes. For Alibaba, waiting for the next round of the green light incurred a loss of more than two minutes, which proved to be not only significant by itself, but also responsible for further complications in the rush-hour traffic. The sixth discriminator against Alibaba was a courteous driver who held the traffic on his lane while perhaps enjoying some amount of salutation from the throngs of drivers making a left turn in front of him. The traffic arena at this particular occasion is a clear zero-sum game. The time gained or the joy experienced by one group of drivers equals exactly the time lost or anxiety borne by another. The seventh discrimination against Alibaba came from a car illegally parked on the roadside lane. The car is a participating object in the traffic. It stands as an obstacle to the flow of traffic when it is left on the roadside by its operator in knowing or unknowing disregard for traffic regulations. Finally, Alibaba was discriminated by two drivers who well qualify as inconsiderate, impatient, or inexperienced players in the traffic arena. When a driver backs from an alley or turns left from a side driveway into a main road, he or she needs to yield to the moving subjects and objects in either direction he or she intends to enter. When he or she ignores these basic codes of conduct, he or she holds other traffic participants in discriminatory positions.

It is apparent that participating subjects and objects in the traffic arena must follow rules, observe codes of conduct, and keep to their legitimate space. They can change from normal players into discriminators when they break rules of road, ignore traffic directions, disregard driving etiquettes, or go beyond their due space of maneuver. The traffic system itself may also be set up in a way to discriminate one group of traffic participants against another.

The Victim

The effect of discrimination does not necessarily translate into victimization. However, when discrimination takes place systematically, consistently, or in considerable severity, it will create self-conscious victims, leaving them with a clear sense of victimization, unfairness, and injustice.

At each of the eight episodes in his journey through the traffic, Alibaba was clearly as well as technically a victim. He was forced to give up his right of way, suffered a rapid increase in heartbeats, idled at the intersection for too long, applied the brake pedal repeatedly or suddenly, and/or experienced an intense moment of anxiety or panic. With focus on each episode, there was either loss of time, deprivation of privileges, damage to the vehicle, pressure to the nerve, injury to the body, or a combination thereof. From a long-term point of view, negligible damages to the vehicle from event to event may add up to a major repair, an early replacement of parts, more services in smaller intervals, or an overall faster aging or depreciation process. Similarly, forgivable stressors to life from time to time may crystallize into medical conditions, affecting one's quality of everyday experience. Suppose that Alibaba has developed hypertension, heart illness, or other physical problems years later. Alibaba might then have a reason to connect some of these qualitative problems to his suffering of increased heartbeats in the traffic on that typical morning.

On the day of incidence, of course, Alibaba was unlikely to wander far into all possible ramifications of each discriminatory encounter he had in the traffic arena. Naturally, he would only know that his daughter was late for school, that he missed his appointment, and that he and his daughter both have to make an extra effort just to get back to normal. In fact, had all episodes not happened in a close sequence toward a noticeable consequence, they each would have automatically dissolved and disappeared from Alibaba's consciousness. Being sequential, consistent, cumulative, and systematic, therefore, is what essentially makes often randomly occurring discriminatory experiences a clear case for attention and action in the real world.

Another factor contributing to self-awareness about victimization is spillover. That is, discrimination inflicted upon one has consequence beyond oneself. For a large part, what made Alibaba feel victimized in the traffic arena on that typical morning is that he left his daughter late for school. Indeed, when individuals face discriminations by themselves, they may take those discriminations as naturally occurring misfortunes. They are likely to put up with those unfortunate experiences without any open reaction. However, when they see discrimination spill over to their neighbors or significant others, individuals may then have a heightened consciousness of the discriminatory act and hence a strong reaction to it.

To move beyond himself and his daughter, Alibaba might have a flashy moment of concern and sympathy for other victims who were unnecessarily thrown into a similar experience as he had at each incidence. Traffic involves participating subjects and objects in a flow of movement. When Alibaba had to wait behind a signal, miss an entry, apply the brakes suddenly, or idle on a traffic lane, he had one, two, several, or a whole line of drivers behind or around facing similar hurdles. The situation manifests best in the freeway pileups where one driver, by his or her own miscalculation, mistake, or misfortune, may cause dozens of other innocent drivers significant human injuries and property damages, and even tragic losses of life.

The Compromise

There was not much compromise that Alibaba could make with his direct discriminator to regain a fair position or minimize loss at each discriminatory situation into which he was forced. In the traffic arena, where subjects and objects move from one another constantly, there is indeed neither occasion to engage in negotiation nor moment to fashion a compromise between instantly passing parties. Discriminators come and go. Victims appear and disappear. While most participants remain to be regular players most of the time, they can turn into discriminators at one occasion while serving as unwilling victims at another.

In the mind of each participant in the traffic arena, however, a sense of compromise seems to remain present all the time. The sense of compromise each participant has is key to his or her continuing participation because it helps him or her properly channel any feelings of discrimination he or she may have developed from his or her involvement. In the case of Alibaba, it was primarily his sense of compromise that made him timely invoke his understanding about, sympathy for, or practically useful cynical attitude toward his discriminators. He calmed down, felt okay, and kept moving on when he was able to say some compromising words or flash some compromising ideas to himself: "The delivery driver has to deliver so many items by 10:00 a.m."; "Some people just feel they have to risk a red light to be ahead early in the morning"; "Truckers are afraid of losing each other in sight when they travel through an unfamiliar place"; "Not all traffic lights are well synchronized"; "There are drivers who are confused and do not know where to go at certain moments"; "Some drivers are just too polite so that they are often taken advantage of"; "People do not always pay close attention to when and there they can park their cars"; and "Not all drivers are considerate or experienced." Imagine that Alibaba did not have any sense of compromise when he was faced with each episode of discrimination. He then was likely to honk his horn or yell at his discriminator. He might even follow a specific discriminator, launching some kind of revenge against the person or vehicle involved. Consequently, there would be fights, collisions, disruptions to the traffic, and/or larger losses of time, labor, money, or property.

Obviously, a sense of compromise prevents particular experiences of victimization from accumulating into a general feeling of injustice. With a sense of compromise, participants in the traffic arena can take the role of others (I sometimes do the same), shrug off an unfavorable encounter or explain away a discriminatory incidence (It just happens, from time to time), and keep a proper perspective of the large picture (You gain here and now. You lose there and then. It is all too natural).

The Universal

The traffic is an arena for human interaction. Individual participants are supposed to possess adequate vehicle-operating competency, follow traffic rules, exercise personal cautions, observe social etiquettes, and show mutual respect. When some players fall short of any of these expectations, they can turn into instant discriminators, pushing other players into disadvantageous positions. Student drivers or drivers in training are likely to hold the traffic. Drivers who speed through a red light may collide with vehicles moving from other directions. Vehicle operators who eat food, comb hair, or talk on the phone behind the wheel often make other traffic participants stopped and scared. One subject may feel threatened, offended, or annoyed when another screams at, points fingers to, or cuts in front of him or her.

Discrimination in the traffic arena is mostly void of evil intentionality. A discriminating driver who steals someone else's right of way does not necessarily have a bad intent to hurt the deprived. In fact, one plows ahead often because one does not think one would hurt anybody else. Associated with this feature, discrimination in the traffic seems to be target-unspecific. To some degree, the vehicle serves as a shield to make its operating subject feel that he or she can discriminate against others because he or she does not face those others directly. In terms of effect, discrimination in the traffic arena can either even out amid randomly indiscriminative forces or reinforce itself by way of discriminative accumulation. For example, one misses a would-be collision simply because one is held several cars behind by a trucker who backs up his vehicle inconsiderately from a side road. Or one runs into a series of delays and mishaps when one misses a left turn arrow because a SUV jumps ahead suddenly from the center lane of the main road.

Individual reactions to discrimination in the traffic may range from revenge, road rage, and compromise to withdrawal. While acts of revenge lead to confrontation, road rage, and violence, spirits of compromise are what keep people willing participants in the traffic arena. There are rare cases where individuals say they withdraw totally from driving or moving through the public transportation system simply because they are so fed up with so many discriminatory subjects and objects therein. Indeed, from a long-term point of view, one can always get even when one continues in the arena. Or one can undo one's victimization only when one participates long enough in the traffic.

At the system level, while discrimination occurs inevitably in the traffic arena, it can lessen, decline, and become unnoticeable when a culture of civility, law, patience, and mutual respect prevails among the general public.

SITUATION 2

Lunch is an important ritual for working professionals. It is precious to find at lunch a break from work in the middle of a long day. During the lunch break, one refuels body and refreshes mind so that one can remain productive for the second half of one's daily work. For some working individuals, lunch also affords them either a good time to run errands or a prime opportunity to make friends.

The Particular

As usual, Alibaba has a few things on the list for his one-hour lunch break: mailing a letter in the post office located one block away from his office building, making a payment at the bank across the street, and having lunch at an eatery he goes to most of the time.

   With a busy plan in mind, Alibaba stepped out of his office at noon exactly. He arrived in the post office five minutes later. The line was normal, with seven customers waiting for service by three clerks. Alibaba took the eighth position in the queue, expecting to have his turn in a few minutes. However, when he moved up to the first position of the queue, Alibaba found he had already waited for fifteen minutes. Under his anxious watch, one postal clerk kept chatting with each of his customers about matters unrelated to postal transactions, such as pets and gambling in Las Vegas. For one chat, the clerk was so involved with his customer that he seemed to have forgotten that there were a dozen people in the room listening to him. Next to this talkative clerk, another postal counter service agent was working patiently with a customer who seemed to have so many questions and worries about what she was about to send. The customer filled out one form after another, tore them apart altogether, and finally decided to go with registered but not insured mail. The third postal worker waved Alibaba to her for service at 12:17 p.m. She murmured a few words and then quickly ran to the rear office. By the time she was back, Alibaba had watched three persons lining behind him already attended to by the other two clerks. He wondered why she had called him forward if she knew she was not able to serve him right away. Alibaba stepped out of the postal office at 12:25 p.m.

   Next, Alibaba ran to the bank across the street. There again was a line of customers waiting for service. Alibaba stood in the queue for a while. Then a bank representative walked to the line, asking if any customer came in for noncash transactions only. Alibaba raised his hand and was led by the representative toward an office cubicle. Knowing the little time he had, Alibaba told the representative directly what he needed to do: depositing a check and transferring money from his savings account to pay for the entire balance on a credit card. The representative said she could help him with those two needs fast. However, what followed proved to be the opposite.

First, she sat Alibaba courteously, with a seeming intent to keep him comfortable and long. Second, she attempted to make a connection to Alibaba when she saw Alibaba's company-issued check. She said she used to work there as well and started mentioning some names, units, and physical features of the company as references. Third, she tried to introduce some of her bank products to Alibaba when she looked at his accounts. By thanking her for her information while turning his eyesight to his watch, Alibaba tactfully refocused her on the transactions he had to complete at the time. Finally, when Alibaba took the receipts from her, he found that the payment made to his credit card was not the whole balance, but the minimum amount required. Alibaba pointed out the difference to her. She said she was sorry but had to take him back to a teller to correct the error. Alibaba spent another five minutes taking care of the matter. It was 12:50 p.m. when he was finished with his banking business.

With only ten minutes left, Alibaba just purchased a sandwich and a drink from a convenience store on his way back to the office. He thought he could eat his simple lunch quickly before he set out to work for the afternoon. Unexpectedly, he received a phone call when he was about to unpack his sandwich. After the call, he ran to an emergency meeting. It was then uncertain when he would be able to get back for his lunch.

The Discriminator

Most service agencies know that working-class customers use lunch breaks to attend to their banking, mailing, and other business needs. When these service agencies open fewer windows for customer service during the peak lunch break or after-work hours, they hold de facto discrimination against many of their clients. In the case of Alibaba, institutional discriminators include the postal office and the bank branch. Both of them can study their business flows and make proper adjustments to their assignments of clerks or tellers to the customer service counters or windows by the time of the day, the nature of transaction, and the number of clients waiting in the lobby. Unfortunately, many service agencies defy the logic of business, becoming undisguised discriminators against their clientele. They let employees out for lunch at the same time many of their working-class clients come in to make needed transactions. The line for service is long. Customers waiting in line are often nervous, worried, and stressed. Especially when service agencies close their offices or branches at the same time as other institutional establishments, many working-class customers have to call in sick, take off a whole workday, or leave the job earlier just to attend to some simple yet necessary matters in life.

Most service agents understand that they need to move fast during certain hours of their work. When they see a long line of customers and still take enjoyment in chatting with their fellow workers or each of their clients or walk away to attend to other discretionary job duties or even non-job matters, they lodge actual discrimination against innocent customers who are in need of service. For Alibaba, individual discriminators first involve a customer service agent who talked to each of his clients unnecessarily on non-transaction matters, another who waved him forward to the counter and then left him waiting in idleness, and still another who lured him with a seeming promise of expedited service yet intended to keep him as a target for sales. A customer service agent may genuinely hope to personalize service with each of his or her clients, may indeed have something urgent to take care of, or may honestly consider it natural to ask his or her clients about their other service needs while attending to their current requests. However, there are also impudently discriminatory agents in the field of customer service who like showing off their sociable or popular personality or chatting skills in front of a larger waiting crowd, who are eager to cash in a favor offered for the opportunity of sales intended, and who even take pleasure in seeing an increase of their own importance in contrast to a throng of anxious and stressful customers waiting for service.

Individual discriminators against Alibaba were not limited to customer service agents. The customer who changed her mind for service repeatedly obviously took an unwarranted amount of time from her serving agent and hence acted discriminatorily against Alibaba and all other customers who were waiting for service in the postal office. It is not uncommon in the field of customer service that one customer makes many other customers waiting in queue uneasy at least and frustrated most of the time with inconsiderate pleas for accommodation, unreasonable requests, or voluminous orders. Imagine a checkout line in a grocery store where a customer asks Alibaba whether she can cut in front of him because of an excusable reason. Suppose a service queue at an eatery for lunch where Alibaba has to wait more than five times longer than he normally does since one of the customers ahead stands to make six different takeout orders for himself and his colleagues. Occasionally, there are even bored idlers who say they make nominal purchases just to see holiday mailing or buying crowds in postal offices or elsewhere or downright pranksters who intentionally take time from customer service agents with unnecessary questions or orders when they see a long line behind.

The Victim

In the field of customer service, since a discriminatory or victimizing act is likely to ripple through from one particular customer to all others following, victims can be general versus specific and direct versus indirect. The talkative postal clerk made everyone in the lobby a general victim because people could be easily annoyed as they were listening to his unnecessary chats and perceptively viewing him as a culprit who has wasted time from assisting customers and facilitating the movement of a long waiting line. His fellow clerks could say in their minds: "Please be considerate; talk when there are fewer customers waiting in queue; you stress us out when you keep your leisurely pace in front of a throng of customers in need of service; and you make us look bad by way of association." On the part of waiting customers like Alibaba, most of them might plead in silence: "Please stop talking about those non-transaction matters; please help us faster; and I beg you to get me out of here sooner!"

The customer who filled out and then tore one form after another made it difficult for the helping agent to execute a transaction. As a direct victim, the agent had to explain one procedure after another, spending more time than that warranted by the transaction itself. Without knowing the details, the agent's fellow workers might begrudge him or her for being not clear or fast enough in his or her response to customer queries. If the number of customers served and the nature of transactions executed figure significantly in job performance, the agent may have to suffer some loss in his or her periodical evaluations due to an incident like this. Also, in the process of dealing with a difficult customer, an agent is likely to look unfavorable in the eyes of other customers in presence. Even when the agent is patient and acts professionally, other customers might still think of him or her as being too patient, untactful, or as having a lack of commonsensical smartness. Indeed, other customers as indirect victims who have to wait longer for service are likely to blame both a troublemaking customer and this customer's direct victim, the service agent, for holding up the line.

The postal clerk who called Alibaba forward and then left him waiting at the counter created a specific as well as a direct victim. Alibaba was a specific victim because he happened to be the one whom the agent intentionally or unintentionally targeted for victimization. Alibaba was a direct victim because he bore all the effects of the agent's unexplained, inexcusable walk-away from service. Given the fact that the agent could and should have been in service facilitating the movement of the waiting line, all other customers queuing behind Alibaba are general and indirect victims.

The same is true in the bank branch. Alibaba volunteered for a seeming offer of expedited service, yet unknowingly became a specific target for the banking specialist's sales effort. In direct terms, Alibaba lost valuable lunch-break time to the sales ploys the specialist attempted to set up for potential customers to buy additional products and services available at the bank. In contrast to Alibaba as a specific victim, general victims are all other customers waiting in line in the sense that any one of them could fall into the trap as well. In the peak time when a banking specialist is advised to put aside his or her regular duty to help ordinary customers with their needed transactions, he or she should just perform the expedited service so that the line can move up faster. Other customers in queue are also indirect victims because each of them could have waited shorter in line had the banking specialist not intended more to find potential customers for sales opportunities than to genuinely assist customers with their needed services.

The Compromise

It is clear that Alibaba made a series of compromises with individual agents, agencies, and service as a whole throughout his lunch break. At the individual level, Alibaba could have approached the talkative postal clerk, asking him to focus on his job at the peak time of service. He could have patted the annoyingly time-taking customer, tossing out a suggestion, a reminder, or even a reprimand, such as this remark: "Hi, guy, didn't you see the line of people waiting behind you? Shouldn't you have most of your stuff ready when you came up for service?" Alibaba could have stopped his serving postal clerk from leaving the counter by simply saying: "Wait a minute! You called me forward now. And you must take care of me before you leave!" Similarly at the bank branch office, Alibaba could have made it clear to the specialist as soon as he noticed the latter's intent to draw his interest in other bank products with an upfront statement that "I am sorry I have no time for all these sales pitches today. Please just help me get out of here as soon as possible." In reality, like most other customers, Alibaba wanted to keep his conformity to normality or his commitment to civility. He did not want to become someone who behaves as a police officer or who makes everyone else feel that only he or she knows the right thing to do under the circumstance. Instead, he took whatever came out in the situation, putting up with all unnecessary yet nerve-breaking delays and holdups.

At the level of agency, Alibaba could have walked out of the line, out of the postal office, or out of the bank branch had he not compromised. Indeed, if he had a choice, Alibaba would have gone to a different postal office or another branch of his bank. Understandably, there would be no other postal office within the walking distance from his workplace. He might be able to mail his letter through a commercial carrier nearby, but the cost can be either undesirable or inhibitive. The same holds true for banking. If one has to drive ten minutes to an outlying branch of the same bank where one could have all one's transactions completed in two minutes, one would still choose to wait in queue for fifteen minutes or even longer at a local office of service. Or even if one can find another bank for faster or better services, one might still opt to stick to one's existing bank because one feels more comfortable with what one knows now. Taking into account cost, quality, reliability, and other relevant factors, one may not only compromise on time, convenience, or access, but also gain a sense of comfort with one's compromise. For Alibaba, he may well cherish the fact that there is a postal office near his work and that he can take care of his banking needs during the lunch break.

Taking service as a whole, an uncompromising person could pledge to himself or herself or declare to the rest of the world that he or she would never use commercial or noncommercial services again in his or her life because he or she is so fed up with waiting in line for service, pleading with service agents and agencies for care and speed, or worrying about his or her items being serviced. When one has a message to share with one's friends, one will carry it directly to them. When one has money to save for the future, one will hide it in a jar buried underground. In doing so, one will have to compromise dearly on one's quality of life and may eventually have to give up one's whole life in contemporary society.

The Universal

Service is an integral part of contemporary life. It is common that one has to wait in line for service in both commercial and noncommercial, both public and private, or both small and large agencies.

Queuing for service, one may feel discriminated against by a customer service agent if that agent is technically incompetent, plainly inconsiderate, or deliberately sluggish. In reaction to a presumptively discriminatory agent, one can show disrespect, express anger, file a customer complaint, or take avoidance. In the service line, one may also feel discriminated by one's fellow customers who jump in line, who ask too many questions, who fulfill an unwarrantedly excessive order, who take too much of a serving agent's time because of confusion, carelessness, or stupidity, or who intentionally place obstacles in others' way. Toward perceived or potential discriminators on their own side, customers are likely to act collectively by keeping the waiting line tight and straight so that no one can cut in line illegitimately or by making unfriendly or disapproving stares at outliers so that everyone may move through the line quickly. Beyond a specific setting of customer service, one may take a whole service branch, office, or store as a discriminatory agency that does not open a sufficient number of counters or windows to meet peak demands, that does not handle customer complaints timely to earn patron trust, or that does not treat employees or customers well to build a positive communal image. As part of a general response, people may boycott the store, develop unfavorable opinions about the office, or even make public protests against an entire corporate agency that owns the office or the store.

Compromise, however, seems to be the prevailing rule of the game. When there is a queue, people will wait in line. Not a great many customers opt for avoidance. Customers may become anxious and frustrated when they see no or little movement in line. They may blame some service agents or fellow customers in their minds for delays and holdups. But rarely would one break silence to yell at another customer, challenge a service clerk, or forgo one's turn of service with an agent one deems to be an irritating cause for the slow movement of the line. Indeed, it is compromise that keeps the apparent appearance of patience, civility, and order in markets and public places.

SITUATION 3

People work hard and take life seriously. They need vacations, hobbies, and other breaks to recreate, refresh, and rejuvenate themselves. Hearing concerts, watching sports, or attending sociocultural events can often serve in various functions as a diversion from job stress, a lifting of spirits in everyday affairs, or an enrichment of life overall.

The Particular

It was meant to be a special day today. Alibaba had planned and waited for an exciting event of the day for a long time and with a great deal of effort. The expected event was a widely acclaimed show by a famous performance troupe. The troupe was on its worldwide tour through the metropolis.

Alibaba spent handsomely on the tickets for his family a few months ago. Upon receipt of the tickets by mail, he made arrangement for half a day off from work on the day of the show. His wife struck a similar deal with her employer, a full-day absence without pay. One day before the show, Alibaba checked information about the sponsor, the venue, and the troupe. Everything seemed to be in order for the show.

With a whole day off from work, Alibaba's wife went to the beauty salon in the morning. She left home early in the afternoon. She first picked up her daughter from school. They then met with Alibaba at his workplace. About one hour later, Alibaba had his son come aboard from a local college. Now the entire family was on its way to the great event of the day.

After a one-and-a-half-hour drive through the metropolitan traffic, Alibaba's arrived in the venue, about one hour before the show. They parked the car, bought fast food for dinner, and found their seats in the stadium. The show was scheduled to begin at 6:30 p.m. But it was not until 6:45 p.m. that a host came to the stage and made an announcement to the audience. The announcement was all but shocking: "The two key performers of the troupe are not able to appear tonight due to an unpreventable event; the troupe and its sponsor sincerely apologize for this surprising change and will make every effort to optimize the experience of the audience with the troupe and its renowned performances in the evening although the program will have to be dramatically altered to reconcile the absence of some of its flagship elements."

The audience became obviously upset. Some screamed and some left, but most stayed. Alibaba's remained seated for the whole program, yet as everyone else in the stadium, carried an overwhelming sense of disappointment throughout the night. They regretted missing the core of the show for a long time afterward.

The Discriminator

There were both primary and secondary perpetrators in this incident. The primary perpetrators were the two major performers who failed to show up for performance onstage. Holding essential acting roles, they should make their utmost effort to fulfill their contracted obligations with the troupe and its sponsor, and essentially their assumed promise with the audience. They should stay healthy: eat what they are supposed to eat while avoiding any substances that may negatively impact their artistic functionality. They should be active: practice what they are supposed to practice yet stay away from any strenuous exercises that may push them off performance. They should remain available: follow whatever rule members of the troupe are supposed to follow and report to the troupe always on time. On a world-wide tour, members of the troupe should be especially cautious about leaving the troupe out of necessity: they must keep their troupe abreast of their individual schedules and, most important, have a secure plan for on-time return to the troupe.

The secondary perpetrators were the troupe and the local organizer of the show. The troupe should have explicit rules for its members and keep close contact with each of its performers, especially principal ones. The troupe must have a backup plan should it run into an unexpected situation. For example, it keeps a qualified pool of surrogate actors and actresses. Or it only lets its principal performers leave the premium one at a time. In the unlikely event it exhausts all possible options for keeping a scheduled performance, the troupe should notify the local organizer immediately. The local organizer, on the other hand, should stay on top of everything surrounding the show. It first needs to keep pressure on as well as provide support for the troupe so that the latter is able to deliver what it promises to do in the locale. The local organizer then should take decisive yet appropriate actions when it is notified of an abrupt change in program. In the incident experienced by Alibaba's, the local organizer could have alerted all ticket-holders at the time of check-in about the unfortunate alteration to the show and graciously offered a full refund to anyone who did not want to compromise on a watered-down version of the show. Even if it was notified at the last minute, the local organizer could still be able to compensate and comfort the audience by pledging in the 6:45 p.m. announcement an issuance of a meaningful discount coupon applicable toward a future event at the time of exit.

The Victim

Alibaba and his family were clearly victimized in this incident. Financially, Alibaba took half a day off from work, his wife had a whole day absence without pay, they spent a considerable amount of money on the tickets, they paid higher than normal prices on fast food at the stadium, and they had to bear the dear cost of driving to reach and come back from the venue. In indirect terms, Alibaba's wife might not have necessarily spent money at the beauty salon had she not expected to watch the show.

Of course, the major loss was on the part of cultural consumption. Alibaba's expected to see the key actors and actresses on stage, enjoy the flagship performance of the troupe at its best, and get most out of the time and money they were so willing to spend on the show. Perhaps they had a sufficient glimpse of the troupe and its worldwide tour performance by watching a watered-down version in the evening. However, thinking of the fact that the two lead performers did not appear for a couple of the defining episodes of the show, Alibaba, his wife, his son, and his daughter, each and all, are likely to keep some regret in their respective memory about the event. Indeed, without the ultimate feeling of perfection or consummation, one would naturally find it an incidence of unfortunate discrimination or victimization.

Along with Alibaba's, there were hundreds of other individuals or families implicated in this little misfortune. Obviously each victim had his or her own story. The actual experience of victimization one had from the event varied in accordance with how much one invested in time, how much one spent monetarily, what one expected from such a typical entertainment event, and even what kind of person one is. It might not matter much at all if one walked to the venue after dinner from one's apartment nearby or if one had seen similar cancellations of or alterations to art or sport events and hence did not take this one as particularly out of the ordinary.

The Compromise

Compromise was inevitable to the troupe, the organizer, and the audience as it was forced upon each of them by the circumstance of the two lead performers. Originally, it was supposed to be a smooth show for every party involved. Without the two major players, the troupe now scrambled to reorganize and rearm so that it could retain the balance of the program and keep the reputation of its worldwide tour. There were likely complaints from members who were present to do all necessary impression managements both onstage and backstage. Financial incentives might have to be offered to minimize inner tension. To the outside, the troupe had to do a lot of explanations to the organizer as well as the audience. Financial concessions might have to be surrendered according to the terms of the contract or just to pacify some confrontational viewers.

The local organizer could not simply terminate its contract with the troupe, denying payment to and logistical support for the troupe. Instead, it had to work compromisingly in even closer cooperation with the troupe to manage the impact of the untimely change. To assist the troupe in its realignment of performers and performances, the organizer might have to mobilize necessary equipment, materials, or personnel from different sources. Depending upon the reputation of the troupe and the relative strength it had with the troupe, the local organizer might have to face the unhappy audience all on its own, absorbing the total monetary loss due to refunds, cancellations, and/or offerings of future discounts.

The audience could not just walk out of the venue, demanding a full compensation from the troupe or the local organizer for all the expenses incurred for the sake of the show. In fact, Alibaba, along with most of the other viewers in the audience, chose to stay to watch the altered program.

Although they were not thrilled as they expected to be normally, they managed to make some out of what they had invested in for the evening. For those who angrily walked away, it was unlikely that they would recoup all the money and time they had spent in their preparation for watching the show. They might receive a full refund of the ticket price they paid, but had to forever keep the memory of their compromise on a permanent loss of all the collateral expenses, such as no pay for time off from work, cost on driving, fees for parking, and other miscellanies.

The Universal

Arts, concerts, sports, and other cultural events play a significant part in the lives of contemporaries. People seem to be willing to make extraordinary efforts in both time and money just to watch some artists perform, some athletes play, or some luminaries speak. Public fascination gives celebrity figures tremendous clout over their audiences. As a result, fans, followers, and other innocent members of the audience can easily fall into a situation where they have to face loss of money, loss of time, and even unfair treatment.

Indeed, a concert, a game, a show, or a public event involves hundreds, even thousands, of ticket-paying viewers. When lead performers, players, or speakers fail to show up because of their personal choices or troubles, they hold a large number of people in discrimination for altered programs, watered-down performances, and compromised experiences. Organizers may offer an apology, issue a refund, or do a rerun. But nothing can actually make up for what is lost in a circumstance of program cancellation or alteration. For example, an apology may make people feel better but would offer no help in removing regret from one's memory. A refund may cover the loss of a paid ticket but would never take care of all the costs incurred for making it to the show at the venue. And a program rerun would only double the expenses for those viewers who are willing or able to come back.

Despite some unfortunate experience they may have left for a considerable number of viewers in a particular locale, many teams or troupes are likely to march on with their planned countrywide or global performance tours. As performers or players keep their fame and grow their influence, they surely raise the possibility that they will panic another local organizer and audience with unscrupulous change as well as the consequentiality that they will give people a more intense feeling of loss, disappointment, or stress when they misbehave or fall short of their own performance.

SITUATION 4

Society becomes more and more open for participation by common people in the contemporary era. In democratic countries, there exist various channels and forums through which ordinary citizens can voice their concerns and opinions on specific community affairs, general social issues, and even critical public policies.

The Particular

It was marked on Alibaba's calendar about a month ago. In preparation, Alibaba had read books, visited websites, compared statistics, and even written down a few paragraphs for what he might say tonight at the community meeting on a new development project. To make it there on time, Alibaba had to skip his formal dinner with the family. In fact, driving directly from his office after work, Alibaba had only half an hour to swallow a sandwich at a neighborhood eatery before the meeting started at 7:00 p.m.

Alibaba sat in the fifth row of a 250-person auditorium. There were about 150 people in attendance. After a series of formal presentations by city planners, developers, and neighborhood council members, the community forum opened up for public discussion in which concerned residents could ask questions or make some kind of statement. A moderator stood in the forefront of the stage to pick who would speak and decide how much a chosen speaker may talk for his or her turn.

Alibaba raised his hand soon after the public discussion was under way. He kept his hand up every time a new person was to be chosen. For some reason, however, the moderator seemed to have ignored Alibaba for quite a number of turns. A person sitting in the back of Alibaba was chosen. A person sitting two seats next to Alibaba had spoken even though she raised her hand after Alibaba first did. People around Alibaba started to notice the fact that he continually raised his hand while being bypassed repeatedly by the moderator for somebody else. Sympathy developed. Some kind of collective signaling followed. As a matter of fact, Alibaba felt that it was not his own hand-raising but some hand-directing toward him by other people in the audience that secured him a speaking turn after an embarrassingly long wait.

For his hard-earned turn, Alibaba stood up from his seat. He first introduced himself as required of every voluntary speaker. He then made a brief comment on the two sides and their respective positions toward the development. With the stage properly set, Alibaba went on to present his points of view, using the data he had gathered from different sources during his preparation study. The audience was quite receptive. There was even applause for a couple of instances. The major speakers on the stage seemed pretty impressed as well. A few of them nodded their heads at various points. The moderator, however, stepped in abruptly, asking Alibaba to stop because of the time limit placed on each unscheduled speaker from the audience. In the middle of it, Alibaba terminated his presentation of a seemingly unique approach to the development project.

As far as the moderator was concerned, he saw at least three speakers go beyond the time limit under his watch throughout the public discussion. For one speaker before Alibaba spoke, the moderator did not intervene at all. It was a member of the audience who put a brake on the speaker's aimless, rambling words. Another speaker ignored the moderator and went on to have finished her talk in another three minutes. The third speaker pleaded with the moderator for more time and was granted almost an extra turn to complete his rather long remarks. Interestingly, Alibaba also asked the moderator for a little more time but was firmly denied his request.

The Discriminator

The moderator seemed to be the one and only clear discriminator for what Alibaba received at the community forum. He ignored Alibaba. He kept Alibaba raising his hand and waiting in anxiety. He placed Alibaba behind those who showed their intent to speak later or with less effort. As a moderator, one is supposed to be fair, open, and objective. One treats everyone the same. One picks voluntary speakers simply by the order of time they raise their hands. In the case when a number of people volunteer simultaneously, one can follow a convenient rule from left to right or from back to front.

When it comes to the enforcement of a time limit, as a moderator one should be consistent. One may let all chosen speakers freely express their ideas if time allows. One may impose a limit without any exception if time is tight. One may grant each request the same extension when one has some leeway in managing a discussion session. In the case of Alibaba, the moderator obviously committed discrimination against one or more persons in the audience. He interrupted Alibaba while letting another speaker ramble off limit. He rejected Alibaba's request for a little more time while giving twice as much time for another speaker to finish. He succumbed to nonconformity while showing little appreciation of a conforming plea for accommodation.

In the real world, unfortunately, there is no lack of moderators like the one who treated Alibaba badly. They act unprofessionally or incompetently, discriminating some while benefiting others in academic exploration, legal deliberation, public debates, or political expressions. For instance, some moderators pick their colleagues, friends, or superiors first. In a college colloquium, a moderator from sociology may allow the dean to ask questions or make comments before everyone else or let his or her colleagues in sociology speak before people from anthropology, psychology, or political science. Some moderators select people by their known positions or points of view. Popular ideology is promoted while unique perspectives are suppressed. Some moderators even use sex, gender, race, ethnicity, or physical appearance as key variables for their choices. Majorities have their way all the time, whereas minority groups often stay in the shadow.

The Victim

Alibaba was an obvious victim. He knew he was not treated well at the time and afterward. People in the audience also noticed in the process of discussion that something irregular, inconsistent, or unusual happened to one or more persons who volunteered to express their opinions.

What exactly went on in the mind of Alibaba as a victim? First, he kept raising his hand for a chance to speak. There is physical fatigue when someone keeps trying something without success. There is mental stress when someone wants to do something but is repeatedly pushed aside. In front of an audience, being ignored time and again makes one feel embarrassed, discouraged, and even self-pitying. One naturally wonders if anything is wrong with oneself or whether one is worthy of any attention or opportunity to speak at all.

Second, Alibaba was cut short in his presentation. Telling half of a story may make a rather good story look bad. Indeed, expressing half of his position, Alibaba felt that he did not leave people with any position or any alternative to think about the development project. Even if he had left something, that something was likely to be incomplete and hard to understand, and therefore useless. Such a public impression could feed back on the initial treatment that Alibaba received. That is, people might feel that the moderator did right by not allowing Alibaba to speak in the order he raised his hand and by stopping him immediately when the limit of time was reached.

More subtly, Alibaba did not know why he was treated differently than everybody else. He dressed professionally at the time. There is no irritable mark or trace in his physical appearance. He has an accent but speaks English always in a clear, confident, and understandable manner. He is an ordinary person, holding neither fame nor notoriety for any outlying act, awkward position, or outrageous point of view. Of course, Alibaba comes from an ethnic minority. However, the public forum was supposed to be an occasion where all concerned residents in the community could hear information and express their opinions regardless of age, gender, race, and ethnicity. Being treated unfairly while having no clue about its cause, one may feel an experience of double victimization. In other words, one suffers the pain of victimization as it occurs in the first instance, and one carries the burden of victimization as it lingers in one's consciousness without a settlement.

The Compromise

Alibaba could have stood up from his seat and made a loud voice of protest when he felt clearly that he was intentionally ignored by the moderator. Instead, he kept raising his hand every time the moderator was about to choose a new volunteer to speak. With a cooperative attitude, he had earned sympathy from people around him. For the community forum as a whole, nobody was distracted from a possible protest against its format or procedure. Everyone was able to concentrate on substantive issues or the content of the forum.

With pressure from the audience, the moderator finally gave Alibaba a chance to speak. In principle, one could use the full strength of one's discretion as a moderator to block a particular person from speaking in a public forum. One could pretend not to have noticed the person in a sizable auditorium. One could even make it clear that one would not let the person have the chance to speak as long as one is in charge of moderating the program. By intentionally and repeatedly denying a person's request to speak, one as a moderator may make oneself look prejudiced in front of the audience or cause unnecessary intensity to one's job of maintaining order for public discussion.

On the matter of time, Alibaba could have held on to his turn of speech firmly until he had completed all he wanted to say. In other words, he could have ignored the moderator's warning to stop or he could have unyieldingly insisted that he be given extra time to finish his presentation. Instead, Alibaba asked for more time only gently. When he was denied, he terminated his speech courteously. By doing so, Alibaba demonstrated his conformity to the rule of procedure, his respect for the moderator, and perhaps his character as a gentleman. Although he was not able to inform the audience of the whole detail of his position, he might still have impressed the audience with his unique approach to the development project. It is possible that more people would seek to talk to Alibaba after the forum because of their lingering interest in his unfinished presentation.

The Universal

Academic panels, professional workshops, community forums, town hall meetings, and other discussion groups are common occasions where professionals communicate with each other, citizens express themselves, officials gather public input, and concerned participants make an impact on opinions and policies regarding their fundamental interests.

A moderator presides over the occasion. In moderating public discussion, one holds power over the audience. On the one hand, one can be neutral, granting everyone equal and fair opportunities to present his or her points of view. On the other hand, one can be partial, partisan, and even prejudiced, discriminating against one person, one group, or one position while advocating, advancing, and promoting another. There are also moderators who themselves are confused or overwhelmed. Pushed by different waves and tides from open discussion, they may in default allow one opinion or ideology to dominate a show while holding another under stress and repression.

People may not necessarily give much weight to a particular public discussion. However, as far as an individual is concerned, being given an opportunity to speak in front of an audience may help build confidence, cultivate an expression habit, or develop an outreaching career style for him or her. On the opposite, being denied a request for expression may once and forever raise one's sense of anxiety, fear, or reluctance, making one a person of acquiescence, silence, or passive acceptance. The same holds true for a specific point of view. When it is expressed in an appropriate occasion, a particular idea or ideology can catch instant attention, spread rapidly among groups, and even turn into a fashionable pursuit throughout the population. In contrast, when it is suppressed at its debut, a rather creative, useful, or revolutionary finding or product may never have a chance to gain access to public arenas to make its potential contributions to social welfare or human progress.

SITUATION 5

People experience stress from different dimensions of life. While they can manage stress at its source, they may willingly or unwillingly allow it to spill over to other areas. For example, one receives an unfavorable evaluation or even a reprimand for one's work. Instead of correcting it, fighting it, or at least containing it at the workplace, one may find an innocent target elsewhere to vent one's dissatisfaction, disappointment, and anger. Displacement is indeed seen in common use by contemporaries as a natural defense mechanism against anxiety in their often stressful everyday life (Freud 1965, 2003).

The Particular

It was a quite eventful day for Alibaba. In the morning, he dropped off his daughter at school only a couple of minutes before the bell rang. He did not know if his daughter would run quickly enough to make it to her homeroom on time. When he rushed to work, he almost hit a car from behind. The moment was nerve-breaking although he escaped it unscathed.

At work, Alibaba had a dispute with one of his coworkers. He did not intend to bring the matter to the attention of his supervisor. But the supervisor happened to have taken notice of the matter when he walked through the office. Despite the fact that Alibaba settled the dispute in his favor, the supervisor did not seem to be happy with the whole issue. In the mind of the supervisor, as Alibaba knew so well, the best thing was always this: nothing ever happened in the first place.

Later in the afternoon, Alibaba answered a few calls. From one of those calls, he got an ominous warning that one of the project proposals into which he had put so much effort might not overcome a major administrative hurdle that it was facing now. Suddenly, Alibaba felt as if he were crawling under an overcast sky in his world of work.

On his way home, Alibaba listened to the radio. From the news headlines, he learned that the stock market had tumbled for the day. He immediately moved to the side of the road and checked two of the stocks he had in a brokerage account. Upon hearing the results, he wished in helpless regret that he had sold those stocks a few days ago when they had hit their high marks in trading.

Alibaba arrived home about half an hour later than he usually did after work. His wife opened the door, asking if he was okay and why he was late. He did not answer his wife and appeared to be mad on his face. A few minutes later at the dinner table when he noticed a couple of more dishes than usual, he broke out in anger toward his wife: "Why did you cook more than we could possibly consume for the night? Didn't you know that eating leftovers on the following day is not good to personal health? Didn't you know how to sequence our weekly family food supply in a rational order? Didn't you know how to save family resources?" Alibaba kept on yelling, screaming, and hitting the table while watching his wife in tears.

The Discriminator

Alibaba might have borne some unfair discrimination on different occasions of the day himself. But with respect to what he did to his spouse in the evening, he was unequivocally a discriminator.

Upon a late return, at the doorstep, Alibaba should first have explained to his wife what kept him from getting home in time. He understood that his wife had already had some worry about him under the circumstances. Unfortunately, he remained indifferent when he was greeted by his wife. He did not show any sign of appreciation when he was let into the house with concern and assistance by his wife. He did not answer his wife's questions. Most important, he kept all unhappiness on his face, making his wife feel as if she did something wrong at home.

The dinner was made ready for Alibaba at the table. It was a bounty dinner with more dishes prepared heartedly by his wife. His wife and daughter have been waiting for him, perhaps with some degree of hunger. They both could have had their dinner some time earlier. Alibaba had every reason to say thanks, offer an apology, or at least show some self-feeling of comfort or relaxation in front of his loved ones. Instead, he yelled at his wife for preparing a bountiful family dinner, that is, for doing something nice and kind for him.

In his discriminatory act, Alibaba hurt his wife, scared his daughter, and created unnecessary tension for his family. That night, his daughter did not finish her homework, his wife wept in sorrow and went to bed late in a separate room, and he himself struggled with pain and regret for a long time until a few sleeping pills took him to rest.

The Victim

The immediate victim of Alibaba's act of displacement was his wife. She used her heart to prepare a hearty dinner in the hope that she would perhaps give her husband a happy surprise, a pleasing comfort, or a feeling of home after a long day of work. She waited for about half an hour in some degree of anxiety. She ran to open the door when she heard her husband arriving in the garage. She even lent her hands, assisting Alibaba to get his stuff out of the car and into the house. Instead of being reciprocated by her husband, she became a final target for Alibaba to vent the anger he had accumulated during the day. Without a clue for Alibaba's discriminative behavior, she shed tears. Bearing an inexplicable sorrow, she skipped the dinner and had a restless night in bed.

Besides his wife, Alibaba indirectly hurt his daughter. First, she could have had her dinner earlier had Alibaba arrived home in time. Second, she swallowed her dinner in the shortest time possible when she watched in fear her parents in the middle of an argument. Supposedly, she had a bounty dinner to enjoy for the night! Third, she ran to her room quickly but had difficulty concentrating on her homework. Fourth, she needed help on her math assignments. Being fearful, she did not ask either of her parents and just left her homework unfinished. Finally, what could Alibaba's daughter expect for her night? With a memory of parents still in dispute and math problems unsolved, she could only wish that she would not wake up in a nightmare.

At a subtle and abstract level, Alibaba put his marriage and family through an unnecessary test. Marriage sustains through times of trust, love, and unity between husband and wife. Days of discord, tension, and stress can only lessen the total amount of happiness derivable from marriage for a couple. The same holds true for family. The overall quality of family life builds upon each moment, each day, each month, and each year of encouragement, empowerment, and mutual support among family members for their individual pursuits.

The Compromise

There were still compromises made between Alibaba and his wife, daughter, and family in spite of the incident that had happened. These compromises kept the incident in proper perspective although they did not prevent it from occurring in the first place.

On the part of Alibaba's wife, she probably knew that Alibaba had carried some deep displeasure from work. Instead of talking back to possibly fuel her husband's anger, she remained basically unresponsive. She gave up her turn to offer an explanation. The tactic was appropriate because Alibaba would not be able to hear any explanation at all when he just wanted to pick holes in what his wife did. She took all the verbal bombardments from Alibaba. While she could, she did not stay away from him totally. In fact, she uttered a few words now and then so that Alibaba could keep going until he felt emptied. The strategy was proper because complete avoidance would make Alibaba equally unhappy as would direct confrontation under the circumstance.

As a third party, Alibaba's daughter could have confronted her father directly or with a diplomatic overture. For example, she could have said: "Daddy, you are so unfair to yell at Mommy. Mommy picked me up from school, helped me with my homework, and spent a whole hour in the kitchen for this nice dinner. She even told me she wanted to cook you a huge meal because you have been working hard recently. You owe a big apology to Mommy. And you should give my mommy a big hug!" Had she so confronted her father, she could have thrown Alibaba into greater anger with a thought like this: "What a lousy day! Even my own child could find fault with me!" Of course, Alibaba could have also calmed down when he heard those words from his innocent daughter.

With his wife's forbearance and his daughter's avoidance, Alibaba saw more clearly his total lack of a justifiable cause for the whole skirmish. Although he was not able to stop immediately or turn around suddenly, he started making sensible adjustments in his expressive output. He focused on the triviality of the issue with which he initially found fault. He did not attack his wife with regard to her character, her beliefs, and her fundamental approach to family life. In fact, he seemingly attempted to make his wife know that he was just acting out with his anger from elsewhere and therefore was more than usual in need of her accommodation and forgiveness.

The Universal

As one of the most common defense mechanisms used by people to cope with anxiety in life, displacement begins with an original source of anxiety, where one's fundamental interest lies. Lectured by a teacher in school or reprimanded by a supervisor at the workplace, one is likely to find non-threatening targets somewhere else to vent one's disappointment, frustration, and anger. Friends, relatives, loved ones, and even unrelated drivers, sales clerks, or bystanders could well become innocent victims either at a wrong time or in a wrong place.

Discrimination in the form of displacement can be either random or habitual. A random discriminator may pick up any easy target for his or her expressive output. A habitual discriminator, on the other hand, may turn to the same target for release of anxiety every time he or she experiences it. Whereas a habitual discriminator may consciously keep a proper perspective with his or her regular target, a random discriminator can become quite explosive toward his or her onetime victim. Indeed, the consequence from random displacement may even include a tragic loss of human life. As a real-life example, two autoworkers in the United States beat a Chinese draftsman to death because they blamed the Japanese for the loss of employment in the American automobile industry and mistook the Chinese man as a Japanese person (Zia 2000).

Reaction to victimization due to displacement varies widely from forced acceptance, passive acknowledgment, and codependency to universal compromise. A random victim may naturally attribute his or her victimization to a matter of bad luck. With some awareness about hierarchical order in society, he or she may realize that people in lower levels are more likely to bear unfairly displaced blames by those in higher social echelons. In the spirit of forgiveness, he or she may take a form of universal compromise on his or her suffering as a onetime random victim: "I myself do the same thing sometimes to people who are younger, in lower positions, or of nicer character. I'll get even in the long run." A habitual victim, in contrast, may in the initial phase of his or her victimization just passively acknowledge that it is yet another time he or she has to serve to give vent to his or her known discriminator's anger. As it continues, habitual victimization may progress to codependency, where a habitual victim takes his or her own suffering as inevitable, necessary, and even indispensable to the normal functioning of his or her familiar discriminator.

3   At Home

Home evokes a general feeling of peace, comfort, and happiness. Whereas some may take home as a tranquil refuge or a protecting shelter from work and social competition, others may view home as a safe haven or a relaxing retreat, where they can cultivate their personal interests and enjoy their private lives (Friberg 1993; Gallagher 1994; Booth, Carver, and Granger 2000; Lefebvre 2000; Hill et al. 2004; Marcus 2006; Hardie 2008; White and Klein 2008; Bryson 2010; McGoldrick, Carter, and Garcia-Preto 2010; Settles, Sheng, and Zhao 2011; Arnold et al. 2012; Pink 2012).

Home, however, can also be a site of conflict, tension, and struggle. A critical observation is this: people often keep their home affairs to themselves even when they suffer from neglect, discrimination, and abuse at home.

SITUATION 1

Women have assumed primary roles and responsibilities in childcare and housework. The division of labor was natural and justifiable in history when the husband was usually the main breadwinner of the family. In contemporary society, it has become increasingly an unfair and unreasonable arrangement as working women put similar efforts into jobs that bring home similar levels of income as men while in the role of wife they are still expected to take a greater share in homemaking and childrearing than the husband.

The Particular

Alibaba met his wife as an undergraduate in college. While he went on to earn a master's degree in computer science, his wife finished her law school with a J.D. Now they both work full-time, one as a computer specialist in the municipal government and the other as a lawyer for a private firm. Insofar as income is concerned, Alibaba has to do some out-of-job consulting work to be on a par with his wife.

At home, however, the division of labor seems to be always at Alibaba's favor. On a day-to-day basis, Alibaba cleans the table after each meal, drops his daughter at school, and dumps the trashes, whereas his wife prepares meals, picks up his daughter from school, and washes dishes. Weekly, biweekly, or monthly, Alibaba works on the yard, fixes problems around the house, and shops for groceries, daily articles, or home improvement items, whereas his wife washes clothes, cleans the house, and visits stores or malls for apparel, shoes, or family supply miscellanies. With regard to childrearing, Alibaba searches for information about school, but it is often his wife who checks homework, deals with school, and reads bedtime stories. Of course, Alibaba only looks on and lends a helping hand when his wife has to go through a ten-month pregnancy, a cesarean section, and a six-month breastfeeding period for each of their two children. On the matter of family management, Alibaba plans for excursions, vacations, and long-distance trips, but it is his wife who visits banks, monitors investments, and tracks retirement accounts.

The Discriminator

By either the amount of time required or the intensity of labor demanded, Alibaba overall is on the lighter side of housekeeping and family responsibilities. For example, compared to the normally hour-long time his wife has to spend on cooking and dishwashing, Alibaba just needs a few minutes to wipe the table and to remove the trash. In contrast to the laborious research, planning, and strategizing his wife has to put into the family finances, Alibaba can simply count on commercials, words of mouth, and chats among acquaintances to pick a vacation destination or to grab a fantastic travel deal.

Family labor is supposedly shared between husband and wife, especially when both husband and wife work full-time and make comparable contributions to the family income. Discrimination occurs in actuality if one spouse does more labor than the other. Specifically, there are voluntary versus involuntary, chronic versus situational, and conventional versus fashionable discriminations surrounding family labor. Voluntary discrimination happens when one spouse is more capable, conscientious, or energetic than the other and hence voluntarily takes a greater share of family labor from time to time. Involuntary discrimination falls upon one when one's spouse fails to partake of a particular housekeeping job or a general family responsibility that has to be addressed as part of everyday life. Chronic discrimination persists in a family when one voluntarily or involuntarily does more housekeeping and other family maintenance work because one's spouse is always lazy, often sick, or habitually elusive. Situational discrimination takes place now and then in a family when one suddenly finds a reason to go away, leaving an unfinished or yet-to-do piece of housework to one's spouse. Conventional discrimination has to do with established tradition, culture, or customs, whereas fashionable discrimination comes and goes along with trendy social fashions and vogues. For instance, some cultures take it for granted that women do more housework regardless of their professional status. In the meantime, there are also uniquely cultured groups, communities, or even cities where high fashion catches on, making men do most of everything at home for their loved women.

In the case of Alibaba, he is a de facto discriminator against his wife because he overall does much less work than his wife for the maintenance of their family. First and foremost, Alibaba is a conventional discriminator. Although he is educated and holds the public view of equality between men and women, he seems to nonetheless enjoy the fact that working women are still made to do more housework by deep-rooted social conventions. Second, as a conventional discriminator, Alibaba automatically becomes a chronic discriminator because he consistently takes advantage of a dominant convention regarding men and women to place more housework on the shoulders of his wife. Moreover, Alibaba makes excuses time and again for even not doing his duly assigned housework to an extent that he will eventually progress to a chronic discriminator from his multiplying perpetrations as a situational discriminator. Finally, Alibaba takes his role of a discriminator in both voluntary and involuntary forms. As a voluntary discriminator, he often teases his wife with these words "I just like what you cook" and "You do such a fabulous job in managing our family finances!" With a little trick perhaps, Alibaba sometimes appears to be an involuntary discriminator in front of his wife by saying, "I am sorry I have to leave all these housekeeping chores to you when I am preoccupied with this consulting project" or "I just feel ashamed I can never do a better job in cooking and dishwashing."

The Victim

Willingly or unwillingly, Alibaba's wife is a victim of this unequal share of household labor at her home. On a particular day, Alibaba may feel that it is no big deal to have his wife do some more housework here and there. Over a particular household chore, Alibaba's wife herself may not think much about taking care of it in her husband's favor or to the benefit of her whole family. However, day by day, one housekeeping chore after another, Alibaba's wife will end up losing dearly in a variety of fronts throughout her life.

Physically, cooking meals, washing dishes, and ironing clothes are hard labor. They each demand time and can lead to the development of certain health conditions on hands and body joints, such as arthritis and skin dryness or roughening. As a good-looking woman who is highly conscious of her appearance and style in the public, she would love it if she could visit beauty salons often and keep her hands young, fresh, and pretty away from water and dishwashing liquids!

Professionally, Alibaba's wife has to give up many opportunities for expansion and growth as she puts a great deal of time and energy into her family. Keeping the house neat and clean on a daily basis, she no longer thinks as often as she used to before marriage or as intensely as some of her single colleagues about extraordinary careers and career achievements. Managing family affairs year after year, she now seems to be at ease with the reality that she must take good care of her family from time to time while at work she just needs to stay on track until retirement.

Besides sacrifices of beauty, youth, and professional success, who knows if Alibaba's wife will age sooner and hence live a shorter life than she would otherwise as she has to continuously bear a heavy load of housework at home while working full-time outside? It is nevertheless certain that the overall quality of life matters, and that Alibaba's wife would only have a higher quality of life could she afford to do the same as Alibaba for her share of hard labor at home.

The Compromise

On many specific occasions, Alibaba's wife takes the route of compromise out of no choice. When dishes pile up in the sink, she has no alternative other than washing them. When clothes smell in the laundry room, she cannot pretend that she has not taken notice of the effect. When guests come to the house, she knows she will have to bear most of the blame if she has not spent enough time getting everything in order.

In general, Alibaba's wife compromises on her unfairly heavier share of housework for both personal and social reasons. At the personal level, she always tells herself that Alibaba is a good man, that he loves her and their children, and that he puts his heart over no other place than their family. She even feels a considerable sense of satisfaction by thinking of those negative cases she has heard so often from the media and her personal circle where husbands become abusive, disloyal, or violent to wives. In the social level, Alibaba's wife seems to accept those culturally established views about men and their assumed privileges in comparison to women. For instance, she tends to believe that a man of ambition, courage, vision, or success would not mess about too much in the kitchen or around the house. Instead, he should do those men's things outside the house with other men.

Alibaba's compromise, on the other hand, echoes well in his wife's self-feelings about their marriage and family. Knowing that his wife takes a greater share of the housework and makes considerable sacrifice in her own professional career, Alibaba never misses opportunities to acknowledge and praise his wife's good deeds to him, to their children, and to their family in front of relatives, friends, and colleagues. Whenever possible, he follows his wife around when she cooks dinners, washes dishes, and irons clothes with nice chats and a helping hand. Most important, Alibaba always says to himself that I have such a wonderful wife and my children have such a caring mother, which critically and subtly keeps him off all the lures and seductions he sees from work and everyday life. Indeed, he is a devoted husband and a dedicated family man.

The Universal

In spite of the governmental legislation that mandates same rights between men and women, women still hold less power while performing more labor in almost every social arena. Regardless of the organizational regulations that require equal treatment of men and women, women still receive fewer opportunities for upward mobility while making no less effort. Despite report after report in the mass media that more and more women work full-time and bring home income comparable to what is made by men, women are still considered the keeper of the house, the caretaker of the child, and the sympathizer of the husband in the core of secular opinions, social customs, and the general culture.

As a result, many working women carry two full loads of labor on their shoulders. At work, some organizations accommodate child-raising and family-caring female employees but then use the accommodations provided as excuses to bypass women in promotions and opportunities for career growth. Some organizations ignore female employees and their needs for family-related assistance outright. Working women hence either lose their jobs immediately or end their professional careers prematurely. At home, some husbands watch their working wife's sacrifices but rarely take any action to alleviate her from the heavy burden of the family. Some husbands even take advantage of the existing bias against women and throw all the housework into the hands of their fully employed wife. The case of Alibaba, who appreciates the greater share his wife takes in family responsibilities, seemingly represents a not-so-bad situation for a professional woman.

Although the issue is being raised, it will be a long time before working women become completely equal with men in their share of all family responsibilities, privileges, and rewards.

SITUATION 2

It is a mixture in contemporary society as far as how husband and wife relate to each other in a family. There are modern families, where both husband and wife work outside and share household responsibilities inside the home. There are traditional families, where husband serves as the sole breadwinner for the whole family. There are even "postmodern" families, where husband stays home to take care of children and housework with support from his working wife.

The Particular

Alibaba has a close colleague and friend at work named Daniel. They go to lunch together often. They even engage in joint activities, such as excursions and sports, over the weekend sometimes. Daniel shares many of his family life stories with Alibaba over time.

The biggest frustration Daniel has with his family seems to center around his wife, June. June does not have a job. In fact, she has rarely worked in her whole life. The burden of supporting the family falls totally on the shoulders of Daniel. Indeed, Daniel not only works hard, putting in an excessive amount of overtime, but he also lives in fear, keeping a constant eye on the job market. Listening to Daniel almost day by day, Alibaba understands Daniel and his worries: "I have so many bills to pay every month" and "I am scared to imagine when one day I am given a pink slip. June and our two children depend on me!"

A private complaint that Daniel always makes against his wife in front of Alibaba is June's nearly addictive behavior of shopping for the sake of shopping or spending money without a purpose. After dropping off their children at school, June likes shopping with her jobless housewife friends from store to store and from mall to mall across the metropolitan region. From Daniel's telling, Alibaba can clearly paint a picture about some of the dire consequences from June's shopping habits: unused or unusable items piled up in closets and throughout the garage; dishes left in the sink until the next meal, dinners skipped from time to time, attention to children delayed for days, or house thrown into disorder or uncleanness for an unbearable period; and, most critically, considerable payments to make to various credit card accounts every month.

Alibaba also hears an unusual secret from Daniel: June seems to be quite demanding on her sexual gratifications. After working hard, Daniel tends to fall asleep as soon as he lies in bed. Living in fear and worry, Daniel does not seem to have a great deal of interest in sex. As a habit of avoidance or an unconscious strategy of defense, Daniel likes working late and sneaking into bed when June is already in deep sleep. However, there are still weekly nightmares, according to Daniel, when he is somehow manipulated, played, or hypnotized into sex by June in the middle of the night. Exhausted from such horrific experiences, Daniel sometimes feels as if he were sleepwalking on his way to work or daydreaming over his duty in the workplace.

The Discriminator

Daniel's wife, June, seems to be a discriminator in this case. Whether it is a situation Daniel and June are thrown into unavoidably, economic dependence of June and their children upon Daniel and his job-derived income puts tremendous pressure upon Daniel. Daniel needs a wife who shoulders everyday care for the children, who pursues shrewd and thrifty practices in family affairs, and who insulates husband from all household chores. Whether it is a circumstance Daniel and June agree to or embrace, the choice by June to stay home explicitly or implicitly stipulates that she manages and keeps home as a safe haven, a comfort zone, or a backstage of total relaxation for Daniel. Instead, June presents Daniel with mountains of bills to pay month after month, disorganized family scenes to face here and there, and seemingly uncultured demands for sexual gratification to meet now and then.

On close examination, June does not work; she lets Daniel face all the stress in the world of competition: looking for a job, keeping a job, and coping with fear of losing the job. June does not bring in any income; she sets the stage for Daniel to work overtime, take on multiple assignments, and struggle hard to remain completely employed. June does not exercise proper caution and necessary discipline in family expenditure; she makes Daniel bear a constant pressure to keep the family out of debt. June does not always keep the house in order; she frustrates Daniel sometimes with no dinner at the table, kids watching TV or playing games late in the night, or no clean clothes for the next working day.

Emotionally, June hardly takes Daniel's perspective as a salaried worker; she often complains to Daniel: "Why are you always so busy with, so tired of, and so stressed out from work?" June rarely understands the persistent effort Daniel makes in supporting the family; she likes presenting Daniel with one comparison after another: "Diana's husband gets a promotion, April's husband takes home a big bonus, and Virginia's husband makes three times as you do!" June seldom commits time to Daniel for some heart-to-heart conversations or just an after-dinner walk; she rushes to shop with her friends whenever she figures that she can count on Daniel to look after the children or clean the house. June pays little attention to Daniel, his physique, and his affection; she threatens Daniel a few times that she would seek a boyfriend when Daniel seems so overwhelmed by her in bed.

The Victim

Daniel becomes a clear victim in the relationship he has with June. First, Daniel is pushed into a corner where he has no choice but work, working hard to obtain promotions, working overtime to increase the amount of his paycheck, and working in fear to prevent loss of employment. While Daniel knows and understands his financial responsibilities to support June and their two children in the best terms possible, he sometimes feels that he is to some degree exploited by his wife, who by all means could and should make an effective effort in stemming her wasteful shopping habits, curbing overall family spending, and practicing a frugal lifestyle in tune to their economic situation.

Second, Daniel is maximized in his utility for housework. Daniel does not have much free time from work after all. However, whenever he is home, June would waste no time putting him in immediate use. For example, soon after he arrives home from work, June would ask him to check homework for their children, wash laundry, or make the table for dinner. Most critically, June leaves a whole messy house to Daniel every time she knows that Daniel will stay home in the next several hours or over a week-end day. Indeed, the time when Daniel wishes to breathe freely from work always turns into the time he has to clean and reorganize things at home. Put in different words, Daniel's time of release from work is his time of hard labor at home, and Daniel's time of labor at home is June's time of freedom from the house, specifically, her time of fun in shopping, visiting friends, or idling in a beauty salon.

Third, Daniel is stretched thin, and at times beyond limit, in his libidinal energy. Work, stress, and fear take a heavy toll on Daniel. In his early forties, Daniel already experiences frequent lack of desire for sex and occasional erectile dysfunction while in bed with his wife. Although he is reluctant to blame June for channeling much of her bodily energy through sexual gratification, Daniel still wishes that his wife would not so bluntly use him as a sort of sex machine. Instead, he wishes that his wife would cultivate and maintain with him a joint interest in sex and intimacy for the lifetime of their love and marriage.

THE COMPROMISE

Daniel and June are both committed to their marriage although they each sometimes wish that they had a better spouse, making more money or taking better care of the family.

On the part of June, she feels she has given up much she sees some of her friends enjoying in their lives. She loves shopping, but does in her mind struggle hard not to buy many items she wants to have dearly, purchase things with discounts or smart-savings coupons as much as possible, and return merchandise once she realizes that she can live without it. She feels a strong sense of guilt and offers to comfort her husband when she sees Daniel wresting with bills. In the matter of housework, June chooses not to use any cleaning service, cook home meals most of the time, transport children to and from school, and manage family affairs with various economically sensible measures. With regard to sex, June understands that Daniel is five years older, works hard, faces a considerable amount of stress, and experiences some kind of chronic fatigue. Only she knows in her own consciousness that she has on many times and occasions made serious efforts to hold back, divert, or conceal her desires for intimacy with her husband.

Daniel also has June's perspective in mind from time to time. June is an intelligent, life-loving, and energetic person. It is not easy for her to stay home in the first place. Indeed, with proper training and opportunities, June could have a successful career in a variety of professions. As a home-maker though, June is not perfect in keeping everything in prime shape. But by no means should she be imprisoned at home all the time like a cleaning lady, a nanny, a cook, or an all-way housekeeper. She deserves time to be out shopping, being with her friends, or just relaxing in beauty salons. The question is not about whether June should do all those womanly things, but rather about how much Daniel as an able husband makes those things available to his wife. In a similar line, Daniel can only thank his wife for her lively sexual interest in him. What is life? Life is not being a workaholic. With due conscience, Daniel knows that to a large degree it is June, her active interest, and her refreshing energy that keep him what he should be, a husband, a father, and ultimately a man in life.

The Universal

Every marriage is unique. The give-and-take between husband and wife cannot be precisely measured, methodically calculated, and absolutely equaled. There are, however, families where contributions or sacrifices by one spouse are so apparently out of his or her due proportion that he or she may be considered and sympathized by the community of neighbors, workmates, relatives, and friends as an unfortunate victim of relationship, circumstance, or fate.

In a society of middle-class self-sufficiency, a nonworking spouse who spends out of necessity the other spouse's sole income, who does not adequately perform the job of a homemaker, and who does not have many other choices than sex to channel the idleness of unemployment and the boredom or tiredness of housekeeping routines can be easily singled out as to blame or even a heartless discriminator. The working spouse, on the other hand, is often praised as a nobleperson of sacrifice because he or she has to triumph in the world of competition, shoulder the financial responsibility for his or her loved ones, and serve as a de facto pillar of support and stability in his or her family. The stress he or she bears from work, the tiredness he or she shows at the dinner table, and the sexual ineptitude he or she suffers in bed can all be counted as specifics of his or her overall victimization experience in the marital and familial relationship.

Feelings of discrimination or victimization can obviously translate into arguments, fights, and other forms of tension between husband and wife. Nevertheless, negotiation, compromise, and understanding often gain force and currency, keeping many families phenomenally intact despite some of their common and essential flaws, such as emotional incompatibility and economic inequality between spouses.

SITUATION 3

The United States has for generations been one of the most popular destinations for emigration in the world. Immigrants come to the country first by themselves through work, by way of study, or in the name of political asylum or business travel. Once they secure a standing on their own, many immigrants work to bring their spouse, children, parents, and even relatives for reunion in America.

The Particular

In graduate school, Alibaba got to know Jung by sharing office with him. Jung came from a foreign country, living on meager research assistantship while working on his Ph.D. in a discipline of science.

Beginning the second semester into his doctoral study, Jung petitioned to the university to provide all necessary documents for his wife to join him in the United States. He visited offices and officers on and off campus, advised his wife over the phone, and wrote to some of the officials at his former employer, where his wife was working at the time as well. With months of serious work and coordination, he was finally able to send his wife to the U.S. embassy to obtain her visa in the capital of his home country. He saved money creatively and relentlessly so that he had enough savings to show in his bank statement to defray most of the cost incurred in the process of the application and to purchase the air ticket for his wife to travel to North America.

As soon as his wife reunited with him, Jung took her to the church, the university, and many other occasions to make new friends and to gain exposure to various facets of American society. He also helped her apply for school, look for temporary employment, and build a network of everyday contacts. Life was hectic and simple yet meaningful and with hope for both of them.

Less than one year after their reunion, Jung's wife was admitted to a graduate program at another university for herself. Young, pretty, and intelligent, she quickly became a favorite of her chief advisor. The research assistantship she was initially offered soon changed into full-time employment as a research associate. She started bringing home more income than Jung. Most noticeably, she seemed to have quite a few opportunities to travel with her chief advisor to academic conferences in various places.

One day following a conference trip with her chief advisor, Jung's wife told him that she needed to move out to an apartment close to her own university. Jung was shocked in disbelief but nonetheless had to take the harsh reality of her unchangeable mind. Separation lasted a few months, dotted by meetings of fierce arguments and fights. As the relationship deteriorated, Jung eventually signed the paperwork for divorce filed by his wife.

Haunted by the emotional trauma of divorce, Jung struggled for a considerable time as a poor doctoral candidate. While still with an uncertain future in the fourth year of breakup, Jung coincidentally learned that his former wife had just landed a tenure-track position in a local liberal arts college, had recently married her former chief advisor, and was expecting a child with her new husband in a few months.

The Discriminator

According to the story told by Jung, Alibaba felt that Jung's wife was a discriminating opportunist. She used Jung first to leave her unpromising past when she worked on a regular job in their home country and then to adapt to a new environment when she landed in the United States as a first-year alien. She abandoned Jung when she found a man of greater utility toward her personal gain and success.

Specifically, Jung's wife exploited her marriage with Jung in three dimensions. First on the financial dimension, Jung's wife used the money earned by Jung with his "blood and sweat" when she applied for her passport and visa, when she traveled from their home country, and when she looked for school and employment in the United States. She received and spent Jung's money as if she were deservedly entitled to it in the role of his rightful wife. She neither offered to return any money nor reached out to somehow assist Jung at the time when she lived in affluence, yet she watched her former husband struggling economically.

In terms of time, Jung's wife made Jung spend hour after hour searching for information for her visa, job, and school, calling for assistance with her various applications, advising her, or just comforting her. For countless times, Jung messed up course assignments, missed appointments with advisors, or postponed prescheduled commitments because he had to work on a document for his wife, prepare her for an interview, or take her to a meeting. Jung's wife drew a lot of attention from Jung while with him but never bothered to inquire about Jung after divorce from him.

Emotionally, Jung's wife never spared her words in saying how much she missed Jung day and night when she was still back in their home country, how much she wanted to fly to Jung's side when she obtained her visa, and how much she loved Jung when she saw him make one serious effort after another helping her gain ground in the United States. However, she gave Jung only a few simple words when she suddenly said she wanted to move out. In the following months of separation, she even bitterly suggested to Jung that he was not good enough for her and that for the good of her life could he please leave her alone.

The Victim

Jung shared his story with Alibaba and other people who were close to him to a large degree because he wished to express his sense of being victimized. Abandoned by a woman in whom he had invested so much of his income, time, and emotion, Jung would need a lifetime to understand and recover from this misfortune.

First, Jung was pushed behind his graduate studies and career pursuits. During the months of separation, Jung could barely stay focused to do any coursework. In the aftermath of divorce, Jung even thought of pulling out of school to go back to his home country or just to disappear from everyone he knew in the land that was so foreign to him. It was through many sleepless nights of soul-searching struggle that Jung finally got back to normal. However, the grand dream of working toward a successful professional career was gone. Jung seemed to be only capable of handling one thing at a time in everyday routines.

Second, Jung was forced out of his planned life course to become a supportive husband and a caring father. Since marriage to his wife, Jung had not thought of anything other than loving her, living with her, assisting her with school, work, and career, and making her feel all happy. He dreamed of raising a few children and striving side by side with her toward a common goal of both successful professional career and prosperous family life. Now with divorce, Jung was left in pain and total loss of hope.

Third, Jung was forever changed in his views about women, people, and life. For a long time, he was afraid of talking to any woman around. He was even instinctually inclined to shun people in general. Life to him was no longer promising, but rather seemed in every term tricky and treacherous. Perhaps this drastic change of view helped Jung later become a more careful person in everyday life. However, wouldn't it be nice and like a fairy tale if someone could always feel freely that people are mostly trustworthy in the world?

Of course, if he were stronger in character or had a more easygoing attitude toward marriage, Jung could have a totally different experience of what happened between him and his wife. Regardless of intensity, though, victimization did fall upon Jung, with its source pointing all toward the woman whom he loved out of innocence and in purity.

The Compromise

Despite the shock he felt initially and the pain he experienced for a considerable amount of time, Jung eventually forgave his former wife and went on with his own life. Even at the height of divorce, Jung did not set any demanding condition that his wife return all the money he accountably spent on her from application of travel documents, purchase of air and other transportation tickets, and preparation of job and school materials to maintenance of everyday life between reunion and separation. Nor did Jung make any suggestion that his wife explicitly or implicitly compensate him for all the time and emotion he had unselfishly invested in her so that she could come to the United States and find a professional career and a private life she perceived to be good for herself. In fact, Jung never bothered his former wife, even when he still struggled financially in graduate school and when she already lived in comfort and affluence.

Jung's wife, according to people in the network to which both of them have access, never said any negative words about Jung. In her mind, Jung is a gentleman of kindness. She forever is grateful for what Jung did for her, her career, and her life. Although she had not done anything in actuality, she sincerely wishes that she could somehow pay back Jung. Perhaps as she grows older, she could find more meaningful ways to express her inner feelings or at least she could wander more in memory of the time she had with Jung, striving for their once joint dream of career success and real-life happiness.

The Universal

It is common that someone follows a person of close relationship toward a widely known or generally perceived destination of professional success, material affluence, or secular happiness. It is also not uncommon that the beneficiary of such a following would later change his or her attitude or position, walking away from, turning against, or even becoming a bitter enemy to the original benefactor. The paired roles in question could range from husband–wife in marriage, master–apprentice in craftsmanship, and advisor–student in academe to patron–protégé across various social arenas.

The sense of discrimination or victimization felt by a benefactor in the case of his or her beneficiary's transgression or betrayal can be generally warranted by both fact and assumption. At an assumptive level, it is taken for granted that wife submit to husband, apprentice yield to master, student listen to advisor, and protégé remain loyal to patron in their mutual relationships. As long as the latter is present, the former should exercise proper caution, restraint, and respect in voicing opinions, assuming positions, forging new relations, or adventuring into new areas. As a matter of fact, many benefactors out of their self-perceived obligations may indeed invest heavily in their counterparts. In the case of Jung, he did everything he felt he ought to do for his wife as a caring, loving, and responsible husband without ever thinking what if she would one day leave him permanently.

Although there is no lack of famous cases of total animosity and bitterness from history or in the celebrity circle, compromise can always take place, keeping a now broken pair at least in good memory of their former close relationship.

SITUATION 4

Sex not only divides men from women in general, but it also differentiates both sides of the sexual divide into privileged men versus disadvantaged women in particular. While it is common that older men take younger women as wife, mistress, or even concubine, it is rare that aged women can ever secure junior men as spouse, lover, or just cohabitant.

The Particular

Alibaba and his family live in an affluent community. Among the neighbors they know, there are quite a few couples where the husband is years older than the wife. For example, Couple "A" involves a state legislator who married his twenty-year-younger wife when she worked in his district office as a field representative; Couple "B" combines a widowed professor with his fifteen-year-junior graduate student; and Couple "C" features a small business owner who, upon separation from his former wife at the age of fifty-five, went back to his home country to marry a young girl just out of high school.

The most interesting combination, however, is Couple "D," whom Alibaba knows well. The couple met at a business conference ten years ago when the husband, John, was an upper-level manager of a sizable corporation and the wife, Sarah, was a trainee of a smaller company in the city. They started dating as John was seemingly able to mentor Sarah into the profession of business management. A few months later, Sarah at age twenty-four married John in his middle forties, a divorcé with two children.

Life after marriage has been a challenge for Sarah. In the first two years, Sarah worked hard with John's two children to get them accept her as their stepmother. She put a great deal of her heart and time into the caring of them while hearing an earful of swear words from them. In the beginning, she even cried when her stepchildren became so wickedly uncooperative, especially after they visited their mother and maternal relatives every other weekend. Soon after she had her stepchildren under control, Sarah started seeing John struggling with erectile dysfunction. Out of fear or shame, John would make various excuses to go to bed late when she had already fallen asleep, to sleep in his home office, or to take unnecessary business or nonbusiness trips out of town. Beginning in her middle to late twenties, Sarah knew she suffered dearly from an acute hunger for sex. Now after years of unsatisfying sex amid often long periods of no sex, Sarah wonders whether she still has her natural instinct for carnal gratification at all.

Most shockingly, John was found to have diabetes and a heart condition following a comprehensive physical examination last month. In addition to making a range of necessary changes in diet, exercise, and everyday life, John was advised to reduce both the load and the intensity of work on his job. Coincidentally in the company where John has for years climbed to its higher echelon, there are ongoing chats and gossips about various cost-cutting measures, including replacement of highly paid management personnel with new hires of similar qualifications at a much lower salary. Fearful of becoming such a casualty, John feels he needs to work harder and more to prove his worth to the company.

In contrast, Sarah has just entered the golden period of her professional career. With effort, intelligence, and luck, she can achieve considerable upward mobility within the company she works for now and beyond in the future. However, in the prospect of an aging, ailing husband who may soon end his working life either through early retirement or untimely termination, Sarah will surely have to give up or pass by many opportunities that come naturally her way.

The Discriminator

In a close relationship like marriage, it can never be clear and precise to document and measure how much one side takes unfair, unwarranted advantage of the other. On the very surface, it is nonetheless apparent that John discriminates Sarah in three dimensions.

First and foremost, John steals youth, the often neglected yet most valuable asset an individual possesses in his or her life, from Sarah. While there is nothing wrong with older men dating, loving, and having sex with younger women once in a while, much can go unnatural, unjust, and even evil when a politically powerful, economically bountiful, intellectually knowledgeable, or otherwise resourceful male takes custody, ownership, or possession of an innocent, generation-younger girl as his wife in the name of family. John was more than twenty years older than Sarah when he locked her into his second marriage. Did he care enough to ever imagine that he would not be able to work compatibly with Sarah in bed and many other areas, making her enjoy and appreciate what she deserves to enjoy and appreciate as a woman of her early, middle, and late twenties, thirties, forties, so on and so forth?

Second, John burdens Sarah with the care of his two children. John did not miss or compromise his experience as a man of his twenties, thirties, and early forties. He enjoyed sex, in all its intensity, colorfulness, and excitement, with his first wife through late youth, early adulthood, and the mature middle-age. He had two children calling and embracing him as father. Then he somehow became bored and tired. He bowed out of marriage. As he looked for new excitement in life, he also had a clear intent to get the burden from the past out of his hand to someone else. Ironically, this essentially selfish intent often figures in the court of public opinion as an unselfish attempt for the sake of children: "He needs to marry someone and restart a family in the best interest of his kids." John found Sarah. The responsibility of taking care of his two children from the past marriage thereby fell rightfully and gloriously upon Sarah.

Third, John now needs Sarah to comfort him as he wrestles with the fear of being forced into early retirement or terminated untimely for the company to save salary payment and to make way for new talents. Most critically, he depends upon Sarah to care for him as he ages with chronic diseases. To assist John with his health, Sarah has consulted a variety of sources for a new family diet. She often makes phone calls to remind John to check his blood sugar after lunch at work or following each meal when John is away on a trip. The call of reminder applies to all the medications John has to take on a daily basis as well. In bed, Sarah has now totally shut down her own desires. She only responds to John. And even in those rare occasions when John makes an advance, Sarah will have to pause to see if she can comfortably take it given John's medical conditions. It is sad and awkward that at her golden age Sarah has to withhold all her natural wants and feelings, acting rather like a nanny, mother, or grandmother for her older husband.

The Victim

No matter how Sarah perceives and acts upon the exploiting marriage she has with John, taking it as a matter of her fate or embracing it out of a genuine love for her husband, she inevitably and virtually bears all the bruises and wounds inflicted by such a markedly unequal and essentially unfair relationship.

Physically, to John's two children, Sarah feeds them, chauffeurs them from school to extracurricular activities and sometimes even to their maternal relatives, shops for them, reads stories at their bedsides, and comforts them when they have trouble in school or with their own daddy or mommy; for John himself she prepares meals, does laundry, implements health plans, administers medications, and observes various don'ts in bed. Whereas serving as a loving stepmother is strenuous, acting as a caring wife is by no means less labor-intensive. For example, making a series of adjustments such as dampening, diverting, withholding, or forgoing carnal interests and desires in bed to accommodate a generation-older husband can be especially energy-consuming and body-fatiguing. Not typically at her age, Sarah nonetheless has already seen some early aging traces and scars on her hands, face, hair, skin, and even her whole body.

In emotional terms, Sarah has severed a number of boy- and girlfriends at her age. For girls, she somehow felt they were immaturely out of pace with the prevailing sentiments she had right after her marriage with John. For boys, she stopped seeing or communicating with them simply because she did not want to raise any eyebrows from her sensitive husband. Investing heavily in John's two children in the first several years, Sarah did not have much time to experiment with the colorful world people of her age are entitled to enjoy. Because of the same reason, Sarah did not make any plans for raising her own children either. Unfortunately by the time she felt ready to give birth to a child, Sarah found it already too late to become pregnant with John. They consulted with one specialist after another. None of them offered any words of promise upon examination of John's medical conditions. It was a blow to Sarah. For a couple of years, Sarah wrestled to accept the reality while never ceasing her due effort in bed. Obviously, had she married to a man around her age, she would have not faced this deep regret of a lifetime. Most important, she would have been able to procure pleasure from sex at a frequency as well as intensity appropriate to people of her age for decades, not just a few years. Now in the middle ages, Sarah has to throw her heart, many years earlier than her due time, into the dusk of life when worry over declining body functions, deteriorating mind alertness, and even death takes the center stage. Again if it were not for John and his aging and ailing physique, Sarah for herself would and should have all the wonderful feel of life with all its vivacity and vitality.

Professionally, Sarah asked for time off, called in sick with emergencies, and gave up a number of business trips and training opportunities when she struggled in her role as a competent stepmother. The years in which she learned about and coped with the fact that she might not be able to carry any child with John also cast a shadow over her work. Of course, a more critical time has just arrived recently with John's health. The pressure to bend on her career aspiration looms seemingly large in the horizon. Indeed, Sarah worries so much about her husband's medical conditions that she has made up her mind to do whatever necessary to treat, care, and comfort him, including taking a leave from job, forgoing opportunities for upward movements, and even pulling out of her professional career indefinitely. The current state of affairs, as far as her job is concerned, is that Sarah is in the heyday of her working career. With her talents and diligence, she has great potential to move higher up in the top echelon of her company.

The Compromise

In his consciousness and unconsciousness, John holds a sense of guilt toward Sarah for exploiting her youth while rarely satisfying her sexual needs. He makes an effort to compensate Sarah by acting as a seasoned, tempered fatherly figure in their marital relationship. He hears Sarah complain, cry, and sometimes even scream on both work and nonwork issues, making her feel she has a solid shoulder to lean on or an ultimate shelter to seek refuge in during the time of frustration, disappointment, and failure. John also shares his experience, presents his perspectives, and extends his encouragement whenever Sarah has a question or problem at work or in the matter of family affairs. Because he thinks in the best interest of Sarah, John seems to give her the best possible advice, insights, and support in almost everything she faces in life.

Sarah, on the other hand, does not always carry a feeling of sacrifice for the sake of John, his children, his career, and his health. In times when she feels overwhelmed with two uncooperative stepchildren, Sarah reminds herself that she loves John, she made her own choice of marrying him, and as wife she has an alienable responsibility for the family. At moments when she wonders why she has put herself through those difficulties, Sarah convinces herself that the real world does not mean to be perfect; John is her man of choosing, and she has to embrace what she has to fulfill in the meaning of life. As a matter of fact, Sarah never threatens John with words of leaving. She does her duties as wife and stepmother faithfully, methodically, and laboriously.

Of course, the ultimate test of the couple's mutual accommodation inheres in the fact that John and Sarah have been living together as wife and husband for nearly ten years and will by every possible indication remain married for an indefinite time to come, perhaps until the very end of life on one side of the formula.

The Universal

Patriarchal mentality is deeply rooted in societies around the world. Although in industrialized countries patriarchal authority is neither officially recognized nor legally sanctified, it still holds firm and strong, permeating almost every relationship involving men and women.

With a ubiquitous presence of patriarchal influence, men of power, wealth, knowledge, or experience prove not only priceless, but also irresistible to women, oftentimes regardless of the latter's social backgrounds, professional pursuits, and personal lifestyles. Whereas women of lower socioeconomic status sell nakedly their youth and beauty to rich men in the form of marriage for a perceived better life, women of political, entrepreneurial, intellectual, artistic, or other promise and potentiality also seek men of expertise, connection, or influence as familial life partners toward success. There are even situations, including some widely known celebrity cases, where women of professional success are so indebted to or mind-controlled by their masters, mentors, advisors, coaches, or business managers that they dedicate their much younger life to these male figures in the name of wife or even without a socially legitimate name as in the pernicious role of a mistress.

As illustrated by the marriage of John and Sarah, common discriminations falling upon a generation-younger wife include forced service as stepmother, compromised experience in bed, assumed failure in bearing children, and superimposed early onset of senior age and fear of declining health. With each and all of these likely victimizations in sight, can women be risk-taking, flexible, and forbearing enough to compromise? Hopefully, as society changes in the direction of a waning patriarchal influence, it will see less and less, eventually no, need to ask anybody in one half of its population to make such a compromise in life.

SITUATION 5

Despite stories of negligent and abusive caretakers from the mass media and in everyday life, most parents raise and support their children with all their hearts. In contrast, while adults are not often exposed in the public when they fail to take care of their elderly parents in the industrial age, a great majority of them do not actually assume much responsibility for those who reared them and facilitated their growth and progress in various stages of life.

The Particular

Alibaba has a family friend who runs a private nursing home business for senior citizens. Because they are often asked to assist with birthday or holiday celebration parties at the facility, Alibaba and his wife get to know almost all of those elderly people under their friend's care.

Some common characteristics shared by all these residents that strike Alibaba and his wife are: they have adult children; they miss seeing but hardly receive visits from their family members; and none of their care is paid for by adult children. In fact, there are residents whose adult children work as doctors, lawyers, professors, corporate executives, business owners, or in other professional capacities. Although they take pride in talking about their children, most of these elderly people also express regret explicitly or implicitly that they are often forgotten or virtually abandoned by the ones they have cared and loved so much all in their lives.

Gene is one of them. He and his wife raised three children, John, Aileen, and George. They worked diligently, saved smartly, and invested heavily in each of their children. To send their children to one of the best schools in the area, Gene commuted a long time every day, his wife quit her job of promise, and the whole family lived in a crowded apartment instead of a spacious house. To prevent one of their children from biting off his tongue in a seizure, Gene's wife instinctually put her fingers in between his teeth. In difficult economic times, Gene and his wife yielded to their children in food, clothing, and other daily articles. It was once a family routine that Gene and his wife ate after each of their children filled their ever-insatiable stomachs of their growing bodies.

With careful planning and unwavering support, Gene and his wife oversaw all their children graduate from elite schools into high-paying jobs, with the first being a doctor at a university hospital, the second becoming a partner of an established law firm, and the third working as a research scientist at a leading pharmaceutical company. Since each of their children is preoccupied with a professional career, Gene and his wife never expected to burden any of them with care when they entered their senior ages. Ten years ago, Gene retired from his job to join his wife, who quit working at sixty. In the following seven years of retirement, Gene and his wife enjoyed quite a leisurely life. They visited their children, volunteered to look after some of their grandkids, and entertained all or most of their children and grandkids in their own home on birthdays or major holidays.

Three years ago, Gene's wife was diagnosed with stomach cancer. Although calls were frequently made and visits were occasionally paid by their children and grandkids, it was Gene who accompanied and cared for her through tests, the surgery, and postoperative treatments. Most sadly, Gene's wife was not even able to see any of their children at her bedside when she passed away.

Gene experienced a sharp decline in health in the aftermath of his wife's death. With difficulty living on his own and without a viable option of staying with any one of his own children, he moved to the nursing home run by Alibaba's friend. In the past one and half years since he took residency, Gene has received only a few occasional visits from his children and grandkids. There were important anniversaries and holidays Gene quietly observed all by himself. The last time his three children came together to see him was an occasion where they talked about how Gene would leave his wealth divided among them after death.

The Discriminator

Although it is no longer the case that people take complete care of their elderly parents in industrial societies, it is still a laudable deed that adult children support and comfort their aging mother and father in various sensible ways until the end of life.

First, while Gene and his wife raised their children with a whole heart, none of their children seems to throw much passion behind their parents over health care and medical treatment. For their mother in particular, a better health plan might have caught her cancer earlier, a more experienced surgeon might have done a better job in operation, and a more advanced medical facility might have rendered a higher-quality postoperative care, all of which could have lessened her sufferings and perhaps lengthened her life. In fact, Gene's s first child as a practicing physician at a reputable university hospital did not even bother to tap into his own professional knowledge and network for possibly far better care of his mother. In consideration of cost and other complications, he stood idle just to let his mother live and die with the much poorer local health plan she had had for most of her life.

Second, whereas Gene and his wife tightened their belts for the best possible future of their children, none of their children seems to be so ready to contribute to a relatively homey life for their parents. Following his wife's death, Gene wished dearly that he could stay in his own house, where he and his wife lived for a long time. He also dreamed that he would be invited to live with one of his children or rotate from one child to another. And in the very least he hoped that he would stay in a scaled nursing home facility, where he could participate in a variety of activities with a spectrum of senior peers. Indeed, with the fortune each of his children has made from professional work, any of them, needless to say the three of them in combination, could handily hire a qualified homecare service person to live with Gene at his own home or make proper arrangements in their individual houses for Gene to live with them. Instead, they chose to let Gene go where his own savings could take him, that is, the small-sized nursing home run by Alibaba's friend.

Third, despite the fact that Gene and his wife made every effort in work and life to meet their children's desires, wants, and needs, none of their children seems to be so willing to take time to call, visit, and accompany their parents. Gene notified each of their children when he knew his wife had only days to live. Two of their children came home but went out to dealing with their own things in town on the following day. As a result, only Gene remained at her bedside when she forever closed her eyes. Now at the nursing home operated by Alibaba's friend, Gene is left with a prevailing feeling of loneliness. There are telephone calls from children and grandkids, but these calls are all brief and come only a few times in a long month. There are visits by children and grandkids, but these visits are all flashy and happen like some random spots throughout a whole year.

It ought to be pointed out nonetheless that Gene's three children are by all means normal contemporaries. They fall in the category of discriminators against their own parents to a large degree because they are culturally, professionally, and socially set up to be so. In other words, homecare, nursing home, insurance, and governmental programs, such as Medicare and Social Security in the United States, are so laid out to aid senior citizens so that most adult children can choose to do the minimum in the care of their elderly parents.

The Victim

As parents, Gene and his wife never expected to reap every penny, plus a calculable profit, that they had invested in their children. In fact, they made conscionable efforts in planning their senior life so that they would not burden their children in any foreseeable way. On the other hand, are there any parents in the world who would not wish to have frequent visits from their children when they live alone in nursing homes, who would not hope to have best possible treatments when they fight serious diseases, and who would not crave attention and companionship from their children as they move toward the end of life? For Gene and his wife, there were unfortunately many moments of disappointment and sadness in their late-age experience with children.

An unforgettable incident in Gene's memory was when he asked his first child, the practicing physician, to look for and transfer his wife to a better medical facility for treatment when she was diagnosed with stomach cancer. The response from his son sounded irrefutable but to Gene was just a series of excuses to dodge a reasonable plea for support: "Treatment for stomach cancer is fairly standard from hospital to hospital; neither a more reputable hospital nor a more famous doctor has a magical wand to cure a disease that is essentially incurable; the personal physician Mommy has had for years should have a deeper understanding for and therefore a better treatment plan for her; and it is not good to remove a terminal ill person from his or her familiar environment to an unfamiliar setting where he or she has to make an additional effort to adapt." When Gene complained to his other two children, he was surprised that they both said only this: "Trust the brother. He is a doctor." As a result, Gene had to comfort his wife to rest with her current care, removing an almost sensational hope from her struggling mind.

Another unforgettable incident took place when Gene suggested to his three children that he could live with them on a rotating basis or if they each would help find and fund a reliable homecare service so that he could stay in his own home. With regard to his first suggestion, Gene gathered these responses: "Daddy, you probably don't want to mess around with my four little kids"; "You know Diana turned down a similar request from her mommy, my mother-in-law"; and "Daddy, you won't be happy to move from place to place. You will end up without any feel of home at all." Gene's second suggestion did not fare any better either: "Daddy, I am pretty overwhelmed with my work now. Check with Aileen and George to see if they can help"; "It's no easy task to find a reliable homecare person. In addition, you will have to worry about all those bills you pay continuously for the maintenance of the house"; and "Daddy, you and Mommy think of us all the time. You both always want us to focus on our job and take care of our own life and family. I think it's best to move into a nursing home so that you won't worry a bit about burdening any of us in your last years." Reluctantly, Gene sold his home to take residency in the nursing home operated by Alibaba's friend.

Now a salient feeling hanging around in Gene's mind is whether his children and grandkids will answer the plea he made for a sooner comeback when they visited him last time. Gene remembers the birthdays of all his children and grandkids. He extends his congratulatory greetings over the phone or by mail on days of personal importance to all of them. But he is not sure if each of his children and grandkids remembers his birthday because he only receives a few calls or postcards on that day. Insofar as face-to-face visit is concerned, he can only wish that he would be the happiest father and grandfather in the world when all his children and grandkids come to celebrate his birthday next time.

The Compromise

Like most other parents, Gene and his wife adopted a philosophy that forever keeps them on the side of their children. When they hear children talk back harshly without due appreciation for their sacrifice, they would comfort themselves with these words: "They are growing up with a lot of frustrations to face at this time"; "They are career professionals having various pressures to deal with all the time"; and "They just have a bad moment." When they see children act selfishly without basic regard for their interests, they would convince themselves with these lines of reasoning: "Isn't it our hope that they take care of themselves?"; "Don't we wish that they know what they want and work hard for what they aim for?"; or "Aren't we happy that they prosper and triumph in their own terms?" Suppose some of their children engaged in criminal wrongdoings, tarnishing the reputation they have in the community. Gene and his wife would with no doubt have rushed to the defense of their children, at least with this public statement: "Nothing can change the fact that they are our kids. We love them regardless of what they do and have done."

In action, Gene and his wife never make their giving of care and support to children and grandkids conditional to what they have garnered from the latter. Suppose they just had a bitter argument with John. Gene and his wife would still look after grandkids if John left the kids with them. Suppose they just had a negative experience in their visit with Aileen and her family. Gene and his wife would still loan or give her money if Aileen made such a request. Suppose they just received a negative response from George to their plea for assistance. Gene and his wife would still attend his house if George counted on them to do so. Toward his last years of life, although he has quite mixed feelings about his children in their handling of his wife's treatment and his own care, Gene still takes every limited visit he has with John, Aileen, and George to talk about how they may benefit from the inheritances he and his wife have left for them, how they shall take care of their own careers and families, and how they must keep their mutual bonds as brother and sister.

Gene's children, for their part, have various plausible explanations in their minds as well. On the one hand, they seem to be ready to say: "They are our parents. We love them. We will definitely do something if they are really serious about it." For example, John might claim: "I would have transferred my mommy to a better medical facility had my daddy insisted me to do so just to give my mommy a stronger sense of hope." On the other hand, Gene's children may resort to this justification: "Nobody else than us knows our parents better. They would not feel comfortable at all if they know we have to pay a large amount of money or spend a great deal of time for this kind of care or treatment. They have been living a simple life. It's best to let them continue what they are so accustomed to in their senior age." Perhaps Aileen can note this at her daddy's funeral in the future: "Daddy spent his last years in a small nursing home. He did not ask anything from us children. He can now forever take comfort in seeing that he and Mommy have never burdened us children whom they cared, supported, and loved so wholeheartedly in their lives." Most important, Gene's children can make themselves feel at peace with the minimal care and support they give to their parents because they reason that they have put their maximal efforts in living up to the full expectations of their parents as successful career professionals and happy family persons. Isn't it a great irony that children consciously or unconsciously view faithfully fulfilling parents' dreams for children's success as the ultimate reason why they may compromise on care and support for parents who have wished and done all the best for children?

The Universal

While there are parents who abandon their offspring or demand more than they have invested in their children, there are far more adult children who fail or are not able to offer their elderly parents the kind of care and support they used to receive early in life.

A full gamut of situations exists in the contemporary era. On the one extreme, adult children fail to attend their aging parents because they themselves are homeless vagrants, drug addicts, incarcerated inmates, hospitalized mental patients, or otherwise disabled dependents. On the other extreme, adult children do not come to the aid of their ailing parents because they have abandoned, severed relationships with, never been on speaking terms with, or are simply lacking in filial affection for their parents. However, most significant are normal cases where adult children are able to take care of, embrace basic filial sentiments toward, and remain in regular contact with their parents. As clearly and subtly illustrated by the case of Gene, his wife, and their children, neither cultural mentality nor social arrangement in postmodern conditions seems to place much emphasis on optimal care and support from children to parents at the time when the former strive for career success and the latter wane from active contributions to society.

Perhaps it is the law of social progress that necessitates this universal surplus from one generation to another: parents invest more in than they harvest from children. Imagine the opposite, when the older generation takes more than it gives to the younger generation. Society will then run into a deficit, becoming mired in no or negative movement toward a better future.

4   Over the Workplace

The workplace is where one translates one's talents, knowledge, and skills into creation, performance, and productivity; where one compares to others to see how competitive one is; and where one reflects upon one's career-making journey to feel whether one has succeeded in one's professional pursuits (Tilly and Tilly 1998; Kirchmeyer 2002; Hill et al. 2004; Tomaskovic-Devey and Stainback 2007; Vallas, Finlay, and Wharton 2009; Bosanac and Jacobs 2010; Miedaner 2010; Rubin and Brody 2011; Templar 2010; Settles, Sheng, and Zhao 2011; Volti 2011; Ballman 2012; Weisbord 2012).

It is obvious that the workplace involves constant comparisons and contrasts by individuals. Conspicuous discriminations can occur in various organizational aspects, such as recruitment, retention, and promotion, whereas inconspicuous victimizations may take place over personal characteristics, from age, race, and sex to practice in culture, religion, or lifestyle.

SITUATION 1

Employees are hired by companies or organizations for the use of their labor. Karl Marx (1990) argues that workers are exploited because they can never be paid by employers at their labor's full worth. From an employer's point of view, however, while most employees make positive contributions, a few may just drain business resources, strain customer relations, tarnish institutional reputations, or pose as grave liabilities in legal, financial, or political terms.

The Particular

With an advanced degree in his field, Alibaba teaches one course a semester in a local university besides his regular job. In his capacity as a part-time instructor, he knows a few full-time faculty members at the university. One of them is Gregory.

Gregory has been with the university for more than twenty years. In classroom instruction, he is a mediocre performer. He goes to class late often and cancels classes sometimes. Having taught the same set of courses for years, Gregory does not have much new and challenging to offer to students. As a matter of fact, he habitually spends quite a bit of class time talking about news, telling his personal stories, complaining against the university and other establishments, or even admonishing students for coming to the university out of an undeserving academic record. If it were just for his classes, a student with a normal ego would walk out of the university once and forever because for one reason he or she does not learn much from Gregory, and for another he or she gets enough belittlement about the university as well as himself or herself who unfortunately has to attend the university.

In research, Gregory published a few articles years ago when he struggled for tenure. Now as a full professor, he barely reads any current literature and has not published in the scholarly media for a long time. In the name of research, nonetheless, Gregory maintains a whole contingent of laboratory equipment, experimental agents, student assistants, data and software contracts, journal subscriptions, computers, printing devices, and office supplies, all at cost to the university. One time when Alibaba saw him push a large case of copying paper into his office, he heard this from Gregory: "I am going to write a book." But as far as Alibaba knows, he has never seen a book in print by Gregory. Perhaps Gregory can write a book about his only famous or infamous piece of work that brought much negative publicity to the university because of unsubstantiated evidence. Unfortunately, that's Gregory: he does not have many publications to add to the university's academic reputation overall; in one of his few published articles where he lists the university as his affiliated institution, he makes people question the university and its credibility in sponsoring serious academic research.

With regard to service, Gregory has his name on several committees in his department and college within the university. He does not usually attend all the committee meetings and rarely bothers to understand what issue or task he needs to tackle as a committee member. One time when he chaired the faculty recruitment committee in the department, he sarcastically told candidates so many stories of a more negative than positive nature about the department and its standing within the university that none of the finalists took the job. The faculty search hence collapsed despite all the cost it incurred to the department and college.

Now toward his retirement, Gregory has been handpicked by the dean as the acting chair of the department. With the advantage of incumbency, he is by all indications likely to win a formal appointment in that capacity for a full three-year term. As he honestly admits, he assumes the chair's position simply because he will receive a higher annual salary and can further apply it as his peak employment income in the calculation of monthly retirement paychecks provided by the university retirement plan.

The Discriminator

In the era of organizations, there are perceptively smart members who play with institutional rules or the system for self-comfort, hierarchically privileged stakeholders who utilize institutional resources or a whole organizational entity as means or tools toward personal goals, or plainly greedy individuals who contribute as little as possible while taking as much as they can from employers or workplaces.

Gregory appears to be one of those greedy individuals who take advantage of or hold discrimination against institutions. Like many customer-oriented businesses, colleges and universities serve students and their learning needs. Gregory, in his dealings with students inside and outside the classroom, seems to intentionally make them feel that they come to this university because they are not good enough and have nowhere else to go for school. He alienates students, making them develop or keep a negative attitude toward the university. The university obviously hurts when some of its students do not take it seriously, hold no respect for its offerings, or leave it because of unfavorable experiences with the faculty.

Of course, the reputation of a university goes beyond students and their reactions. For the urban comprehensive university in which Gregory works, part of its reputation inheres in faculty contributions to scholarship in various fields. Gregory does little research and has published only a few articles in his lifetime association with the university. While it is questionable how much, if any, Gregory has added to the university and its standing in the academic community with the rest of his publications, it is certain that the one controversial work he put out in the name of the university caused it considerable damage. Insomuch as net contribution to scholarship and the university's academic reputation is concerned, Gregory is definitely in deficit.

In routine contacts with the outside, Gregory does not fare any better in his de facto representation of the university. He habitually complains about his department, college, and university when he converses with scholars and other professionals in academic conferences. He likes making derogative comments about or poking fun at his students, colleagues, and leaders when he engages in casual communications with relatives, friends, neighbors, or even strangers in the community. The recruitment he took to complete failure is one of the most consequential incidents through which Gregory erratically yet consistently speaks of his underlying mindset. Ironically, Gregory receives funding from the university to attend academic conferences or takes credit for running a committee of service. In other words, he deals the university double losses: not just over the court of public opinion, but also financially.

Further, over the financial terms Gregory has with the university, he started off with a salary that was a few steps higher than the average since he skillfully used an offer from another institution as his bargaining chip. Over the years, Gregory exploited quite successfully some organizational loopholes, including a grievance procedure, to push up his salary out of his cohort a few times. Now drawing a twelve-month salary as a department chair instead of a nine-month salary as a regular member of the faculty, he has a nice peak salary in his employment history to make the university pay him handsomely in the years of retirement to come.

The Victim

Organizations employ people to contribute to their causes, goals, or missions. While they already pay employees for the use of labor, they may still have to assume ultimate responsibilities for various liabilities intentionally or unintentionally brought by individual members.

In the case of Gregory, the university becomes a definite victim, not so clearly noticeable, though, of his acts over years of employment. First, the university pays far more than average in salary to Gregory as a regular member of the faculty. Despite a proportionally higher investment in Gregory, however, the university receives much lower than normal in contributions from him. In financial terms, the university might well have suffered a net loss from Gregory's employment. An institution will obviously run aground if it bears losses rather than gains from above a certain number of its employees.

Second, the university might lose some of its existing students when Gregory cultivates in them a negative feeling about it from class to class, from semester to semester, and from year to year. An utterance, such as "you wouldn't be here if you were good," that is so habitually addressed by Gregory can send a powerful message to students, making them drop school or transfer to somewhere else. For prospective students and their parents, guardians, or sponsors who consider enrolling in the university, what else can be more revealing and convincing than these words so readily spoken about the university by a professor who teaches there: "Don't go there unless you absolutely have nowhere else to go"? As a matter of fact, none of Gregory's relatives, friends, and neighbors sends their children to the university. Moreover, by word of mouth, who knows how many other people within and beyond the reach of Gregory and his negative messages about the university do not attend yet could have otherwise applied for admission to it?

Third, the university was caught in negative media coverage when Gregory published his research with questionable evidence. A considerable amount of institutional resources were dispensed to put out the controversy. Another recorded incident was obviously when Gregory blew the recruitment effort he himself was in charge of at his department. The university in a sense lost its face to all academic job seekers who came to see it by way of application. There are, however, far more consequential or inconsequential occasions where Gregory might have prevented or discouraged interested scholars from attending academic events sponsored by, seeking collaboration from faculty members affiliated with, or accepting students graduated from the university. Indeed, while the university might be technically able to calculate its loss of academic reputation from some particular incidents, it has no way to measure how much it has suffered from Gregory's negative expressions about it through day-to-day communications with other scholars as well as over major academic conferences or gatherings in his field.

The Compromise

In many circumstances, an organization cannot simply fire an employee as soon as it realizes that the employee has done or is doing harm to its reputation, its goal or mission, or even its very existence. Compromise often figures in as the best possible approach to prevent further complications.

For Gregory, the university could have terminated him when controversy broke out over his questionable research. The university decided to keep him instead because it figured that firing could shake its position in the eyes of the faculty, bring about intervention from the faculty union and other interest groups, or prompt Gregory to take legal actions. In times when students filed formal complaints against Gregory for his negative comments, the department, the college, or the higher level of administration involved could have censured him or used some of those complaints to affect his tenure and promotion. Nonetheless, they all chose to only communicate student complaints to the attention of Gregory in the hope that he would make necessary corrections on his own. With regard to stories about Gregory making negative expressions or representations about the university in professional and nonprofessional occasions off campus, leaders in different levels frowned initially but essentially shrugged off with comments such as "We cannot follow him to every occasion with some kind of warnings,"; "After all, it is his right to freedom of speech"; "It does not reflect well on himself either when he says bad things about us"; and "You never know, it may make us look good or at least prompt people to take a serious look at us when he attempts to spread a bad image about the university."

From Gregory's point of view, he has stayed with the university even though he has a considerable degree of dissatisfaction with it. In a sense, complaining against it, making negative comments about it, or talking it down serves as a coping mechanism or a working compromise for him to continue his relationship with the university. The university needs instructors to run classes. Gregory has taught all those classes assigned to him semester after semester. The university needs the faculty to maintain laboratories for research and instruction. Gregory spends most of his time on campus in his laboratory year after year. The university aims at productivity and visibility in scholarship. Gregory has published a few articles and is not among the least productive members of the faculty. Now in the position of the department chair, Gregory starts expressing regrets about spreading so much negativity about the university on various occasions. He seriously hopes that he will be able to make up some of the damages he might have caused earlier in the rest of his employment with the university and beyond.

The Universal

An organization hires employees or recruits members, placing them in different positions throughout its hierarchy. Individual employees or members, while trusted with specific duties to make specific contributions, could nonetheless cause various harms, conspicuous or inconspicuous, to the organization.

Conspicuously, employees or members of an organization may steal raw materials, final products, or critical services; they may embezzle money, put organizational resources into personal use, or bill the organization with unwarranted expenses; they may expose the organization unfavorably to the public, take it to the court of law, or demand outrageous compensations or severance packages; they may use the organization to realize their individual dreams, gamble it on their immature ideas or fantasies, or take it to bankruptcy or total breakdown with their ill-conceived agendas or plans. While conspicuous harms and harm-doers can easily catch the limelight from the mass media, inconspicuous harms and harm-doers, such as employees playing on the job, sales clerks whispering money-saving secrets to customers, or members spreading unfavorable news about their home organizations, may often sneak away from public scrutiny. However, as inconspicuous harms can be perpetrated by a whole spectrum of employees or members in different levels or positions on their day-to-day work, they can add up to a fundamental problem or mushroom to a system-wide crisis to an organization.

In direct terms, an organization compromises by approaching member-initiated predatory acts as part of its routine operation, by absorbing costs associated with employee-perpetrated harmful acts, and by still keeping employees who commit discriminatory behavior against it. Individual employees or members, on the other hand, may not be seen offering any immediate concessions to or compensations for the organization to which they may have done harm intentionally or unintentionally through employment. But as buying customers of organizational products or services in the general population, all individuals have to compromise with organizations eventually when the latter pass on higher operational costs in the form of higher prices.

SITUATION 2

The principle of the mean states that people tend to move around the middle in their personal position, fluctuate along the average in their individual performance, or equilibrate toward a modal point in their collective activities. However, when an organizational employer uses the principle of the mean to guide its personnel policies and procedures, a few outstanding performers or so-called "rate busters" can be held in disadvantage at the service of the average, the ordinary, or the regular.

The Particular

Alibaba has a friend named Nathan who works at a research institute. Nathan is a talented intellectual and seems to have an incessant spring of fresh ideas out of his mind all the time. He is energetic and works diligently as well.

In his first year on the job, Nathan initiated two research projects, obtained a prestigious grant, and published three articles in first-rate journals. He accelerated his pace of work and scholarly outputs as he settled fully into his institute through the second year. By the middle of his third year, the middle of the year being when one has to submit one's file for personnel action effective in the following year, Nathan had already in every aspect far exceeded the amount of work required normally over a period of six years for promotion from assistant to associate scientist. He talked to his unit leader about his intent to apply for early promotion. His leader said: "It's way too early. Besides the amount of work you have accomplished, you need to serve enough of your time as well." Heeding the unit leader's warning, Nathan gave up his first attempt at upward mobility.

With a continuous momentum in performance, Nathan added more to his personnel record. Although he still received informal discouragement from his unit leadership, he formally decided to put himself forward for early promotion. The process did not sail smoothly, with a mixture of support and nonsupport from all recommending agencies involved. As a result, Nathan had to go through a procedure of appeal in which he pointedly argued that a candidate is much more deserving for promotion when he or she has accomplished over a shorter period of employment far more than what is expected of a regular employee through the normal duration of progression in rank. The appeal, however, did not come in his favor. Nathan failed in his second attempt.

Despite these setbacks in upward movement, Nathan did not experience any slowdown in his research activity and output. There were more projects executed, grants secured, publications completed, services offered, and academic activities involved in his record. With the same kind of persistence he had demonstrated in research and scholarship, Nathan made his third attempt at promotion. While he believed he had a stronger than ever case in light of meritocracy and universal justice, he nevertheless started hearing from some of the recommending agents ominous words as these in the early stage of the process: "Nathan keeps asking us to consider him for early promotion. We advised him not to apply too early. We turned him down. Does he take us seriously? Well, he obviously thinks he is better than everybody else." The end result was again negative: Nathan failed in his last attempt for early movement in rank.

In the following year when he was supposed to move up in rank normally, Nathan became an associate scientist without any incident, yet with a record of accomplishments that is several times more than his average peers, who all seem to have taken greater comfort in making the same movement over their individual research careers.

The Discriminator

When one experiences clear discriminations from an organization, one may not necessarily find it clear and easy to report where discriminations originate specifically and who discriminators are exactly. In the case of Nathan, he can only point to his whole institute as a major source of discrimination or a principal discriminator at the surface. Perhaps the institute is currently in the hands of academic administrators who themselves have switched to management because of a lackluster or mediocre performance in research and scholarship. The institute may have a tradition of discouraging the exceptional in the service of the average. It may have a prevailing atmosphere that favors comparable work and progress among members in similar cohorts or groups. Or the institute may pursue a personnel policy that implicitly or explicitly applies the principle of the mean to pull or push extremes toward a modal point in productivity and performance.

Within the institute, Nathan has to screen each agency or agent involved in personnel evaluation, recommendation, and decision to find out who may have discriminated against him. At the unit level, he knows that his unit leader holds biases toward him, not just as an outstanding performer, but also as a member of a minority group. The unit leader first used timing as a reason to prevent Nathan from applying. She then found trivial issues with Nathan's record to argue for her negative recommendation. In the third year when she felt she had nothing substantial to hold back Nathan, she spread gossip among other recommending agents about Nathan as an incompliant, uncooperative, or even defiant member of the unit. The unit personnel committee composed of colleagues in research was generally supportive but at times heavily influenced by the unit leader. In the middle level, the director of the division seemed to side automatically with the unit leader upon whom he relies to carry out his divisional policies in one of the division's units. The division personnel committee composed of representatives from individual research units was supportive all the time. However, the final decision lies in the president of the institute, who, without a clear vision and agenda for the institute, tends to take an easy route along the established lines of authority. In other words, the president embraces recommendations from lower levels of managers, such as unit leader and division director, rather than those by representative committees of the academic staff when there is a split among recommending agencies.

While administrators from lower to higher levels appear to be primary discriminators, average staff researchers in a broader sense seem to serve well in their generalized role as collective accomplices in discriminations against the outstanding, the extraordinary, and the exceptional. First, average staff researchers are the ultimate forces to define and determine the so-called norm in duration of progression from entry to middle to senior ranks. Second, they are the actual population base to produce administrators in various levels from the unit, through the division, to the institute as a whole. Third, they serve as a background of reference against which a discriminatory personnel decision by the administration becomes justifiable. Fourth, they provide a context or an atmosphere of collective sentiments in which rewards for outstanding performance do not necessarily appear desirable. Finally, they form the mean, the golden, sacred, and unbeatable mean, by which outperformers are targeted naturally for discriminatory treatments such as pullback, lack of recognition, and denial of accelerated promotion just as underperformers are identified automatically for additional attention from intensified training, reinforced incentives, and pressurized monitoring to other pushup measures.

The Victim

When one falls prey to discriminations by an organization, one could experience double victimizations. In the case of Nathan, he was not given the kind of recognition and rewards he deserved through his contributions in the first place. Moreover, he was pushed into a trap of unfavorable relationships with his leaders and some of his average colleagues who had intentionally and unintentionally spread words about him as a defiant, self-centered individual.

Specifically, Nathan made three attempts without any gain. At his first attempt, he only put his unit leader on alert so that she could find ways to stage her strong opposition in the following two years. In preparation for his second attempt, Nathan not only worked diligently in expanding his record, but also put hours into organizing his file, presenting his case, and preparing for his appeal. He did the same thing, only broader in scope and further in depth, when he attempted an accelerated promotion in the third year. From a materialistic point of view, Nathan obviously lost in all the efforts he had put into applications year after year. Most important, he lost in what he was deservedly entitled to for all the contributions he had made to his work. As a reference, there were colleagues in other units of his division who were promoted two years earlier. Even right at his own unit, another colleague was given a one-year-earlier promotion at the same time Nathan made his second attempt. When those colleagues were promoted earlier for one year or two years, they were given a higher salary, better access to organizational resources, and higher latitude in dealing with the outside sooner than normal.

Despite his losses in material terms, Nathan was put under unnecessarily close and unfairly critical scrutiny. When he was confronted with a few trivial issues his unit leader sinisterly found with his record, he had to clarify and explain as if he had done something wrong or inappropriate. When he met with various recommending agencies and agents along the way, he had to plead and convince as if he were a weak or vulnerable candidate who needed special consideration and protection. When he went through the procedure of appeal, he had to demonstrate and justify as if he had not done good enough with his far more than the average contributions to the institute. More detrimentally in the court of public opinion, Nathan started hearing gossip about his failure in accelerated promotion year after year, his troubled relationships with leaders of different levels within the institute, and his misperceived self-importance with regard to work. Even some of his close colleagues said: "I know you deserve it. But I would not put myself forward if I knew in the beginning I'd have to face this irrational opposition. People cheer on those who succeed, no matter how. They turn away from or even against you when you fail. It's not smart to drag on this unfair game only to see more negativity spread throughout the institute about yourself. "

The toll of double victimizations proved heavy, if not devastating, to Nathan. In those three years which he in retrospect viewed as the darkest time in his career, he questioned the worth of his contributions, the sanity of his mind, the soundness of his choice, the trustworthiness of fellow humans, and the attainableness of professional justice. There were sleepless nights when he was overwhelmed with hope for success, anxiety in waiting, or regret over some misstep. There were workless days when he was thrown into anger, disappointment, or hopelessness. The outer pressure to keep up his work and the inner motivation to expand his record for the following year were beyond imagination. Looking at the mirror, Nathan saw more gray hairs growing on his head almost every day. As observed by his wife, Nathan aged about ten years earlier or faster in those three difficult years.

The Compromise

Having a solid record of accomplishments, Nathan could be much more aggressive in his pursuit of accelerated movement through the ranks. With existing cases of accelerated promotion as reference, Nathan could be much more confrontational in dealing with administrators at different levels. For example, he could pay visit after visit to his unit leader, asking the leader to analyze his file item by item in reference to each of the corresponding clauses on promotion in the administrative manual; he could stage a sit-in in the office of his division director, challenging the director to compare him category by category with each of those whom he had recommended for promotion in the past several years; he could make an appointment with the president of the institute, pleading with the president to provide specific reasons for denying his application for the higher rank. Institutionally, Nathan could appeal to the grapevine by sharing his record with a larger audience or spreading words about the unreasonableness of some of the recommending agents. He could take his case to some of the activist groups within the institute. Most critically, he could ask the union to intervene in the process. In the third year, he was even on firm ground to take the institute to court.

In reality, Nathan did not resort to any one of these individual or institutional means available to him. He chose compromise and opted for the route of forbearance instead. He took recommendations from recommending agencies as they were because he believed with all his scholarly innocence that it is ultimately subjective appreciation rather than objective standard that makes a leader or a recommending agent support a candidate for accelerated movement through the ranks. When he received a negative recommendation from a recommending agent, Nathan felt he just needed to work harder to make that agent appreciate what he has done in the future. On a practical note, Nathan knew he had to keep all his attempts for early promotion in perspective with his long-term employment career in the institute. He accepted each of the final decisions from the president as it was because he understood with all his commonsense pragmatism that it is not wise to let an aborted early promotion attempt abort the scheduled normal progression through the personnel process.

All the nonsupport recommending agencies or agents and the institute as a whole, on the other hand, seemed to have skillfully, if not mischievously, walked a fine line on the case of Nathan. Despite the fact that they discouraged Nathan from ever making his first attempt, and disapproved him of his second and third attempts for accelerated promotion, they all acknowledged in their letters that Nathan was making satisfactory progress toward promotion as normally expected of his cohort. In everyday dealings at work, they greeted Nathan with apparent warmness and regard. Whether it is hypocrisy or friendliness, the unit leader even made efforts in finding occasions to give Nathan her signature hugs whenever possible. In other words, none of them crossed the line to make Nathan feel he had to leave the institute once and forever or he had to take the institute to the court of law for a verdict of ultimate justice.

The Universal

Discrimination against the extraordinary in the workplace often goes unnoticed because in the eyes of the ordinary, the extraordinary already receive more recognition and rewards ahead of the game or at least will obtain what everyone else gets on normal schedule.

While discriminators against the extraordinary can refer to the tradition, the norm, or the mean to justify their acts and actions, victims may find it necessary to back down or compromise in the name of nobility, peace, and unity. For example, victims may feel they are so blessed with a higher level of energy, intelligence, or luck that they should be only happy to make more contributions without recognition and material rewards. They may like Nathan take a fairy-tale belief that it is a matter of voluntary appreciation rather than inalienable obligation for an institution to acknowledge and reward exceptional contributions to its mission through material and nonmaterial means. Victims may also choose to wait, concede, and suffer when they fear alienation from the average, ostracism by the top, and turbulence through their own professional career.

As in any case of institutions versus individuals, discrimination against the extraordinary involves clearly identifiable individuals who consciously anguish with mistreatment and injustice while not always knowing exactly who and what are ultimately responsible for their victimizations. There are leaders or recommending agents. But they can mischievously hide behind their positions within the institutional hierarchy. There are units, divisions, or the whole organizational leadership. But they are just empty offices or abstract concepts when they are separated from people. The great irony, of course, is that individual victims can be trapped with discriminatory treatments by the enforcers of the mean. As illustrated by the case of Nathan, he was kept in peace with his institute by all recommending agencies' mentioning of a satisfactory progress toward promotion on normal schedule. Yet his continuous stay in forbearance was just a sheer experience of discrimination in the stark form of repeated denials of his entitlement to the kind of recognition and rewards he had deservedly earned through his outstanding performance.

SITUATION 3

Organizations in the contemporary era are supposed to operate on the principles of productivity, effectiveness, and meritocracy. Organizational leaders are expected to emerge from competitive performance and move up through the hierarchical order on the basis of expert knowledge, managerial experience, and substantive contributions.

The Particular

Alibaba plays tennis with Frank and Ronald almost every weekend. Frank teaches as a professor in a private university. Ronald serves as a staff engineer in a sizable public agency. Within and outside the tennis court, the three share a great deal of their working experiences.

Frank is a widely published scholar, an effective classroom teacher, and an active participant in faculty governance at his university. By academic record, he is indisputably the most qualified and deserving member of his department to become the next chair. However, when the election of a new permanent chair was held among the faculty through secret balloting,

Frank lost to a colleague who in every comparable category is less contributory to the department. In retrospect, Frank realizes that his academic colleagues seem to be naturally in favor of an average, if not mediocre, person as their leader because they feel they can relate to that kind of a person better, they can trust that kind of a person more in sticking to the mean, or at least they do not have to worry about that kind of a person possibly raising performance standards.

Ronald is one of the most celebrated staff engineers at his unit. By either seniority or experience, he is inarguably the best-positioned member to lead his unit in the next term. Unfortunately, when the existing unit leader left his position unexpectedly, the upper management appointed a little-accomplished member as the acting head of the unit. By the time the selection of a permanent unit leader was launched, the acting head not only had the advantage of incumbency, but also the honeymoon effect of new headship. Ronald applied for the position but lost to his acting head in a seemingly open, fair, and merit-based screening and recruitment process. Reflecting upon his failed attempt, Ronald comes to the conclusions that people who spend time on interpersonal relations are more likely to gain attention from leaders or win a favorable impression from the general public; that leaders are more likely to eye those who are similar to them as their subordinates, surrogates, or successors; and that leaders become leaders more through day-to-day dealings with people rather than substantive contributions to the organization or profession.

Indeed as a general background, it is important to point out that, in both Frank's private university and Ronald's public agency, professional leadership usually takes a bottom-up pattern of emergence, development, and growth. Experience as a department chair or a unit head prepares one for the dean of a college or the director of a division. Experience as a college dean or a division director paves the way for one to become the president of the university or the executive officer of the whole agency. In other words, many professional organizations are not necessarily under the leadership or in the hands of the most talented, most accomplished, and therefore most deserving members they have under their institutional roof.

The Discriminator

As a subtle hence often unnoticeable case of discrimination by individuals against organizations, de facto discriminators are people who are not necessarily most qualified or deserving yet somehow by way of political dynamics, personal connection, or the principle of the mean are pushed into leadership positions.

Once they take charge of their unit, division, or organization, these leaders are likely to use institutional resources to make up what they lack or fall short on professional track. For example, an associate professor who becomes the chair of an academic department may use his leadership position to obtain released time from teaching to work on scholarship, to secure funding from local coffers to attend conferences or to carry out research projects, or to persuade some graduate students or members of the faculty to coauthor articles. In the personnel process, he or she may skillfully apply a close working relationship with the dean, the provost, the president, and faculty self-governance groups to benefit his or her movement through the ranks. These self-interest efforts can obviously cause harm to the general atmosphere of standard, competition, and integrity at a professional unit. Moreover, these efforts can prevent one from doing fully what one is supposed to do as a unit leader.

Compared to those who are most qualified and should have become leaders originally, de facto discriminators in this case may not be able to represent a unit, a division, or a whole organization with the kind of rank, stature, honor, or reputation necessary and appropriate to the positions they hold officially. For example, a novice scholar leading an academic association is not likely to give a highly positive image to the association; the association can suffer in various aspects both within its membership and in larger academia. A little-known engineer or scientist with inadequate credentials heading a think tank, a research institute, or a consulting firm is not likely to add much, if any, competitive edge to his or her organization; the organization may find itself in disadvantage over grant application, contract negotiation, and other business dealings with different agencies. Even in the community of nations, an unwise, unintelligent, or unpopular leader can put a country under unfavorable limelight or make it bear critical losses in economic, diplomatic, or military terms when he or she takes the helm of state, either by way of democratic selection or undemocratic maneuvering.

Most important, an unqualified, unprepared, or undeserving leader may discriminate a unit, a division, or an entire institution with a full spectrum of leadership defects, deficiencies, or disorders, from lack of vision, ill-conceived plans, poor judgment, corruption, deflated employee morale, waste of resources, policy inconsistency, and mismanagement to operational dysfunction. The end results can be either naught profit, flat productivity, or zero progress in best scenarios or deep debt, complete breakdown, or total bankruptcy in worst scenarios. Of course, since history cannot be reversed or replayed for any organization with regard to any of its chosen courses of action, it is never possible to categorize exactly what and calculate precisely how much discrimination, harm, or loss its current leadership might have caused in contrast to an assumed yet never-existent team of leaders composed of its most able members.

The Victim

A unit, a division, or a whole organization whose leadership does not necessarily consist of the best of its membership may experience a variety of tangible or intangible victimizations in terms of productivity, effectiveness, morale, and public image.

Productivity depends upon membership performance. When best-performing members take leadership roles, they are likely to emphasize performance and place the focus of their group or organization on substantive tasks that the group or organization is set up to tackle. On the other hand, a group or organization may divert its due attention to trivial matters when leaders emerge from average or mediocre-performing members and do not find any strong point on their own records to talk about performance standards. The group or organization can therefore slip into a decline in productivity. Of course, it may also experience no change at all as it hovers historically in the level of low or nonoptimal productivity under a leadership team that one after another draws from and works for the average.

Effectiveness requires that leaders set clear goals, give unambiguous orders, provide timely reinforcements through reward or punishment, and deliver accurate policy executions. It is questionable that a group or organization could ever attain an optimal level of effectiveness when it embraces as its leaders those who are not necessarily sharpest, most talented, and best experienced across its membership. Although it can make its members feel the difference made by effective leaders in their everyday working experience, the group or organization may never know how much it might have suffered in organizational effectiveness and efficiency from leaders who often do not think rationally, speak pointedly, act promptly, and distinguish clearly right from wrong, productive from counterproductive, and contributive from exploitative among various employees and employee behaviors.

Morale correlates with employee job satisfaction and membership perception of fairness or justice over work assignment, resource allocation, performance evaluation, and reward delivery. Nothing else can deal a more devastating blow to morale than the fact that a top-performing member is passed over by his or her lower-performing counterparts in ascendance to leadership. First, top performers will lose motivation to take the lead in work and productivity. Second, average performers will consolidate their middle position to avoid any possible sense of injustice as experienced by top performers. Third, people will look beyond performance to find ways and means for material rewards and upward movements. Most important, as members feel anyone can be a leader or even worse only those average, mediocre, or leader-following people can usurp leadership positions, leaders will not have the full moral authority to lead a group or organization at all. Again, how much does a group or organization know it could have lost in productivity or other critical elements when it is plagued with a low morale across its membership?

Public image of a group or organization inheres in the way its customer services agents, public relations representatives, and leadership positions holders conduct themselves, speak on its behalf, and act for its sake on public stages or occasions. More than anyone else, leaders communicate to the outside critically and summarily what kind of people a group or organization has under its umbrella, talented, experienced, or trustworthy; what kind of products or services it offers, poor quality, low price, or no-frills;

and what kind of respect or reputation it deserves, prestige, disgrace, or no class at all. It is common that people boycott products of a country, dump stocks of a corporation, cease sending children to a school, and sever relations with an association when major leaders of the concerned group, organization, or state perform poorly in larger contexts, casting doubts or creating negativity through the general public about its legitimacy, standing, and even existence. Similarly, loss or victimization over public image a group or organization may have suffered because of leadership can be only second-guessed against an imaginary scenario: if it were led and represented by the best of its membership population.

The Compromise

A group or organization may have no choice other than accommodation and compromise when it bears tangible and intangible harms caused intentionally or unintentionally by a not-so-competent leadership.

First of all, leaders run the group or organization. When they cause harm, they are likely to use the group or organization to hide, absorb, or contain it. In other words, an organization is automatically made to accept and accommodate whatever leaders have done on its behalf. There is not much chance for any group to stand up instantly to challenge its leaders for something immediately consequential. It usually takes a long time before harm has spread throughout the group or organization in a critically sensible degree to generate a collective sentiment for change in leadership.

Besides this structural setup for compromise, a group or organization is likely to fall into division when it faces an unfavorable situation brought about by its leadership. There are people who want to hold leaders accountable. There are segments of the membership who rally behind leaders. The end result is often this: leaders are given time to make corrections, and the whole group or organization is kept to take what it is now for what it is to come in the future. People in the general membership will then rationalize their experience: we choose or produce our leaders; although they did not represent the best of us, they indeed reflect the realest of us; and if we do not like what they have done in the past, we should think about what we do now.

On the part of leaders, they may make a conscientious effort to expand their knowledge, sharpen their skills, raise their profile, polish their images, and improve their day-to-day leadership functions as soon as they are thrown into power-holding and decision-making positions. When they make a mistake, they take quick actions to correct it. When they realize they have caused injury or harm to their constituents or constituency, they openly offer explanations or apologies to comfort the audience or quietly mobilize necessary resources to make up the loss or compensate the victims. As a matter of fact, individuals who are originally unqualified and undeserving for leadership positions do learn and grow on the job. Many of them eventually become competent leaders in their profession or organization. This, of course, is exactly why it is so unfair to those originally better-qualified and more deserving people who were passed over in ascendance to leadership as well as why it is such a discrimination to the organization itself that could have been better served by the best of its members in leadership positions in the first place.

The Universal

Leaders of a group, organization, or state run it inside and represent it outside. When they do not do well in their leadership positions because of ability, knowledge, and experience, they hold the group, organization, or state hostage for serious discriminations from both within and without.

Although it is generally assumed or perceived that leaders of a group, organization, or state emerge from competition and therefore represent the best of the membership or population, it is often true that leaders are at best average people who come into power out of political compromise or take leadership positions due to the work of the principle of the mean. There is no lack of leaders who are not even as good as the average people, in terms of ability or morality, whom they lead and represent for a group, organization, or state. As a result, it is common in history that countries fall, organizations go bankrupt, and groups disappear in the hands of incompetent or morally unfit leaders. In the contemporary era of bureaucracy, however, it is most significant yet ironically often goes unnoticed that many public or private, professional or nonprofessional, and manufacturing or service organizations, small or large, suffer loss constantly, sustain damage from day to day, or bear harm routinely in productivity, effectiveness, morale, and public image when they operate under a leadership that so typically does not draw from the best of their membership.

While it is a valid point that most talented and experienced members of a group, organization, or state are best qualified and deserving to take leadership positions, it might be wishful thinking that these people are most likely to lead their group, organization, or state toward optimal functionality and maximal success. In reality, when average members of a group, organization, or state serve as leaders, they may provide a better bridge between extreme elements or positions in various dimensions and hence make more tangible contributions to organizational stability, sustainability, and longevity.

SITUATION 4

Organizations are rule-coded systems that are presumed to run automatically under normal operation conditions. Products come out of the production line. Services reach the intended clientele. Employees assume positions, play roles, take rewards or face penalties, and navigate up or down the organizational hierarchy. However, just as some products become defective and some services fail to materialize, a few organizational members may not receive the kind of treatment or placement they deserve in a supposedly automatic and fair organizational process. The irony is that when a mistreated or misplaced member stands up to make a complaint or to address an injustice, he or she is often automatically seen as a troublemaker by the organizational authority or even worse as an outlier by the majority of the general membership.

The Particular

Alibaba works with Jeffrey from one project team to another. Jeffrey takes his fair share of team labor, does quality work in his specialty, completes his job assignments on time, attends group meetings, participates in joint activities, and relates to other team members well. However, Jeffrey somehow did not receive as strong an evaluation as other members on a few project team reviews. These project team evaluations not only affect Jeffrey's entitlement to team-specific rewards, but also impact his periodic reviews for promotion and salary adjustment. When he talked to some of those team leaders, Jeffrey felt that everyone treated him as an incompliant, if not rebellious, member. They asked Jeffrey to document what he did, making him look defensive, incompetent, or as if he did something wrong. Consequentially, when they changed their erroneous evaluations, Jeffrey had to thank them as if they did a huge favor to him. On the other hand, when they refused to change their mistaken positions, Jeffrey had to fear them because they could write his action of complaining as something negative in a future evaluation.

Related to the case of Jeffrey, Alibaba's former colleague Maryann blew the whistle on her unit leader to the upper management of the company. The upper management praised Maryann for her courageous action that had prevented a critical unit of the company from falling into trouble. It also meted out a series of disciplinary penalties against her unit leadership. However, when all these dusts settled back to normal, Maryann started experiencing considerable hostility from within her unit. She appealed to the upper management to see if they could intervene on her behalf, extend her a necessary level of protection, or transfer her to some other unit. The upper management offered its sympathy but declined to render any practical assistance. As a result, Maryann left the company. Upon her departure, Alibaba heard these comments by a major member of the company leadership: "We know she did a good thing to the benefit of this company. But we are all normal human beings concerned with ordinary issues such as loyalty and betrayal. Who wouldn't be wary and worrisome with a coworker who used to expose all of us to the outside?"

In reflecting upon Jeffrey, Maryann, and their respective experiences, Alibaba automatically recalls two of his own encounters in a department store. One was when he had to return an originally damaged item in a sealed box he purchased from the store: he had to drive back to the store in the first place; he then had to swear to the customer service agent that it was not him who broke the item; and finally he felt obliged to thank the customer service agent when she had processed the return. The other was when he gave back ten dollars he found a cashier had mistakenly undercharged him for a purchase. Instead of thanking him, the cashier seemed apparently unhappy as she felt she was made to look incompetent in front of other customers.

The Discriminator

In all these similar yet different incidents, alleged discriminators are groups, organizations, and their acting agents or representing leaders. What is common and unique about these incidents is that discriminators intentionally and unintentionally engage in double discriminations against their targets.

Against Jeffrey as a competent team member who had made his due contributions to each team project were his team leaders, teams, and the company. In the first instance, they failed to acknowledge Jeffrey's work, giving him less than what he deserved in team evaluation, project reward, and possibly periodic salary adjustment. In the second instance, they made Jeffrey feel defensive by demanding he provide detailed documentation of what he had done for the team and its project when Jeffrey confronted them with their inaccurate evaluations. As word spread about Jeffrey and his challenge to the team decision, public impression developed inside and outside the team about Jeffrey as a complaining, if not troublemaking, person.

Discriminatory to Maryann in particular and to any whistle-blower in general can be deliberate inattention by the stakeholders of a concerned unit, division, or organization. Although leaders of her company praised Maryann for her whistle-blowing report, they discriminated against her when they declined to offer her any concrete assistance for her dealings with coworkers and lower-level managers in the aftermath of the incident. They further discriminated against her by making unfavorable comments about her loyalty and character. The unit, its members and leaders, and perhaps the whole company that had benefited from Maryann's whistle-blowing act were also obvious double discriminators. They not only passively punished her by not acknowledging her courageous act, but also actively penalized her by distancing her, venting hostility toward her, and eventually pushing her to the exit.

Similarly, in Alibaba's own experiences with the department store, the store discriminated against him in the first place when it sold him intentionally or unintentionally a damaged item he had to spend time and bear cost to return. Instead of offering an apology or some kind of compensation, the store as every other merchant has a customer service process that tends to make Alibaba in particular and every other merchandise-returning patron in general look like a troublemaking or exploitative customer. As a result, the store and the agent who handles the return become a second-instance discriminator. They not only make Alibaba explain why he had to return the item, but also prompt him to thank them for accepting the return. Alibaba's encounter with the cashier at the department store bears resemblance to Maryann's whistle-blowing act. First, the sales clerk did not thank Alibaba for returning the ten dollars she mistakenly gave to him. In the end of her shift, she might have had to dig into her own pocket to make the balance had Alibaba not returned it to her. Second, she spilled anger over to Alibaba for she thought Alibaba made her look bad in front of other customers in line. In other words, she unleashed two rounds of discrimination against Alibaba, who only did something in her favor.

The Victim

In incidents aforementioned, victims are made to stand awkwardly off line. As such, they may not necessarily win much sympathy for their victimization experience.

Beginning with Alibaba's encounters with the department store, he sensed some suspicious looks when he moved the damaged box from his car in the parking lot to the front door of the store. Under those looks, he felt as if there was gossip uttered behind him: "Oh, what a poor guy!"; "What's wrong with him? Is he going to make some trouble?"; "Who knows if he is one of those exploitative customers who shamelessly return used merchandize when they no longer need it." Upon entering the store, Alibaba was directed to stand in a special line for merchandise returns, which, compared to other lines for customer purchases, looked certainly not glorious, if not plainly problematic or discriminatory either. Followed were questionings from the service clerk, examination of the item by a technician, and authorization of the return by a supervisor. All these came imaginably at no joy, if not with conspicuous irritation or discrimination as well. Comparably, Alibaba had to stand off line when he waited to return the miscalculated ten dollars to the cashier. The position he took appeared to draw immediate attention from those who were in the regular queue for service by her: "What does this guy want to do? We surely do not want him to cause any trouble to slow us down!" After he finally returned the money, he walked away as if he left behind an image of no Good Samaritan but bad troublemaker. Added to his victimization, Alibaba was even prompted to offer thanks to all those who gave him discriminating stares, screenings, and treatments along the way.

For Maryann as a whistle-blower, she lost her job first and foremost. With a known reputation for whistle-blowing, she may face difficulty finding a new job in her field. Back to where she blew the whistle, Maryann started hearing various gossip about herself even when she was first praised by the upper management: "Who knows what she has in her mind, gaining attention from the top or seeking revenge on her immediate leaders?"; "Look at her, she seems to think in the whole world only she herself knows and holds a higher standard for professional conduct!"; "Let her relish in all these publicities. Tomorrow will be another day." The worst time was certainly when Maryann pleaded for help to no avail within her company. There were tears, nightmares, irregular menstruations, and periodic headaches. In other words, Maryann suffered both internally and externally in her victimization experience.

Finally, in the case of Jeffrey, he was seen as having some issues with each team leader when he was pushed off line to receive a below-average evaluation. It is almost natural that people assume the perspective of organizational leadership or side with the whole organization when an individual member is singled out as a violator or underperformer. They take it for granted that an outlier, once identified, either erroneously or rightfully, must make an effort to document his or her work, defend his or her position, or clear his or her name. The identified outlier should thank his or her organization for redressing injustice when he or she resolved the matter successfully. Or in the case when he or she is not able to change a not necessarily fair decision by his or her leader, he or she ought to do something to overcome any sense of alienation he or she might have developed with the leader. Obviously, all these common perceptions among coworkers and general reactions from within the company only served to heighten his sense of victimization when Jeffrey went through it day by day.

The Compromise

Jeffrey could literally speak to as many people as possible within and without his team to create and spread a public impression that he has made adequate contributions to the team yet was given a subjectively erroneous evaluation by his team leader. He might even go further by making a factual account of personal biases that his leader has consistently showed to him and some of his coworkers on and off record. The team leader, on the other hand, could insist that under no circumstance he would ever change his evaluation because he carried it out on the basis of verifiable evidence. With a hardened position by each side, there then would be no aforementioned situation which itself represents the best possible compromise in organizational settings even though it makes Jeffrey a virtual victim. It is almost an iron law that one has to take some more victimization when one pleads for corrections through institutional procedures for any mistreatment given by one's organization in the first place.

Maryann could confront those who were hostile to her with a detailed list of specific benefits her whistle-blowing action had brought to her unit. She could be a lot more demanding when she asked for intervention from the upper management. Most important, she could take her company and some of its managers to the mass media or even the court of law for avenging on her, if not just failing to protect her. Instead, Maryann quietly took all unfavorable treatments first and left the company when she felt she could not handle any more of them. Perhaps she just wanted to move on with her professional career without seeing any further complication from this one-out-of-a-lifetime whistle-blowing incident. All the discriminators against Maryann, from coworkers, the unit, and managers to the whole company, might come to a state of compromise and regret after they saw her off to somewhere else.

For Alibaba, he could explain to everyone who threw a suspicious look upon him that he was in or off line to return an item that was originally damaged by the store or an amount of money that was mistakenly given to him by the cashier. When he felt he was being wrongfully perceived as a troublemaker or a system-exploiter, he might even complain to bystanders how careless this store was by selling customers damaged merchandises or how bad this cashier was with numbers when she under- or overcharged customers. Obviously, Alibaba did not bother to offer any explanation or make any complaint because he knew anything he did to dispel all these subtle victimizing suspicions would only add to his overall experience of virtual victimization. On the part of the department store, acceptance of return, either money or a damaged item, itself represents the best compromise it can possibly make to a customer. A store would never think much about how a customer might be victimized when he or she has to return an item unknowingly damaged before purchase. The same holds true for its sales or customer service representatives. Would any of them pause to take the role of a subtly victimized customer when he or she has to deal with a long line of customers at the store?

The Universal

It is almost inevitable that individuals will have to endure yet another round of explicit or implicit victimization when they stand up to address or challenge some discriminations, mistreatments, or wrongs they receive from or witness at a group, organization, or system in the first place.

There are a few reasons why individuals tend to suffer from this inherent disadvantage in relation to established institutions. First, people generally assume that established groups, organizations, or systems are designed with rationality, grounded in objectivity, structured for stability, tested by time, and therefore more reliable or trustworthy than individuals. They naturally jump to the conclusion that one must have some problems in personality, morality, qualification, performance, or interpersonal relationship when one fails a routine examination or falls below the average in receipt of some general rewards. It is not so common that people question an organizational authority for possible misconduct. It is quite extraordinary that people challenge a group, organization, or system for institutionalized discrimination against individuals of a particular age, gender, race, and other background.

Second, people take it for granted that organizational processes are automatic, functional, routine, standard, and hence fair to everyone involved. They normally focus their attention on individuals, individual misperception, and individual maladjustment when someone turns out to be an underperformer, a violator, or a general outlier in attitude or behavior. It is not a first thing in order that people eye major organizational stakeholders for possible power abuse or procedural manipulation. It is virtually a defiant act against normal ways of thinking that people point to organizations, organizational dysfunction, and organizational failure for ingrained prejudice or mistreatment faced by certain individuals of the general membership.

Third, individuals live or operate under the overcast of organizational authority, formality, or rigidity. Instead of making any claims or disclaims from their personal points of view, they have to begin with whatever claims or disclaims the group, organization, or system has unilaterally made about them. One has no forum to present one's contributions for some automatic organizational corrections when one does not receive due recognition and rewards for one's work. Instead, one has to go through a subtly discriminatory procedure of grievance even though one deserves a public apology from one's leadership. One has no stage to show one's victimization for some instant public sympathy when one takes home supposedly intact but actually damaged merchandise. Instead, one has to wait in a conspicuously embarrassing line of return even though one deserves some compensation from the store.

Finally, individuals act spontaneously while an organization can strategize its dealings with individual members. One makes a complaint when one receives an unfavorable evaluation. One appeals to stakeholders when one fails to obtain promotion or a salary increase. One thanks one's leaders when one prevails on a grievance procedure or wins an appeal. And one obviously does not always look far back in time or broader across horizon to see what one loses, what one gains, or where one stands. On the other hand, an organization can refer to some historical patterns, a mathematical mean, or a statistical distribution to single out certain deviations, suppress specific complaints, or counter particular resistances by individual members. It takes an apparent appearance of justice and fairness when it loses to some of its members over their individual grievances. It creates a public sentiment of fear and precaution when it wins compliance by some of its rebellious members with a distribution of reward and penalty it imposes upon the membership.

SITUATION 5

When people join an organization as employees or interest-sharing members, they naturally look for those who are similar to socialize, network, or reference with. While they can routinely find comparison, motivation, inspiration, companionship, or friendship from those who are similar to them in personal characteristics, demographic factors, and socioeconomic variables, they may eventually realize that they are often, explicitly or implicitly, discriminated against for access to opportunities, mistreated over job activities, or held back in promotion because of their association with individuals of the same or a similar property, whether it be the same place they come from, the same group they belong to, the same language they speak or do not speak, a similar culture they practice, or a similar lifestyle they maintain.

The Particular

Alibaba knows John and Jenny well in his employment organization. John and Jenny both joined his department at the same time in the same positions with similar backgrounds and qualifications. Or as everyone puts it, they came and progress as a cohort. In personal relations, John and Jenny seem to get along well. They collaborate on projects, meet for lunch from time to time, attend a few professional conferences out of town together, and even have some mutual exchanges in their private family-to-family events or parties.

Over work and job performance, John is clearly ahead of Jenny. John works hard, fast, and with a variety of skills and talents. He relates to colleagues well and makes a highly positive impression upon clients. In fact, besides oral, informal praises by experienced colleagues inside the employment organization, some of his work has even won written, formal accolades from established authorities around the professional field. Jenny, on the other hand, fits perfectly in the image of an ordinary employee. She performs her job duties as assigned, expected, or required. Although she struggles sometimes, she overall has lived up to the challenge of her position.

On the matter of rewards, however, Jenny serves indisputably as a negative reference for John in both upward movement and receipt of material benefits. For what he has accomplished in work, John deserves accelerated promotion through the ranks. Based on what he has contributed to the organization, John deserves special recognition and salary increases. In reality, John obtains none of these tangibles. Publicly or privately, jokingly or seriously, Jenny often says that she is tied with John in a cohort, that she would be upset if John gets something and she does not, and that she would file formal grievances if John gets early promotion and she does not get her promotion by normal schedule. In particular, Jenny has maintained a close relationship with her department leader, so much so that Jenny is able to communicate to him all her feelings of comparison she has with and toward John. Jenny's tie with a key player in the upper administration is also noticeable because one time when John talked to her about a merit-based salary increase, she said directly to John that she wanted to ensure that Jenny would obtain it as well. While nobody knows how much concern over Jenny and her reactions plays in various leaders' decisions on John, everyone understands that leaders at lower, middle, and upper levels prefer not to break peace, order, and the status quo by making one employee moderately happy and another extremely upset or by making one employee happy and a few more unhappy. As a matter of fact, leaders at all three levels seem to be quite canny, shrewd, and right on target in their assessment and belief that John would do all he can regardless of rewards, whereas Jenny would not sit in quietness when she becomes upset with something.

Similar to the case of John and Jenny, where one employee drags the other in a cohort over access to opportunities, receipt of tangible benefits, and upward mobility, Alibaba knows Gabriel and Georgia at a special interest club. Gabriel and Georgia came from the same town in a rural region. Among club members, Gabriel is known to be a person who often speaks raw language, tends to dig into other people's privacy, and does not always follow the fine etiquettes assumed for club members. Founded or unfounded, real or unreal, Georgia remains worried that Gabriel and his public image at the club may tarnish, at least on occasion, her positive reputation throughout the local membership.

The Discriminator

Jenny becomes a de facto discriminator against John simply because she is in the same cohort with John yet does not perform on a par with him. She serves as a comparison by which coworkers might criticize John as a person who does not care enough to synchronize his own professional progress with that of his fellow cohort member or contain John as a rate buster who threatens the sense of comfort shared by the majority. Jenny also provides a reference for administrators to justify their lack of recognition for John's outstanding contributions. Should John apply for accelerated promotion, administrators at various levels can easily discourage him by citing Jenny and her possible reactions. For the good of collegiality and collective peace, John would hold back his attempt naturally.

Beyond this background discrimination, Jenny actively engages in a variety of activities that prove harmful to John and his career. She demands for the same whenever John receives something out of his extraordinary work. She maintains close relationships with leaders at different levels, spreading her often not necessarily favorable feelings about John. In the minds of some administrators, Jenny seems to be a key factor when they evaluate John and decide on important matters regarding him. As far as Jenny and her fundamental interests are concerned, she always benefits from John in her cohort. In fact, she could most likely have waited for a much longer time to obtain her first-level promotion purely on the basis of her own rather mediocre performance had John not been a pulling force as her fellow cohort member.

Similarly, in the case of Gabriel and Georgia, Gabriel could reinforce some stereotypical views, especially negative ones, that club members might generally have about people from his hometown region. Stereotypes develop over various variables, from sex, age, race, ethnicity, culture, socio-economic status, and hometown to country of origin. When an existing stereotype is activated and reinforced by the unfavorable acts or actions of one live person, it can become all too powerful for many co-present individuals perceived to be of the same or similar kind to steer clear of it. Obviously, Gabriel knowingly or unknowingly puts Georgia in a position where she at least has to answer some awkward questions from other club members. For example, one club member might ask: "Do people from your hometown region really act like that?" while the other might say: "Can you help me understand why Gabriel behaved so oddly the other day?"

The Victim

By fate or accident, John becomes a victim simply because he happens to have Jenny as his fellow cohort member. In everyday work, John needs to show his professional collegiality by carefully attending to Jenny's personal feelings. He greets Jenny almost all the time even when Jenny does not seem so willing to see him. He invites Jenny to lunch when appropriate. Since he offered to pay for their meals the first time, John now has to have another lunch with Jenny to bring even his share of payment by the rule of rotation they have implicitly established for themselves. Most important, John shares a great deal of his work experience with Jenny. He offers his best advice and support whenever Jenny has a question or problem at the workplace or outside normal working hours. Ironically, despite all these selfless efforts John makes on his part toward Jenny, he faces a subtle yet potentially damaging risk to his reputation as a conscionable professional: he could be accused of being condescending and womanizing if he remains too close when he attempts to comfort Jenny on matters related to work or life; he could be charged of being paternalistic and sexist when he intends to help bring Jenny in line with the standard of performance he holds for himself in professional undertakings.

Most critically, Jenny serves as an unfavorable comparison to John. Reasonable or unreasonable, John's colleagues view him as comparable to Jenny given the mere fact that they joined the institution in the same positions at the same time. Right or wrong, John's leaders use Jenny as a reference to hold back John from timely receiving all the tangible and intangible benefits he deserves by his contributions. As so commonly seen in many organizations, while people tend to ignore the difference in work performance across the employee population, they seem to open their eyes wide to any gap in benefits or rewards given to individual members they perceive to be in the same cohort or group. The rule of thumb is this: once two parties, "A" and "B," are considered similar, one party, "A" or "B," would have to do extraordinarily more than the other, "A" or "B," should he or she desire different treatment in public opinion, material benefit, and upward mobility. In other words, John faces an extraordinarily heavy burden of proof, because of Jenny as his comparison, to gain access to what he would ordinarily deserve. Trickily, while John may know that he would better forget about any extra recognition or rewards when he does twice as much work as Jenny, he can never know how much more he has to demonstrate in job performance over Jenny so that people would come to an awakening realization that John is indeed different from Jenny and hence undoubtedly entitled to better treatment.

Between Gabriel and Georgia, the latter may know what she bears, because of the former and her association with him by way of origin, if she just acts normally in the interest club as every other member. But she can never know how much extra effort she has to make to create and maintain a positive image for herself to the degree that other club members would deactivate their stereotypical view about people from her home region in general and would not automatically associate her with an oddly behaving Gabriel from her hometown in particular.

The Compromise

John could have used Jenny to his advantage as well. In the professional dimension, John may use Jenny and her performance as a bottom line upon which he can most likely make an effective argument for recognition and rewards. For instance, he can present to his leaders a list of what he has accomplished in comparison to a list of what Jenny has done as one who is supposed to do the same in his cohort. He then may convince his leaders that he is indisputably ahead of his peers and hence deservedly entitled to both accelerated promotion and preferential treatments on the job. Instead, John never thinks of making a reference to Jenny or any of his other colleagues. He just focuses on his own work, with a simple belief that he will receive due recognition if he does exceptionally well. John takes it without any counterargument when he hears his leaders say that Jenny joined the organization at the same time, does a fine job, and has not received any special treatment for her work either. Indeed, using colleagues to advance self-interests or making comments that might put colleagues in disadvantageous positions is not something that John can ever do in his professional career.

Personally, John could have kept some distance from Jenny for three good reasons. First, he can use such a strategy to counter the public perception that he and Jenny are the same or similar in one cohort. Second, he may invoke some awe and fear in Jenny about him as a competitor. Third, he at least can prevent Jenny from ever thinking and treating him as an out-and-out gentleman to whom she can do anything and from whom she can obtain everything. For example, Jenny can always expect warm greetings from John when she draws her comparisons with John in front of her leaders, which in all its likelihood tends to be damaging to John and his positive image throughout the organization. Jenny can even ask John for lunch right after she makes unfavorable comments on John, his work, or mannerisms, among colleagues. Is John deaf and dumb? The answer is no. John knows everything, sooner or later. But John never shakes and falters in his belief that he treats his colleagues with care, kindness, and respect regardless of what he receives from them.

On the part of Jenny, she knows she holds a special feeling toward John. She misses seeing him when John is out of town on meetings or projects. She fills him in or takes things on his behalf when John is not around. She vigorously defends him when she hears criticisms about John from other colleagues despite the fact that she herself makes complaints against him from time to time. When she compares herself to John in the offices of her leaders, Jenny figures that John is simply so outstanding that he would not get hurt much if she uses him to the most of her professional advantage.

Similarly in the case of Gabriel and Georgia, the former often goes the extra mile in defending, protecting, and taking care of the latter within and beyond their interest club. Gradually, Georgia starts taking Gabriel as a big brother from her hometown. She now feels it not just a forced shame to clear her good name from, but also an inalienable duty to throw a positive light upon what Gabriel says and does in front of other club members.

The Universal

While people generally agree that each individual is unique and should receive treatment on the basis of what he or she has done, they naturally place individuals in different categories, groups, or types according to commonsense perceptions, long-held stereotypes, or even widely spread biases. Once an individual is forced into a category, he or she will then have to face or beat all the odds that may arise from either general dynamics across the population or specific interactions among extreme elements within the category.

In a minority of cases, individuals can benefit from this unreasonable, unfair, and unjust organizational or social process if they happen to be in a "right" place at a "wrong" time, or just plainly lucky. For instance, "A" surprisingly receives recognition and rewards "A" does not necessarily expect and deserve simply because "A"'s boss did not treat many other individuals of "A"'s ethnic culture fairly and decided to use "A" as a special case to counter the general impression of bigotry and discrimination he or she had created across the employee population. "B" as a normal performing or behaving individual makes it to the leadership team of a government or organization when some kind of public awakening or social rebellion gains momentum against a historical or systematic discrimination suffered by the population segment or interest group to which "B" belongs.

"C" finds welcome, support, and respect that "C" usually does not see for ordinary individuals of his or her subgroup from the larger membership of a religious congregation or interest club as long as "C" deviates from the subgroup of individuals under which "C" falls by his or her mother tongue, dialect, alma mater, or hometown.

For the majority, experience is most likely discrimination, unfair treatment, pain, and suffering. Imagine how many individual employees of an ethnic culture have to face systematic mistreatment to make a boss feel it imperative to defuse his or her unfavorable impression with one particular case; how many individual citizens of a race or minority population have to bear years of discrimination to see only a few of their sons and daughters co-opted into the mainstream political establishment; and how many individual members of a subgroup have to put up with routine disrespect and disdain to witness only one of their own accorded with normal treatment. It is like the game of lottery: millions of players have to bear a loss in order to make one single million-dollar winner. Ironically, one or a few lucky winners are often used to dampen the gravity of past discrimination and justify a continuation of the practice into the future.

In particular relevance to the case of John and Jenny, while most organizations tend to refer to a low-performance case to hold back a considerable number of high performers from receiving due rewards or material benefits, few allow a duly recognized or rewarded high-performance case to be exploited by the majority of average or below-average employees to their individual advantage. At the micro level, the case of John and Jenny highlights a considerable degree of randomness in organizational life. It is coincidental that two employees join a work unit, a law firm, or an educational institution in comparable positions at the same time. It is, however, of neither necessity nor inevitability that one serves as an unfavorable comparison, dragging the other in promotion and upward mobility. The same holds true for the case of Gabriel and Georgia. It is a random occurrence that two persons in an interest club or professional association come from the same place. But it does not have to be a sure reality that one exists as a negative reference, tarnishing the other's positive image and reputation in routine membership interactions.

5 Across the Profession

With a systematic division of labor, hundreds of professions appear and exist in contemporary society. While individual professions expand in particular fields with specific tasks to tackle, they all involve and invoke a classificatory system, a hierarchy, or a bureaucracy to categorize, organize, and differentiate individual participants or practitioners in terms of access, compensation, professional privilege, power, and fame (Abbott 1988; Hatch 1988; Jones 1991; Macdonald 1995; Coltrane 2004; Lynch 2006; Lattimore et al. 2009; Bureau and Suquet 2009; Saks 2010; Corey, Corey, and Callanan 2011; Hamilton 2011; Jakobsen, Hansen, and Eika 2011; Judson and Harrison 2012; Dzienkowski 2012).

It is no doubt that each profession, due to its content, skill, operational and organizational peculiarities, has different discriminations inherent in its practice. There nevertheless ought to be no surprise that common discriminations emerge from place to place, especially given the hierarchical structure that so ubiquitously and universally remains in force throughout the world of professions.

SITUATION 1

If the old-fashioned respect for knowledge and the knowledgeable still holds true, people in the general public would most likely believe that colleges and universities are cleaner professional institutions as knowledge lifts spirits and that students and professors are more disciplined professional practitioners as learning purifies souls.

In reality, however, discriminations occur with no less frequency and prevalence across the academic profession, not only individually between students and professors, between juniors and seniors of the faculty, and between faculty members and administrators, but also institutionally from department to department, from college to college, and from university to university.

The Particular

With experience as a student and a part-time instructor, Alibaba hears and sees much about colleges and universities. There are students who do not work on course materials and blame a foreign-born professor and his or her accent for their failure in class. There are students who do not behave properly in the classroom and make the instructor impose a harsh rule or requirement upon all class participants. Teaching from one semester to another, Alibaba knows clearly that he often has to spend far more time dealing with one or two academically unprepared or behaviorally misadjusted students in a class than working productively on student learning for the whole class. He sometimes wonders why everywhere in this world the majority of people have to suffer in the hands of a few undeserving and unworthy individuals.

On the part of the faculty, Alibaba finds another question bothers and bugs his conscience. That is, why everywhere in the world are a few privileged individuals able to control, influence, and exploit a mass of less privileged or unprivileged people to gain fame, power, and wealth? In the backdrop of this question, Alibaba has a real-life case. Douglas has served as a professor, the director of a research center, the chair of a department, and the dean of a college in his twenty-five-year academic career with a major university. When he was a regular member of the faculty, Douglas used his graduate students to take care of the bulk of his teaching assignments. Like most of his colleagues, he delivered lectures to undergraduate and graduate classes when he was in town and felt good about doing a lecture. He left everything else, from lecturing on topics not of his interest, one-on-one student advisement, in-class exercise and discussion, and proctoring tests or exams to grading, to his graduate students. When he was in charge of the research center, Douglas acted as a grant dealer. He hired doctoral students, postdoctoral scholars, junior faculty members, statisticians, and professional writers, putting them to work on grant writing, project designing, fieldwork, data analysis, writing, and publication. He set goals, decided on targets, made comments, approved final submissions, and placed his name on almost all grant proposals as principal investigator and research manuscripts as main author.

A few years later, Douglas became the chair of his department. As the chair, Douglas used the office staff to shoulder much of his administrative responsibilities. To the faculty, he promoted those who worked closely with him on grant applications and research projects while holding back and even pushing away those whose research did not seem interesting or beneficial to him. In two terms, Douglas took most credit as one who had streamlined departmental programs and established its reputation as a leading department in the field of his favored subject. When he led the college, Douglas continued his pattern of behavior at the department. Taking advantage of departments, faculty members, and administrative staff in the college, he convened academic conferences for scholars in his field, sponsored a journal and a publication series in his discipline, and was hence able to make considerable advances in the hierarchy of his professional association. During his deanship, the whole college operated to some extent as a vehicle for his academic agenda and career aspirations.

The Discriminator

In academic settings, while students can be discriminators against each other, their instructors or advisors, and a class, a department, a college, or a whole university, professors are the most common actors of discrimination. As illustrated by the case of Douglas, a member of the faculty can engage in discriminatory practices toward his or her students, administrative staff, and colleagues, the rank and position he or she holds, and the unit or division he or she leads.

Against people, Douglas first commits discrimination against the undergraduate and graduate students enrolled in his classes. As an instructor on record, he is supposed to meet with students in all scheduled class sessions, where he can deliver lectures, hold class discussion, and address student concerns or questions. By delegating some critical elements of teaching, including lecturing, class discussion, and grading, to his doctoral students, Douglas throws a potentially compromised education upon those students who register for his classes. To his doctoral students, he ought to give the best possible advice in research and scholarship. Instead, Douglas exploits them for their time and labor in the tedious part of classroom instruction. With his colleagues, he should only collaborate on an equal footing. But, in fact, Douglas puts them to work on the substantive part of grant applications, research projects, data analysis, and publication preparation while placing their names behind his for academic credit and scholarly recognition. Toward his administrative staff, he needs to observe important restraints with a genuine spirit of professional respect. In reality, however, Douglas utilizes his secretary support to its ultimate limit. He orders his secretarial staff to craft letters, copyedit manuscripts, order supplies, arrange meetings, and sometimes even change his dental appointments, buy a birthday cake for his child, or drop him off at the airport.

What does Douglas do to the rank and position he holds? As a member of the faculty, he could make the role of a professor knowledgeable, inspirational, caring, responsible, and respectable in the minds of the students. There is no doubt that Douglas discriminates against the professorial position when he goes to class late, sends graduate students to run a class on his behalf, lectures a class with little preparation, or returns class assignments without critical comments. As the director of a research center, the chair of a department, and the dean of a college, Douglas could add to each leadership position a sense of fairness, respect, integrity, and even sanctity. There is no question that Douglas inflicts damage to the directorship, chairmanship, or deanship during his terms when he exploits people to his own academic benefits, manipulates people for his own administrative advancement, rewards people in his general favor, or penalizes people to his personal dislike. It is apparent that the position of a leadership suffers in the eyes of constituents when a serving leader acts in total or partial inappropriateness, irrationality, or incompetence.

Toward the institution, Douglas behaves as a discriminator in four different ways. First, he spreads corruption at the center he directs. Using grants
to hire and reward people, Douglas creates a general atmosphere at the center that money matters far more than science. It is money that makes people
stay in their position, conduct research, and receive benefits. Second, he
causes alienation among the faculty at the department he chairs. Applying
his version of scholarship, Douglas rallies one faction of the faculty against
the other. Members of the faculty who work with him in his favored areas
of study are granted resources, opportunities, and promotions, while those
whose research does not resonate with his interest are left out of the loop.
Third, he poisons morale in the college he leads. Taking advantage of the
college for his own academic ambitions, Douglas makes people throughout
the college feel that an academic division can be hijacked by its leader to
advance his or her personal agenda or career while being left in dysfunction
or failure to serve the needs of its ordinary members. Finally, he lowers professional ethics and standards in all three organizational levels he serves.
Although an institution and its functional units can sustain physically from
leadership to leadership, the institution as a whole and its units individually
may require a considerable amount of time to recover morally, spiritually,
and substantively from a discriminatory or predatory disservice rendered
by a particular leader.

The Victim

The most visible victims are individuals. Undergraduate students take water
in their education. Doctoral students face delays toward graduation. Secretaries work long hours before they can go home. Members of the faculty
have to find other employment if they are pushed away or look beyond their
home department or institution for resources and opportunities if they are
denied due support. Ironically, hours of time spent, tons of energy dispensed, and pages of work performed by graduate students in classrooms,
administrative staff behind desks, statisticians- or writers-for-hire in front
of computers, and junior faculty members in offices on or for Douglas's
classes, meetings, grants, projects, reports, or manuscripts may not necessarily generate enough credit or recognition that fairly satisfies him in his
professional pursuits. For example, while he clearly knows that it does not
mean much to him to publish a paper in a premier journal with his name as
the lead author, Douglas rarely takes time to think about how much sweat
and blood all his students, staff, and junior colleagues might have put into
the paper in the long process from draft to final manuscript to print.

The harmed but not so often visible in the consequence of their victimization are ranks, positions, and organizational entities, such as a unit, a
department, and a college. The college deviates from its core mission or
runs out of balance and efficiency. The department experiences unnecessary
tumult from factional infightings or outgrows one area while neglecting

many other areas of its service. The center chases money from place to place or overwhelms its research staff with a desperate sense of mercantilism. The position of directorship, chairmanship, and deanship loses its due authority, influence, and respect. The rank of professorship takes an unfavorable look of exploitation, politicking, and neglect. Trickily, while a center, a department, or a college has to bear specific sufferings from day to day for one or two whole terms of office, it may still not appear to serve its purpose in the eyes of an abusive or discriminatory leader. Indeed, Douglas often complains that he can use his college to do so little for his academic ambitions. For instance, how much recognition has he actually obtained by hosting a conference of scholars in his own field of study with thousands of college funds which could be rightfully used to support a dozen of faculty members to attend various national and international conferences to the tangible benefit of their individual careers?

The Compromise

People can literarily object it when they experience any kind of discrimination. But in reality most of them tend to find ways to accommodate and compromise an unfavorable treatment before they ever decide to stand up against it.

In the case of Douglas, undergraduate students may figure that he is the professor, he can do whatever he wants or he is supposed to act this way, or perhaps he will come back to class with some surprisingly inspirational lectures after a few absences from class instruction on serious academic undertakings. Graduate students likely reason that we receive valuable experiences in teaching when we take care of his classes, we benefit from it when he as our academic advisor gains fame, and perhaps we can make him share his research secrets when we do him more and more favors. Administrative staff may convince themselves that he may give us some sweet treats or even a raise in salary when he feels we serve him well. Anyway it is better to stay busy in the service of a leader who is keen to pursue something, personal or public, than to sit idle with a leader who does not know how or does not want to do anything at all. Members of the faculty may justify their cooperation, compliance, and acquiescence with these arguments: Douglas brings in money; this article has a higher chance of acceptance for publication with Douglas as the lead author although he does not do much of the work; this grant is more likely to be funded with Douglas as the principal investigator despite the fact that he did not and will not commit himself substantively to the project; and Douglas is not a villain even though he is self-centered, acts as a grant dealer, and has done harm rather than bringing honor to the center, the department, or the college and its credibility as an academic unit.

Neither a professional role nor an organization entity itself may make any concession or stage any resistance when it is thrown into the hands of a discriminatory person who occupies the role, services the position, or runs the organization. However, in the spirit of compromise, people may contend that Douglas and his actions add a new dimension to the rank of professorship, enrich the role of academic leadership, or make this center, this department, or this college more revealing of its interpersonal dynamics or inner structural complexities.

What does Douglas do to embrace and perhaps reciprocate all these compromising words, gestures, and deeds by his students, colleagues, and organizations? While he might think he could have acted more aggressively and relentlessly in exploiting students and staff, manipulating members of the faculty, and taking advantage of institutions and institutional resources, Douglas does pause sometimes, wondering how he might better advise students, improve working conditions for staff, assist colleagues, and make the center, the department, or the college under his stewardship more productive, efficient, and harmonious. For instance, he holds holiday parties at his home for students, staff, and faculty members; he occasionally gives students and junior colleagues the full opportunity to present a paper, review a manuscript, or publish an article without demanding credit for himself; and he spends time on making a strong case for the center, the department, or the college to obtain funding from within and without the university, which benefits not just himself but the faculty in general.

The Universal

Douglas is by no means an extreme outlier in his self-serving behaviors as a professor, a center director, a department chair, or a college dean. In fact, the point at issue is not much about the fact that he uses his rank, position, and authority to advance individual interests, seek personal fame, and secure academic influence. Instead it is about how he consciously or inadvertently puts a considerable number of people into disadvantageous positions when he does so. Most important, as he moves up to higher positions, he gains greater potentiality to inflict harm to many more individuals within the scope of his control or influence.

On a university campus, besides professors who can throw a class of students into a difficult situation, department chairs who may place a group of faculty members under an awkward position, and college deans who may cause specific harms to individual departments, the president, the provost, and other high-ranking administrators can in one way or the other discriminate against particular constituencies or constituents, the general membership of the university, or the whole university itself. For instance, the president may make remarks to tarnish the positive reputation of the university when he or she seeks and enjoys personal exposures in the mass media. It may take years of conscientious efforts by hundreds of students, staff, and faculty members to repair the damage he or she causes with one remark. The president may commit the whole university to some kind of public service when he or she attempts to smooth and sweeten his or her relationships with politicians, businesspeople, and social luminaries in the local community. The commitment can incur both conspicuous and inconspicuous costs to students in terms of training in knowledge and skills, the faculty by measures of scholarship, and the entire institution in the form of academic excellence. And the president may happen to be a diplomat-like or diehard socialite who likes joining in the fun of every academic and non-academic gathering upon which he or she can put his or her hands. He or she flies on first-class air tickets, stays in luxury hotels, and delegates his or her duties to vice presidents while away from campus. Imagine how many faculty members have to forgo their participation in academic conferences or must cope frugally with their scholarly travels just to make available enough funds in the university budget for one trip by the president.

Throughout academia, a journal editor, an association president, and a few leading scholars may say things that cast clouds over or place under shadows hundreds of students and scholars or do things that cost time and energy without due productivity and creativity to thousands of academic practitioners. For example, a journal editor may scare off or turn away many worthy contributors when he or she declares that he or she has published only 5 percent of all submissions to his or her journal or when he or she rarely acknowledges receipt of manuscripts, allows submissions to sit idle on shelves for months, or tends to find trouble with authors over minor issues such as length, citation style, or grammar. An association president may push a considerable number of students and scholars into an unhopeful direction when he or she uses association resources to advocate or promote his or her misguided academic agenda.

It ought to be pointed out, however, that a reasonable practice or rational policy by a caring, conscionable, or wise person in an important position can benefit a plethora of people as well, although it is always critical to be aware that many might have made unnoticeable sacrifices or have suffered from unnecessary discriminations even under the reputable influence of an honorable individual.

SITUATION 2

Health care is a highly regulated profession. Prospective practitioners in medicine, dentistry, and pharmacy are required to go through years of education, training, apprenticeship, or residency before they are granted professional licenses to work as doctors, dentists, or pharmacists. Somewhat implicit, though, reasons for stringent requirements upon health-care professionals are quite obvious: they take care of individual humans; nobody wants to be messed up with his or her body or mind; and nothing is more important than humans, their physical and mental well-being, in the whole world.

The question then is this: do healthcare professionals, especially doctors and dentists, commit fully to patients and patient care, translating all their training and credentials into ultimate patient experience, in their individual practices?

The Particular

Alibaba is a healthy person. He sees a doctor or a dentist only a few times a year for a routine medical exam, regular dental cleaning, or when he catches a cold, suffers an injury, or does not feel well on some part of his body for some time. Beyond himself, he takes his children to dental and medical offices when they have regular appointments or are in need of dental or medical attention. For his wife, Alibaba has three most important contacts with hospitals and healthcare professionals, one for an open-heart surgery, another due to a cesarean section in childbirth, and still another because of a six-month treatment for a chronic condition.

From his limited experience as patient and patient's family member, Alibaba develops a general yet clear impression about dentists, doctors, and dental or medical facilities. The impression is this: dentists in private practice hire dental assistants, hygienists, or technicians to do much of the dental work, from mouth X-raying, general cleaning, and quadrant scaling to root planing; doctors use nursing aids, licensed practical nurses, licensed vocational nurses, and registered nurses to take care of patients and many of patients' medical needs; hospitals hire nursing practitioners to do part of a physician's job, such as diagnosis, prescription, and treatment; and dental offices and medical facilities employ professional office managers, records filers, practice administrators, patient or treatment coordinators, insurance and financial coordinators, and other staffers to run day-to-day operations.

In particular, Alibaba has experiences with a number of practitioners. Dentist "A" performs every piece of dental work himself. Alibaba forever remembers the quality care he and his family had received until the dentist's retirement. Dentist "B" owns a sizable dental office which he keeps operational with lines of patients by a full team of dental workers and office managers while taking fishing trips in his private yacht or playing golf with his professional friends. Alibaba has rarely seen him work on his teeth since he signed up with the dentist several years ago. The same holds true for his wife and children. With regard to medical treatment, Doctor "A" maintains clinics in three different locations. He hires office and nursing staff to attend patients and their routine medical needs in each of those clinics. A regular patient would have to wait more than an hour to see the doctor for usually just five to ten minutes. Doctor "B" performs a number of surgeries in any typical week. At the operation table, she relies upon a team of assistants, nurses, and technicians to complete each surgery. She does not pay necessary attention to patients and their family members before a surgery nor does she spend much time monitoring a patient's recovery. Over years of practice, she has to some extent become a robotic figure to function inside the operation room. Nursing Practitioner "A" works in a hospital operated by a medical insurance agency as a health maintenance organization (HMO). Alibaba was scheduled to see her a few times. Inasmuch as he can recall it, Alibaba had to make another appointment with a doctor each and every time after he saw her simply because she was not able to fully take care of his medical needs.

The Discriminator

At the first sight, it just appears normal that dentists, doctors, or hospitals employ people of less training and lower credentials to assist with patient care. In critical analysis, however, they all as employment agents or agencies can hold real and potential discriminations against patients, healthcare staff, medical establishments, and even the whole healthcare profession.

Dental or medical doctors become discriminators against patients when they have dental assistants, medical technicians, nursing professionals, or office staff work on healthcare matters to which they are supposed to attend on their own. As they are likely to charge patients at a rate comparable to what a fully licensed dentist or physician is paid for the work, these dentists or physicians commit financial discriminations against patients as well. Similarly in relation to dental or medical aids or nursing staff, doctors are discriminators not only in terms of professional responsibilities and job duties because they put those assistants under challenge, risk, or stress unwarranted by training or experience, but also in terms of salaries and benefits because they are not likely to pay nursing, office, and other staffers comparably to what they have actually earned from patients. Simply put, doctors use their training and license to cover a range of healthcare work performed by nurses and other assistants they hire for their clinics or practices; they profit from patients as well as nursing, technical, and office staffs; they take credit for much of the work they have not done by themselves; and they can act as serious discriminators against patients and various healthcare professionals in the lower echelon of medicine or dentistry.

Hospitals, when they assign physicians in general medicine to perform work that ought to be done by a specialist, place nursing practitioners on schedule to see patients, or hire nursing aids or licensed practical or vocational nurses instead of registered nurses, commit discriminations in different dimensions against different professionals in health care or medicine. For example, against physicians, a hospital involved in such discriminations obviously devaluates in-depth training in medical specialties and could force specialists out of work or dampens the importance or significance of treatment by specialists. Against nursing practitioners, a hospital puts them under unnecessary or unwarranted risk or stress with a physician's job duty while paying them at a rate lower than that for an average doctor. Against registered nurses, a discriminatory hospital alienates them from nursing staff of lower training and fewer qualifications and could tarnish the professional reputation of registered nurses as patients are not necessarily able to distinguish different nursing roles. A hospital engaging in all these hiring practices certainly qualifies as a discriminator against patients. Whereas it virtually compromises the quality of care it affords to patients, the hospital unlikely charges patients less because it employs medical and nursing personnel of less training and experience in the rendering of patient care.

The Victim

Victims are clear in all these practices. On the one hand, there are patients. They can experience double, triple, or even multiple victimizations as they pay more money and spend more time for less patient service or lower-quality health care. For example, Patient "A" has to wait hours to see a doctor for five to ten minutes simply because the doctor feels it necessary and justifiable to schedule a maximum number of patient appointments with support from nurses and other staff. The patient is by no means allowed to pay less when he or she has to wait long for little attention by his or her doctor. Patient "B" is made to see a nursing practitioner. The patient will have to pay another visit with a doctor, request another absence from work, and make another payment if he or she does not find it helpful the treatment received from the nursing practitioner. Patient "C" is supposed to see a specialist for his or her medical condition. The patient will have to bear considerable sufferings in areas from health, work, and finance to the quality of life if he or she experiences one delay after another in referrals to see a specialist by making numerous helpless visits arranged by his or her hospital or health insurance agency with doctors in general medicine.

On the other hand, there are healthcare workers. They include aids, assistants, hygienists, technicians, nurses, and secretaries in dental offices or private clinics. They also can be dentists, physicians, nursing practitioners, or highly specialized medical professionals in sizable hospitals, especially those sponsored or operated by HMO-style insurance corporations. With regard to their experiences as victims, all these individuals seem to face not just one but oftentimes two, three, or even more victimizations. For instance, Nurse "A" receives salaries and fringe benefits from his or her hospital as a licensed practical nurse, lower than those paid to a registered nurse. Since the hospital does not hire as many registered nurses as necessary, he or she is forced to work as a registered nurse on a variety of duties and responsibilities. To meet the challenge of his or her work, Nurse "A" has to spend money to buy nursing books or attend nursing courses in his or her spare time. Physician "A" works at a HMO hospital as a doctor in internal medicine. Because the hospital does not have a liver specialist, he or she is pushed to attend patients with various liver conditions. To satisfy patients in their medical needs, Physician "A" has to spend his or her work and spare time to research diagnostic procedures, treatments, and preventive measures concerning liver and liver diseases. Ironically, he or she receives a reminder by the hospital that he or she needs to see more patients to be not too behind the required or average number of patients to be attended each week or month. Physician "B" spends a few more years on training in an area of medical specialty beyond his or her general practice in medicine. He or she nonetheless works as a physician in internal medicine as he or she has difficulty securing a specialist position with hospitals in the local area. While he or she is the designated person to see patients with medical conditions of his or her specialty, Physician "B" earns just as much as an average doctor in internal medicine at the hospital, far less than what a specialist of his or her qualifications deserves in the region.

Of course, medical establishments and the healthcare profession will ultimately suffer as victims, not only in public opinion or social image, but also in inner integration or self-sustenance, if both patients and medical professionals continue to experience their respective victimizations to a critical extent or in a significant degree.

The Compromise

People usually take what comes in life without any question. Patients may not be aware that they should be attended by the dentist or physician if they have an appointment with a dentist or physician. They may not be knowledgeable, experienced, or sophisticated enough to know if there is any difference in the quality of care when they are seen and treated by someone of less training and qualifications. Dental or medical assistants as well as nursing staff may not necessarily know all the divisions of labor that should rightfully prevail in medical establishments or throughout the healthcare profession. They may take it for granted that they do whatever the dentist or physician assigns and advises them to do in private clinics or practices. Even physicians may not always understand all the technicalities involved in medical specializations. They may feel it natural to research special health conditions and attend patients with peculiar needs even if they are neither trained nor compensated to tackle those medical difficulties.

People adapt to reality. When they see they do not receive what they are supposed to have, they may comfort themselves with some self-explanations or justifications. For example, patients may shrug off their clinical visits with no or limited attention by a dentist, a doctor, or a specialist with these words: "It doesn't matter as long as I have my teeth or illness taken care of"; "I don't care"; or "I actually feel better with the hygienist than the dentist or the nursing practitioner than the doctor." Dental or medical assistants and perhaps nursing staff may rationalize their work with this reasoning: "That is what it is everywhere and all the time"; "We just have to do all this work for the dentist or physician because he or she always has so many patients to see on any typical day"; and "I experience a greater sense of self-worth when I am trusted to do all these things by the dentist or physician." Similarly, a physician may convince him or herself with these arguments: "Medical school does not mean to prepare us to handle every medical situation"; "This affords me a prime opportunity to learn something new or in greater depth"; and "I feel more productive when I move far and beyond the routine medical practice of seeing patients with similar medical issues in endless repetitions."

On the part of discriminators, dentists or physicians may sometimes pause, wondering if they should keep their clinics or practices in proper perspective so that they can spend more time with patients, provide assistants with better working conditions, or render nursing staff greater material benefits. A hospital can engage in critical reflections as well: wouldn't it be in its long-term interest to hire, cultivate, and entertain a medical team of a necessary variety of specializations as well as a nursing staff of a sufficient range of qualifications to deliver optimal health care to the people of the community in which it resides and operates? However, aforementioned discriminations in the healthcare profession continue perhaps because practicing dentists or physicians figure that they can go far and further in the use of their dental or medical licenses as they put so much into their past training through dental or medical school, residency, or specialization; they can stretch thin and thinner in the employment of their dental or medical assistants, nursing staff, and other personnel as they offer the latter jobs to earn a living and opportunities to work as healthcare workers; and they can expand and extend even beyond limit in the operation of their private clinics or practices as they like everybody else deserve to make maximum profits in their earthly callings. The same holds true for medical establishments, such as health insurance agencies and hospitals, that model after business corporations which take money as their bottom lines and pursue profit as their ultimate goals.

The Universal

A few observations seem to be common within the healthcare profession and beyond. First, licenses in dentistry, medicine, nursing, and other professional practices tend to be exhaustively used by individual practitioners. Since they have made heavy investments in school, specialized training, and other licensing requirements, licensed dentists, physicians, nurses, and other professionals feel they have an indisputable mandate or reason to make maximum use of their hard-earned licenses. A dentist may maintain several offices in one area, whereas a nurse may jog between a full-time job in a hospital and a care-for-the-elderly business at home. As they stretch far and thin in catching as many clients as necessary or making as much money as possible, many licensed professionals can only keep doing the same things over and over again in their careers. They spend little time to continually learn new knowledge and update or upgrade professional skills as so designed and expected by licensing.

Second, patients in particular and clients or consumers in general are not necessarily aware of what they receive from their physicians, specialists, hospitals, or other service providers. While in most cases ordinary patients or consumers are not able to distinguish healthcare or other professional services by providers of varying training, qualifications, and experience, in the long run or in the final analysis they are likely to suffer discriminations in their unavoidable dealings with professionals and professional authorities. The discriminations they face in this regard may come doubly, triply, or even multiply, from time, money, and health to the quality of life.

Third, if aids, assistants, technicians, and other workers in the lower echelon of dentistry, medicine, and pharmacy feel they can take exploitative work, working assignments, working conditions, and working compensations, as their ways to move up through the ladder or their dues to pay for a better professional career, they are likely to do the same when they themselves someday become dentists, physicians, and other licensed professionals. Although the whole healthcare profession may thus find its own justifications for discriminatory practices in the dynamics of personal changeover, it still must open up to regulatory review, critical analysis, and institutional reform. While it is true that it takes sacrifices by many dedicated individual practitioners to build and sustain a great profession, it would be heartless that a profession could for so long downplay, blot out, or ignore day-to-day experiences by a large number of its underpaid, overworked, or even stressed-out workers in the service of the more privileged.

SITUATION 3

The world of entertainment is where dramas, fictions, plays, the imaginative, the surreal, or the unreal are made into life-paralleling stories or put on theatre-like stages for people to watch, cheer on, or lament about. Perhaps because of the dramatization entertainment so often evokes in its productions, the profession of entertainment experiences the most dramatic and drastic discrepancies, disjuncture, and discriminations ever witnessed over the history of human civilizations in the ways entertainers, entertaining workers, and various supportive staff receive compensations, attain fame, and gain status.

The Particular

Alibaba is a regular consumer to the cultural industry. He watches movies, attends concerts, visits theatres, views entertainment news, and reads books about the world of entertainment occasionally in his spare time. Through friends and in his personal networks, Alibaba also happens to know a few people who work in entertainment as photographer, stunt actor, writer, and production staff.

Dotted, fragmented, and limited though in his knowledge, Alibaba seems to feel clear, strong, and unequivocal about how people fare in recognition and rewards in the mass media, across the film industry, and throughout the world of entertainment. On television news, an anchorman or anchorwoman reads scripts written by editorial staff, paraphrases reports gathered by field correspondents, or just asks questions to newsmakers in the real world; he or she makes millions while reporters and news writers barely earn enough to support a middle-class lifestyle, and he or she becomes a news personality whereas news reporters and staff writers receive only occasional appearances on television or remain totally unnoticed behind screens. On late-night shows, a comedian utters jokes, tells humorous stories, and makes fun of current events according to what a group of writers have prepared for the program in the day; he or she draws tens of thousands dollars from any typical hour-long show whereas any of his or her writers may only receive at most a few hundreds in salary on any regular day of research, composition, and editing, and he or she turns into a celebrity while individual writers, technicians, and production staff contribute their energy, talents, and time in the backstage without any attention from the public. The same holds true for talk shows and various other radio and televisions programs featuring a major host or hostess.

Most interestingly, an author may take years to complete a novel; a director may plan and work for months on a movie based upon the novel; and an actor or actress may spend days to play a role in the movie. However, when it comes to recognition, an actor or actress may become a star overnight following his or her role in a movie; a director may become a sought-after figure in interviews from talk show to talk show or from news network to news network when his or her film tops weekend box office sales; and an author may not live long enough in total obscurity to see some of his or her work gradually become a masterpiece in public eyes. In terms of wealth, extravagance, and indulgence in life, there are numerous movie stars wearing costly fashions, riding in luxury automobiles, and residing in fancy mansions; there are many film directors or producers flying corporate jets, belonging to exclusive clubs, and living in high societies; and there are a considerable number of authors or writers in the history of literature who struggle for survival all the time in their individual life and never benefit in either profit or materialistic enjoyment from their timeless contributions until death.

The Discriminator

There are seemingly no individuals standing out as clear discriminators. If there are discriminations, sources do not apparently trace to individual players. Tradition, culture, customs, social conventions, or general practices are usually blamed for this unfairness or injustice, while actors, actresses, directors, producers, or media owners are not necessarily viewed as evildoers.

Beginning with general practices, they feature proximity and commercialism in the contemporary era. When a film hits the top of box office sales, producers, directors, actors, and actresses are the first to collect benefits in the form of money, fame, or both. Who would think much of the original author who develops the story in all its meticulous details or of those negligible individuals who work on filmmaking fields, in film-editing rooms, or at sound-recording studios? Social conventions tend to simplify a crowd or a mass of people with a few representatives. Movie viewers do not normally pay much attention to various roles. Instead, they follow one, two, or three major figures in their own portrayal of a rather complex original story from a film. Customs fuel and reinforce public sensations with movie stars and their often surreal lifestyles. People have prescriptions for what movie stars say and do, while movie stars can literally expect how the public view them and cheer them on. Culture justifies and sustains fashions, vogues, and trendy practices inherent in celebrities and their sometimes unreal pursuits in the ages of modernity and postmodernism. People hope to find their lost interest, meaning, and substance in the lives of a few luminaries they constantly as well as instantly produce and reproduce in the mass media and throughout society. And tradition, of course, keeps the momentum of commercialism, fetishism, popular culture, and social trends built and accumulated over time. With fame, wealth, and power concentrated in the hands of a few individuals, servants, supporting staff, and working professionals surrounding those privileged individuals in particular and the mass, the public, or the populace in general have to bear lack of concern, neglect, inadequate compensations, poor working or living conditions, belittlement, and a sense of alienation, loss, or meaninglessness resultant from those actual experiences.

In sharper analysis, individuals, such as news anchormen or anchorwomen, talk show and other program hosts or hostesses, actors or actresses, directors, and producers, can be seen as acute discriminators as well. For example, when actors or actresses negotiate contracts in their favor, they automatically leave an unfavorable portion of a usually fixed pie to all other players, especially little ones, in the filmmaking process. Most noticeably, famous actors or actresses can refuse or choose to avoid unfavorable acts or actions in their role-playing assignments by using so-called stunt actors or actresses on their behalf. In this practice, original actors or actresses turn into direct discriminators against stunt actors or actresses, because the former use the latter not only as a shield from grave dangers, but also as an insurance for a wholesome or incidence-free receipt of fame, compensation, and celebrity treatments.

The Victim

There are definite victims in this irrational worship for stars or celebrity personalities across the literature, the film, the mass media, and the popular culture. They are ordinary yet talented, regular yet skilled, and normal yet diligent professionals who write stories, design costumes, hair, or makeup, create visual images, make production sets, coordinate musicals, manage locations or schedules, and edit scripts, sounds, or images.

First, victims are likely to lose their due share of reward and recognition derivable from a production or inherent in a program because reward or recognition is essentially a zero-sum game. For example, when a television network pays its prime news anchorman or anchorwoman with a high compensation package, it automatically opts for limited salaries for regular reporters, writers, photographers, and other workers. When a film studio signs a contract in favor of one or two star actors or actresses in a movie, it naturally throws itself into a situation where it can only offer meager compensations for many ordinary workers, such as writing, filming, recording, and editing staff, involved in the production process. The same is true for recognition. As limelight centers primarily on a lead actor or actress in a feature film, people rarely know that there is a full army of production staff involved in the making of the film, ranging from assistant director, stunt coordinator, illustrator, set decorator, props builder, carpenter, greensman, hairdresser, costume standby, camera operator, boom operator, dolly grip, gaffer, colorist, and matte painter to Foley artist.

Second, victimization can be gravely aggravated by comparison and contrast. In other words, there is an added effect of relative deprivation, especially so in the world of entertainment and mass media. In newspapers, magazines, and other printed media, authors write about someone or something as a third person to avoid any mentioning of themselves in the story. They put aside their names or leave their names somewhere unnoticeable in the article. On television, viewers can often see images in which reporters, photographers, and other program support staff dodge limelight or sneak from cameras to gather newsworthy materials or catch moments of luminaries from a scene. Besides attention, recognition, and fame, it can be sad and alienating to a writer when he or she has to write a story in his or her small apartment about an interview that he or she has conducted with a movie star in the latter's huge mansion. Most contrastingly, comedians who speak jokes in minutes make many times more monies than writers who create jokes in hours; actors or actresses who act out stories in days earn many times more dollars than authors who compose stories in years; and program hosts or hostesses who read contents or introduce guests in the front stage take many times more payments than production staff who develop contents or secure interviewees in the backstage. Where is fairness? Where is equality? And eventually where is social justice?

Third, although the general public may feel entertained when they watch films, shows, and content programs featuring stars and celebrity personalities, they can be misinformed, misled, and hence victimized by the cultural industry that favors form over content, appearance over substance, or front stage over backstage. A false consciousness may develop, casting doubts on diligence as a cornerstone for social progress or leaving youths with an impression that they can act out or play around toward personal success. A twisty compartmentalization may form, privileging celebrities, luminaries, or stars as a special category of people who can live their lives beyond and above common sense, convention, custom, or even law. It is incalculable how much a society would suffer when it has to give unwarranted influences to a number of overblown celebrities who are not necessarily people with the best knowledge, experience, and judgment in their time. For example, the United States builds upon science and technology for its prosperity and progress. However, instead of honoring science and scientists, the country gives tremendous fame and wealth to stars and celebrities in entertainments and sports, enabling them to serve as role models for youths or to invade different levels of government as power players. Would the United States be far better off if more people looked up to scientists for inspirations and more governments ran in the hands of people who are trained and experienced with scientific knowledge?

The Compromise

There seems to be no lack of excuses or justifications for one side to inflict or take discrimination upon or from the other. Movie stars, television personalities, or other celebrities collect millions in salaries and benefits, feeling that they have entertained millions in the mass. They gather fame insatiably, figuring that the more recognition they have across the populace, the more people they will be able to entertain with their performances. To an original author whose story he acts out in a film, an actor may take credit without any indebtedness if he believes that the original story would have faded into total obscurity without his masterful acting throughout the movie. To a team of creative and productive staff who write scripts, design programs, and make settings behind the scene, a hostess of a television show may enjoy ratings and compensations without much gratitude if she thinks that words composed, contents designed, and programs produced would have turned into garbage had she not caught the audience with her skillful maneuvering and manipulations in front of the camera. In truly conciliatory tones or terms, however, hosts or hostesses, anchormen or anchorwomen, actors or actresses, and other star figures may routinely or on special occasions thank their coaches, mentors, reporters, writers, production staff, or business personnel openly in the mass media or at public gatherings. Substantively, they may issue annual bonuses to their writers, artists, and other supporting staffers, take them to dinners or vacations, or raise salaries for them.

Professional writers, artists, and other supporting staff, on the other hand, may convince themselves to stay behind the scene with relatively meager compensations for a variety of practical reasons. First, although acting on stage or speaking in front of a crowd is not necessarily one of the most precious or productive human skills, it can bring about instant fame and seemingly unlimited wealth in contemporary society to a small number of people who happen to have that talent. Second, although an actor or a host of a show is not necessarily more intelligent than any average member of his staff, he happens to have caught part of the public's attention by luck or by talent in one dimension or another. Third, although an actress or a news anchorwoman does not necessarily have more education than any typical middle-class professional, she happens to have taken her position by seniority or by relationship of some kind. Fourth, professional writers, artists, and other supporting staff know that they benefit directly from the fame their star actors or actresses or celebrity hosts or hostesses have in public eyes. After all, they depend upon that fame to secure their jobs, increase their incomes, diversify their work assignments, and enrich their professional careers. Fifth, professional writers, artists, and other supporting personnel understand that they can only compare to people of similar qualifications who work outside film, entertainment, and the mass media on matters of reward and recognition. Although they may develop a sense of relative deprivation by working closely with stars and celebrity personalities, they should not by any means take that sense of alienation seriously as they have no grounds to use a special category of people such as movie stars and media celebrities as their reference group in any way. Finally, many professional writers, artists, and other supporting staff may feel fortunate to work directly with an established celebrity or a rising star. Through a film star or media personality, though, they may still feel they know quickly how they fare in the mass media with their comedies, news reports, songs, stories, illustrations, or designs. Or in a sense they may even feel they themselves receive more or less public attention when they see their movie star or broadcast personality go up and down in ratings.

The Universal

There is always a team of people, oftentimes highly educated, trained, or specialized professionals, performing hard labor, making blind contributions, and sacrificing unique talents behind every movie star, radio or television personality, and other celebrity in the world of entertainment, sports, and the mass media. The question is then this: does a star figure exploit the labor and steal the talents of writers, artists, and other supporting staff to build his or her fame and wealth? Or does the star provide an umbrella under which his or her professional writers, artists, and other staff make a living, develop a career, and perhaps gain some side attention from the populace?

Centering on discrimination, star figures are not necessarily intentional discriminators. In fact, many individuals of celebrity status may even make conscientious efforts to pay their serving staff with generous compensation packages, provide them with favorable working conditions, and relate to them privately as family members. To a large degree, limelight focuses on stars because of public sensation, fame revolves around celebrities due to cultural convention, and wealth concentrates in the hands of entertainment, media, or sport personalities according to established social practices.

In contrast, writers, artists, musicians, and other professional staff in service of movie stars and other celebrities can be willing victims of institutionalized discriminations. They work in maximum diligence as well as to the best of their training and talents to write scripts, create settings, design sound effects, and make other necessary preparations so that stars can speak intelligently, appear wondrously, and perform entertainingly on stage. They keep secrets so that celebrities can enjoy a unique lifestyle with palpable public sensations and without interference from the law and authority. They dodge the camera and take regular pay so that featured personalities can gain all the attention, keep most program earnings, and have all the opportunities to relate to the populace. In terms of loyalty, there are no lack of moving stories where writers, artists, musicians, and other professionals take pride in serving for a long time a famous figure in film, theatre, literature, radio, television, sports, and other areas of popular culture or find comfort in "drinking soups while watching their celebrity hosts or hostesses eat meat."

The ultimate victim, of course, is the society that feeds, supports, and entertains a special group of stars and celebrities in contrast to ordinary citizens. Society suffers from division and even polarization as it allows a small number of privileged members to gain fame, accumulate wealth, and wield influence on the basis of the hard labor, precious talents, and conscientious contributions by many regular individuals. It keeps and spreads an illusion that luck or opportunity may pull one out of the ordinary into the extraordinary. The illusion may poison the spirit of diligence, dampen the importance of education and cultivated intelligence, threaten the morale of fairness and justice, and send some members of the society, especially youths, to unrealistic professional pursuits, unsuccessful career paths, and unsatisfactory life courses.

SITUATION 4

In the modern and postmodern world of business, while there are still millions of small entrepreneurs who own, run, and manage individual productions, sales, services, or trades with their own hands and heads, there are hundreds of thousands of corporate executives and managers who strike deals on golf courses, make contacts at exclusive clubs, develop plans in office buildings, spread rules via advanced communications, monitor productions behind computer screens, and control movement of materials or flow of people through a complex bureaucracy. With the model of mass production, the magic of scientific management, and the economy of scale, business corporations seem to be capable of running automatically, expanding exponentially, and profiting unlimitedly. Corporate executives make millions with neither much hard labor by hand nor much serious work in head. They enjoy life with luxury, in style, and by measure of extravagance. Using their corporations as bets or baits in domestic security exchanges or global stock markets, they can even tap into consumer savings, public pensions, real estate mortgages, social securities, and other equities invested in corporate notes and stocks in a country or around the world to double, triple, and often multiply their wealth and wealthy lifestyle.

The Particular

Alibaba has a few classmates, from high school to college to graduate school, who have ventured into the world of business with noticeable success. One of them commands as chairman and chief executive officer a multinational corporation whose stocks are traded publicly on a major security exchange in the world. With his classmates in business, Alibaba maintains meaningful contacts. On important holidays, he exchanges greetings with them. Over business or leisure trips, he visits some of them, holding in-depth conversations around issues of mutual interest. So do his classmates in business when they each visit or transit through the city where Alibaba lives. Occasionally, Alibaba consults some of them on important business matters he himself has to deal with or happens to be interested in knowing.

Besides his classmates, Alibaba has a few anecdotal encounters with seemingly important figures in business management. One time, he sat next to the chief executive officer of a major restaurant chain in the first-class cabin on a five-hour flight. He had quite an interesting conversation with the person over various aspects of business and business operation. Another time, Alibaba found a high-level corporate manager as his talking companion in the lobby of a hotel when they both could not fall asleep in the middle of the night due to jet lag. To kill time, they delved pretty deeply into each other's hobbies and professional worlds. Also on a couple of advisory boards, Alibaba served with business owners or operators in his local community. Prior to or after board meetings, he always managed to find time to ask his fellow board members questions about their businesses and business practices.

Furthermore, Alibaba likes watching business news on television. He pays attention to roundtable debates on issues, commentaries by experts, and investigatory reports about companies or lines of business broadcast on major news networks. In particular, he is interested in feature stories about individual businesses and businesspersons. Alibaba also spends time reading business articles in magazines and newspapers. On some Sundays, he would take a considerable part of the morning to follow news, reports, and analyses through a few printed media. Waiting for an appointment in a doctor' clinic or at a dentist's office is another good time when Alibaba can peruse some materials published on business and businesspeople.

The Discriminator

Alibaba doesn't believe that he is a Marxist who views businesses, business owners, and business stakeholders in capitalist societies as profiting from and prospering on discriminations, exploitations, and manipulations of all working-class people. However, based on his knowledge about the world of business as an educated citizen, he seems quite positive that business owners, business executives, and perhaps most upper-level business managers as well are intentional or unintentional discriminators against ordinary employees in particular and regular consumers in general.

Business owners place at the center the return of their capital investment and the profit of their business operation. They make political contributions to ensure that laws are made and regulations are enforced in the interest of capitalist enterprising. They offer charitable donations or provide community services to keep local residents attitudinally favorable toward business. Inside their business, they establish rules, set goals, lay out procedures, apply scientific principles, employ machines, and utilize technologies so that they can maximize profit while minimizing their own effort. To employees, they have an instinct in hiring as few as possible, paying them with least benefits, or using most cost-effective incentives to elicit best performances from them. In front of consumers or clients, business owners have a motivation to catch as many as possible, sell them products at highest prices, or utilize best-working strategies to avoid most difficult services for them. For a multimillion-dollar mansion where he or she resides, a luxury car he or she rides, or an extravagant party he or she holds, how much does a business owner wrench from ordinary employees of his or her business or regular consumers of his or her products? Imagine one who owns a fast-food restaurant chain. How many individual workers have to labor hard day and night for a minimum wage to fund his wedding with a young beauty? Or how many of his stand-alone restaurants have to profit from thousands of regular consumers to support his family life that normally costs a few millions a year?

Corporate executives care about the market share of their products and the stock value of their company. When they cut the price of their products to win competition, they do not necessarily reduce expenditures on their own travels in corporate jets, presidential suites, or executive limousines. Instead, they are likely to squeeze pennies from employee salaries, benefits, or services. When they see their products expand in the share of market, they do not necessarily lower the price, boost the service, or do something else to the benefits of ordinary consumers throughout the market. Instead, they are likely to go to the board of directors for higher salaries and larger bonuses for themselves. Most interestingly, as fewer corporate executives emerge from backstage as original owners or from bottom up as floor workers or frontline supervisors, they tend to have less empathy with ordinary employees and their everyday working experiences. Or as more corporate executives graduate from elite business schools, they tend to create, expand, and maintain a corporate reality that there is a special group of executive talents who can take turns running major corporations around the world, who may deserve the highest compensations on the face of the earth, and who should keep access or entitlement to the most luxurious lifestyles through human civilizations, all at the ultimate cost of individual working and consuming people in contemporary society.

The Victim

The most immediate victims of business discriminations are people who have to sell their labor to a farming facility, a manufacturing firm, a service agency, or other enterprise for a living. If they work closely as chauffeurs, cooks, gardeners, maids, nannies, or secretaries for business owners or corporate executives, they are likely to experience relative deprivations. Who would not feel a sense of the world as somehow being unfair, unjust, or irrational if one sees with one's own eyes the person whom one serves is not necessarily more educated, more intelligent, or more reasonable than any ordinary folk one knows of, yet lives a life of high style one can never imagine possible for people of one's kind? Relatively when they look at their paychecks, service employees to business owners or corporate executives may feel they are well compensated or taken care of by their boss, host, or hostess. In absolute terms, however, they will never know how much they may be owed for their dedicated and loyal service. The same holds true for all general employees who work in offices or on mass production lines for business owners or corporate executives who harvest profit or compensation in millions.

Then come the consumers who pay for products or services by farms, plants, banks, or other business enterprises. Individual consumers may obtain particular goods or services in high or low prices from the market. However, given the fact that every viable agency, company, firm, or other business entity in the market stands to make a profit, ordinary consumers technically have to pay more in prices than what any product or service is worth in its absolute value. The irony is that ordinary consumers, being inevitably or universally discriminated against in the capitalist market, though, are not only willing victims most of the time, but also happy victims sometimes when they feel they land the best deals for some consumer goods or services they want or need in life.

Of particular notability in this institutionalized discrimination are working people in general. Working people create value through labor. The fact that they work hard yet can only support a working-class lifestyle suggests that they receive only part of the value they have created in the form of salary and fringe benefits. Combined with the fact that business owners or corporate executives do not labor much yet can harvest a fortune, working-class people are clear victims in the labor market. Moreover, working-class people constitute the majority of the consumer population. As soon as they receive their paychecks that usually reflect only part of their labor value, they go to the consumer market to buy foods, drinks, and other everyday supplies, which in prices profitable to businesses may not be worth what they pay with their hard-earned salary. In other words, working-class people are bound to face double discriminations, as both laborer and consumer, in the capitalist world system.

The Compromise

Since the system allows business enterprises to profit in piecemeal from large numbers of transactions, it does not leave working people as well as the consuming public much awareness or grounds to challenge particular business owners or corporate executives who can make millions within the premises of the system rule. While Karl Marx hoped for a widespread consciousness awakening and a systematic collective organizing to change the system, most working-class people would seemingly rather seek compromise, peace, and comfort in status quo.

Ordinary employees first of all may feel thankful to have a job with a business. Using comparable references, they may hardly see if they are underpaid in particular or exploited in general. When they happen to have noticed that business owners or corporate executives gather a considerable amount of wealth, they may shrug off the fact with this line of reasoning: they have capitals, and we don't; they take a great deal of risk in running a business, and we might just rest with it if we have money; they are special, lucky, talented, or blessed, and we aren't. The same holds true for regular consumers. First of all, they feel happy to see lower prices brought by the scale of business. With eyes on the consumer market as a whole, they may be able to figure out the relative worth of goods or services in terms of brand, quality, and price. Here then comes the old saying by consumers: you get what you pay for. More interestingly, some consumers may even make an effort to patronize, defend, or protect their favorite merchants or manufacturers when they feel they receive good values from those businesses.

Business owners or corporate executives, on the other hand, may intuitively realize that they can make employees work more productively or in greater dedication and loyalty when they treat each of their managers, frontline supervisors, and floor workers with proper respect and adequate compensations. Similarly, they may understand that they can keep consumers coming back to their agencies, farms, plants, or stores if they provide each of their clients or customers with genuine quality and true value in products or services. In philosophical terms, a few may even recognize their social obligations to aid those who are left out of the system or otherwise in need, knowing that they have benefited from the system that operates inherently to the economic advantage of the propertied and the rich.

The Universal

Business owners and corporate executives as enterprising professionals seem to benefit from an inevitable discrimination that inheres in capitalism from an ideological perspective or any system from a practical point of view. The discrimination is inevitable in the sense that a system has to take more from than it offers to individual parts in order to continue as a viable system. The consumer market automatically holds discriminations against consumers because if it gives all consumers more than they pay for, it would push individual businesses to bankruptcy and then itself to nonexistence. The labor market naturally places individual laborers under discriminatory positions for if it compensates them exactly for what they create out of their labor, it would make every business nonprofit or at a loss and hereto itself cease to operate. There might be legitimate counterarguments. That is, it is not inevitable discrimination but the miracle of integration that makes a system work: the integration of parts in a system is always more than the mechanical summation of individual parts.

With inevitable discrimination in sight, there then appear willing or unwilling victims and intentional or unintentional discriminators. Consumers shop for products and services. Every time they buy something, they willingly take some amount of discrimination in value. If they are aware of such discrimination, they may say this: I am unwilling, but what else can I do? Workers look for employment. When they work on a job, they willingly bear some level of exploitation relative to the worth of labor. When they are conscious of such exploitation, thanks to Karl Marx perhaps, they are likely to utter this: I am unwilling; is there any alternative nonetheless?

On the part of business, business owner, and corporate executive, some would make themselves sound unintentional by saying, "I own this business for a living or hold this executive position as a job, and I have no intention to discriminate or mistreat anyone," whereas others might be straightforward by making their intention unambiguously clear: "I own or run this business for a profit and will have to make some people disadvantaged or discriminated."

It ought to be pointed out that inevitable discrimination discriminates. In other words, it serves as a prompting backdrop or a downward slide to somehow facilitate or support intentional discriminators against unwilling victims. For example, it is easier for an exploitative employer to keep his or her employees working harder, longer, or for less compensation than for an unwilling employee to decline a demand or forgo a requirement without fear. Similarly in the consumer market, it is more plausible for a greedy business owner to suggest costly yet unnecessary post-sale repairs and services than for an unwillingly unsophisticated customer to take some commercially propagandized or otherwise perceived risks with an already purchased product.

SITUATION 5

Government, power, and politics used to be a family affair. An imperial or royal family passed power from generation to generation by blood linkage, continuing an empire or kingdom over time in the name of a dynasty. In the contemporary era, although some countries nominally keep their imperial or royal heritages and some dictators actually transfer power to their children or family members, many more nations in the world seemingly run their political affairs by way of public participation, such as voting and democracy, or bureaucratic mobility, such as recruitment and promotion. Politics is now becoming more and more of a profession, allowing literally any individual who happens to have an aspiration in power to pursue a political career or turn into a professional politician.

The rise of a political profession with involvement from common citizenry, however, does not change much the way discrimination, exploitation, and manipulation take place in politics. As a matter of fact, whereas in imperial, royal, authoritarian, or dictatorial polities, superiors or subjects used subordinates or servants to keep power throughout a closed system, in democracies political aspirants from among entertainment celebrities, business tycoons, professional high achievers, and other social luminaries need herds of advisors and masses of volunteers to run campaigns from place to place and from time to time when they vie for office across an open landscape. Once they are in office, they more than ever need to mobilize and utilize ordinary people as materials and tools to implement their plans, execute their agendas, and reach their goals.

The Particular

Alibaba is a keen political observer. He follows elections one after another at local, statewide, and national levels. At the height of an election, he would spend hours on various forms of the mass media, from newspaper, magazine, and radio to television, to read feature articles about candidates, watch news and news analyses, and listen to campaign speeches by major candidates. He would even drive to local gatherings where nominees from key political parties make campaign appearances.

On reflection, Alibaba tends to believe that politics or political profession steals too much attention from the populace and wastes too many resources from taxpayers. In a closed political system, such as authoritarianism and dictatorship, it is anybody's guess how much common citizens suffer in their forced or repressed attention, contributions, and subordination to the regime. Under democracy, on the other hand, it is everyone's observation that mass media allocate considerable amounts of space or airtime, the government consumes tremendous amounts of tax revenues, political parties draw ample amounts of social resources, and common citizens make immeasurable amounts of labor and time contributions to political affairs, from election to administration, from propaganda to practice, and from the change of a policy to the maintenance of the bureaucracy. For instance, a national election could overtake a whole country with most, if not all, of its attention and resources for months. In the United States, hundreds of media reporters would follow, thousands of political volunteers would work for, and millions of ordinary citizens would participate with a major party candidate and his or her campaign activities for almost one year.

With regard to career politicians, Alibaba tends to consider them as professional manipulators. In open societies, they make public speeches, rally ordinary constituents, seek political alliances, and appeal to the general populace. During election campaigns, candidates hire advisors, recruit volunteers, attract donors or sponsors, and tease supporters. Pledges are made, promises extended, and appearances managed to invite monetary contributions, free service in labor, and sensational response in the form of vote. Once they take office, however, most politicians are likely to follow the order of the existing political machinery. They may please or disappoint some of their supporters on some issues or occasions. But most of the time, they act without any tangible effects to the mass of people who either support or oppose them for their leadership and policy initiatives.

The Discriminator

Most people are made to believe that politicians follow history, represent people, and act upon the collective will of a nation. They rarely take a critical view of large social structures and processes to see how political leaders or career politicians discriminate against the people or constituents they represent and the country or constituencies they serve.

In general, political leaders are discriminators against a constituency, whether it is a city, a county, a province, or a country. As they assume positions in the constituency, career politicians are most likely to use all resources and opportunities within the reach of their leadership to extend social connections, advance communications skills, expand personal profiles, build mass bases of support, and lay political foundations for higher offices of a larger constituency. A mayor works for a city. But residents of the city will soon realize how much he or she utilizes the city as a personal stage to leap into the office of governorship when he or she later becomes the provincial governor. A governor serves a province. Until he or she takes the presidency of the country, people of the province will not see clearly and thoroughly how he or she benefits from the province as a personal vehicle in his or her overall political career. Although not every career politician possesses the luck to proceed linearly from the office of the mayor to governorship to presidency, most of them certainly have ambitions to move up to higher offices while serving lower constituencies. It is therefore no doubt that all politicians qualify as discriminators against local or smaller constituencies they serve now and then across the political landscape. Even when he or she reaches the highest office of a country, a supreme leader may still have a keener interest in making him- or herself an eternal figure in national history or world civilizations rather than leaving something tangibly beneficial for his or her country and countrymen.

In particular, political leaders are discriminators against all individuals who work for them directly or indirectly, voluntarily or involuntarily, and by way of body or mind. For example, political leaders steal ideas from advisors and experts who explore alternatives, make proposals, develop policies, and forecast outcomes. They take authorship of public speeches crafted by professional writers or special presentations prepared by office staff. In physical aspect, political leaders rob the safety and security of bodyguards, police officers, or secret service personnel who shield away all possible dangers, harms, and risks. Most important, political leaders enjoy limelight and support in mass events where volunteers spend hours of free labor on planning and organization. They usurp credit and fame from ordinary constituents who might have suffered or sacrificed for the nominal or actual success of some policy changes or institutional reforms during the term of office. Essentially, politicians use people as means and tools to execute their wills, implement their agendas, reach their goals, and fulfill their ambitions.

The Victim

Political actors can never be neutral. When they take actions, they inevitably benefit one part of a constituency or one segment of a constituent population at the expense of another. In other words, victimization is inherent in political process.

In a broad sense, victims of a political leader can be his or her whole constituency, which could be a city, a county, a province, or a country. For example, a city can be held as a hostage for corruption, nepotism, wasteful extravagance, racial hatred, political divisiveness, financial bankruptcy, environmental disaster, or a partial or full combination of all these problems when the mayor of the city chooses to practice such policies during his or her term of office. A province can be used as a campaign stage for a national office when the governor of the province opts to keep his job while running for a position beyond provincial politics. Instead of being duly served by a dedicated governor, the province may unavoidably bear all unnecessary disruption or negativity amid a typical political campaign. Instead of benefiting from its chief administrator, the province may end up losing resources, productivity, or political leverage to his or her personal ambitions. Similarly, a country can turn into a furnace of useless ideology, a battlefield of national division, or a target of international isolation when the supreme leader of the country decides to use his or her country as a personal vehicle to demonstrate political will, practice a utopian scheme, or reach some self-set goals. It may take years, and sometimes even generations, for a nation to heal from all the wounds it suffers from one leader in history.

More closely, victims of a career politician are often his or her supporters. Supporters make financial donations, put in their time and labor on campaign activities, or offer other material and nonmaterial contributions. They are most likely not to receive any benefits when the politician they support takes office. In other words, most supporters take a hidden victimization simply because they invest in politicians but do not harvest any gains from their political investment. Imagine hundreds of thousands of volunteers who only face difficulty finding employment when the candidate for whom they work diligently toward a national election victory becomes the president. Specifically, all immediate aids, advisors, security guards, and other supporting staff of a political figure, while they have the opportunity to partake in the spotlight, material benefits, and political influence, may not be able to claim full credit for the work they actually do on behalf of the politician. For instance, an expert advisor is likely to become a victim in authorship or intellectual property when he or she chiefly or single-handedly develops a policy only to the public recognition of the leader whom he or she counsels behind the scene.

The Compromise

Politicians may not necessarily have a clear sense about their own abuse of power, dereliction of duty, or discrimination against the constituency, the constituents, or the followers when they engage in certain practices, implement particular policies, or pursue some special goals in office. First of all, they feel they have the authority, capital, or legitimacy to do what they want by public vote, rule of succession, or bureaucratic order. Second, they think they do what is right for their constituency. Third, they believe they follow fundamental principles rather than human contingencies in what they do. Finally, they hope they will be judged eventually by ultimate triumphs there and then rather than concrete gains or losses here and now. With all these in mind, political leaders may find no reason to compromise with any party on anything they do.

However, most career politicians are smart and shrewd enough to make complimentary, conciliatory, or diplomatic gestures to keep their supporters or constituencies in service of their political agendas or personal ambitions. They thank or pay lip service to volunteers who perform hard labor on their campaigns. They grant access and opportunity to high-profile supporters. They promote their close aids and confidants. They find ways to propagandize the benefits of their policies to the constituency. Specifically, a mayor may direct public attention to qualifications and experience when he or she hires one of his or her former classmates as the general manager.

A governor may implicitly or explicitly refer to the national and even international exposure he or she brings to the province when he or she uses his or her current governorship as a political stage to compete for the highest office of the country. And a president may highlight what he or she has achieved from time to time and pinpoint how all his or her political achievements tie to individual supporters from place to place.

Supporters, on the other hand, may come up with various rationalizations to convince themselves to continue all the loyalty, service, and support they have for specific political causes as well as particular leaders. Volunteers may simply say this: "We just want to send our favorite candidate to the office of the mayor, the governor, or the president. We never think of harvesting any benefit from what we do one political campaign or season after another." Close aids or advisors may reason as follows: "I offer ideas, develop plans, and prepare speeches. But all these ideas, plans, and speeches make sense, draw attention, take effect, and leave an impact only because of the political office held by the leader I serve." Residents of a city or citizens of a country may also wonder whether they have any other choice, better or worse, when they have serious doubts about what the current mayor or president does in his or her policies. As they wrestle with reality, people are most likely to compromise on their ideals and expectations and opt for comfort and status quo.

The Universal

Politics discriminates by its nature, while politicians unavoidably perpetrate victimization with what they do. The cause lies in power, especially the differential in power between political establishments and institutions that deal with them as well as between political figures and individuals who work around them. In the past, people who worked for emperors, kings, queens, and other authoritarian or dictatorial masters were called servants or subordinates. Now, people who serve career politicians can be duly characterized as explicit or implicit victims.

Theoretically, discrimination or victimization by political figures is dictated by three common factors. First is the one-versus-a-crowd contrast. There is only one mayor, one governor, or one president in a city, a province, or a country of hundreds, thousands, or millions of people. The mayor, the governor, or the president has the latitude not to treat his or her constituents as individual humans to empathize with but rather as numbers to count, instruments to utilize, or means to achieve ends. While he or she can take enormously from and contributes diminutively to office, he or she does not necessarily make his or her mass of constituents feel much of a difference about what he or she does in victimization. Second is the top-versus-down gravity. A leader may instantly send his whole constituency to serious bickering, intense fear, or general panic when he or she speaks implicitly about a lofty ideal or advocates openly a divisive ideology in the media. When he or she pursues a specific policy agenda, he or she may leave wide-ranging and far-reaching impacts upon numerous individuals across different walks of life. Third is the close-versus-remote effect. Politicians can make people feel approachable, likable, and connectable when they appeal to the populace for support and forgiveness. They may also keep the public in fear, awe, or pure guessing by creating a general impression that they are high in the royal palace, remote in the presidential resort, or solitary in the executive mansion. Obviously, all these factors can potentially amplify the actual consequence of political discrimination or victimization to its victims while lessening the publicly perceived mens rea for its evildoers.

From a practical point of view, explicit or implicit victims of career politicians are oftentimes willing ones. Volunteers who work freely on election campaigns likely do so out of political enthusiasm, party affiliation, communal tradition, or democratic acculturation. Advisors and aids who claim no public credit for their thought work may enjoy some feelings of masterminding control over political processes. And bodyguards who shield political figures from danger may experience some sense of self-importance, albeit ironically, when they stay close to their protected ones under limelight and amid cheering crowds. Also, political victimization can hardly be known until it takes place. A constituency has to wait for quite some time into a term of office to see how it might have been betrayed for its trust in and support for a political leader. Most important, political victimization can never be fully assessed and measured. A constituency may count the amount of money it has spent on a luxury oversea trip by its top administrator but may never fully trace and evaluate all negative versus positive exposures the same office-holder has caused to the city, county, or province by the trip. Or constituents may now feel they have suffered a net loss in both material and nonmaterial dimensions under their current leader but later only find out that they actually benefit from the same leader's unpopular policies in many aspects.

6   In the Community

The community is where people live their lives. Individuals may make similar contributions while taking different gains. Or they may harvest similar benefits while offering different inputs. In more realistic terms, there are people who take more than they contribute, literally stealing from those who rarely or hardly benefit from their contributions in the form of tax payments, charity donations, and other ordinary or extraordinary acts. For example, a large majority of taxpayers in a jurisdiction are forced to pay for treating a small number of drug users or AIDS patients who choose to pursue a risky yet unproductive lifestyle, imprisoning a small number of inmates who choose to commit crime against people or property, or rescuing a few mountain climbers or ocean surfers who choose to seek some adventures in their personal lives.

In a community of mechanical solidarity, individuals relate to one another frequently and closely. When they see differences in the way they take from or contribute to society, they can quickly make necessary adjustments to achieve proper corrections or restore general equilibriums. In the community of organic solidarity typical of contemporary era, however, people compartmentalize themselves in neighborhoods of poverty or affluence, professions of blue collar or white collar, or interest clubs of high status or no privilege. They cannot always make meaningful comparisons on a wide variety of activities in which they participate. When they notice apparent discrepancies in gain or loss for comparable inputs or outputs, they may not be able to do much to make any justifiable change at all (Durkheim 1964; Gallagher 1994; Lefebvre 2000; McDonough 2002, 2009; Tuan 2002; Bruhn 2005; Day 2006; Block 2008; Auge 2009; Parker 2009; Collins 2010; McKnight and Block 2010; Fong and Chang 2011; Gagne 2011; Sommers 2011; Heath 2012; Sumiala 2012).

SITUATION 1

A catastrophic tragedy or a widespread natural disaster raises public consciousness about the importance of law enforcement, firefighting, and other emergency responses in a community, a city, or even a country. In the aftermath of the tragedy or disaster, there is likely a massive buildup or revamp of all related forces. The buildup can sometimes reach an irrational level when it is fueled by public fear or political rhetoric. In a big irony, residents of a city or citizens of a country will soon find they pay more taxes to fund an unnecessarily large police force that only increasingly monitors their normal life routines from time to time, traps them in noncriminal errors from place to place, and ultimately compromises their individual freedom as well as their quality of life.

The Particular

Alibaba lives in the suburb of a greater metropolitan region. Since the September 11 terrorist attacks in New York and Washington, D.C., he has not only seen extensive increases in law enforcement officials and resources in the federal, state, county, and metropolitan levels, but also experienced a considerably more prevalent presence of police officers, firefighters, and other emergency response personnel in his relatively quiet and safe suburban town that maintains, as a self-incorporated city, its own policing and firefighting forces.

First in public domains, Alibaba hears year after year calls for police reinforcement or pledges of support for public safety by all politicians of all levels. Mayors across the greater metropolitan region take it for granted that they cite the recruitment of police officers, firefighters, and other first-responders as a major administrative achievement for each year or term served in office. County supervisors, congressmen and congresswomen, the governor, and the president seem to hold an automatic agreement that public safety is an unquestionable priority, where being enough can never be raised or taken as an appropriate question or answer. Newspaper editors, television anchorpersons, radio hosts, and all news reporters find it fashionable to cheer on what law enforcement does rather than investigate whether it serves in the best interest of taxpayers and their monetary contributions. Even the general populace understands that since nobody would risk an "if," everyone should remain acquiescent about putting far more, no matter how much more, than enough or necessary in the area of safety and security.

As a common citizen, Alibaba now feels as if he were experiencing a ubiquitous presence of safety and security personnel and equipment in his everyday life. For simple accidents where someone suffers just minor injuries, he often sees a few fire trucks, ambulances, and police patrol vehicles rush to the scene, clogging the traffic in different directions for quite some time. For high-profile or celebrity events, he can only expect a more intimidating contingent of police officers, firefighters, and first-responders lining up on the street, sitting in their special vehicles, or blocking the traffic in a larger perimeter around the area and with a longer time before and after the event than he would normally witness a few years ago. More interestingly, Alibaba notices more and more police officers idling at the street corners or hiding in some unnoticeable places to catch traffic violators or to trap personal or business solicitors. One time, he almost fell into one such trap when he habitually used the carpool lane for a moment on his way to enter the freeway: he drives his child on the route to and from school so often that he almost forgot he was driving alone at that particular moment when two officers were sitting in a patrol car to catch would-be violators on the side of the ramp.

As an educated person, Alibaba moves beyond what he observes and feels in his day-to-day experience. He looks at official statistics for a few police departments in the greater metropolitan region. Without surprise, he finds that all police departments have grown significantly in terms of critical numbers, from personnel to salaries to equipment expenses to total budgets. The largest city police department in the region, for example, boasted of an increase in officer salaries by more than 40 percent in the first five years after the September 11 incident. As a result, both per capital and per square mile costs of policing in the city rose by more than 25 percent even though crime went down steadily over the period.

The Discriminator

Firefighters, police officers, and emergency responders, such as paramedics, lifeguards, and rescuers, are specially trained professionals who work in their specific duties to serve the residents of a city or the citizens of a state. They each could, however, turn into discriminators when they outgrow themselves as powerful interest groups at the expense of their serving public.

As illustrated in the particular by Alibaba, the sheer size of a police force in a city may determine whether the force to some extent discriminates against the residents of the city. First, although there is no magical formula to calculate an absolute number of police officers needed to fight crime and maintain peace in a city, there is definite truth to reveal the amount of tax-payers' money wasted for every single law enforcement agent unnecessarily hired and kept above the city's necessities. In other words, an oversized police force holds discrimination against all taxpaying residents of the city simply because it lives on the city budget funded by tax revenues. In terms of net effect, forcing individual residents to pay higher taxes for a larger city budget is no different than robbing them or stealing from them on the street.

Besides money, an overgrown police force is more likely to develop into a self-interest group that tends to fight more fiercely for its own political, eco-nomic, and social positions than for public safety and security. An oversized force is also more prone to abuse, waste, ineffectiveness, and inefficiency. While the scenes seen by Alibaba where far more emergency responses than necessary go to routine traffic accidents on the street represent an effective waste of city resources, situations unknown to ordinary residents where firefighters, police officers, and emergency responders accustomed to over-staff idleness fail to activate themselves quickly or fight over who should get off first may pose grave dangers to the city in various fronts. Of course, as more officers are on the force, they are more likely to disperse in differ-ent beats, catching people in minor errors, finding trouble with people, or plainly inconveniencing public life. As a regular resident, Alibaba can tell in his metropolitan region that there are numerous stories where simple disputes escalate into serious problems because of premature or unnecessary police intervention and that there are countless moments when police patrol vehicles weave through the traffic for no discernible reason, sending shocking waves across the driving public.

The Victim

Victimization falls explicitly and implicitly upon the residents of the city when policing, firefighting, and other emergency responding forces grow beyond necessity.

Explicitly, residents have to pay higher taxes or make sacrifices in other areas of critical service to support an outgrown force. A larger than necessary police department, for example, needs not only a bigger account for employee salaries and benefits, but also a greater budget for expenditures in facility, equipment, and activity. As the force becomes expanded excessively across the city, it soon gains and exerts a heavy clout over municipal operations. The mayor relies upon the police and would never say no to any of its requests. The city council, the city attorney's office, and other municipal entities are fearful of the police and would have to mobilize considerable public resources, eventually at the expense of city residents, in order to counter or contain it and its unwarranted influences.

In implicit terms, residents are more likely to face inconvenience in everyday life when an excessive force becomes so eager to show itself off in the eyes of the public. Individual freedom can be lost as the police stretches its extra muscles in various domains of social affairs. The quality of civilian life can be compromised when residents limit their choices under widening surveillance, deepening crusades against criminal elements, and everfrequenter curfews or crackdowns entertained by surplus law enforcement forces. Ironically, when it comes to crime, disaster, or crisis, residents may not necessarily receive faster responses and better assistance because policing, firefighting, and other emergency forces, when they each are more than enough and therefore not the only one that can and must act, are more likely to ponder or bicker over who should respond first.

The danger of facing a police state is real even in an open society when residents are not only made to believe in the insurmountable importance of public safety and security, but also mandated to support an outgrown law enforcement and emergency response system with their hard-earned income.

The Compromise

Ordinary residents may talk about seeing the police everywhere in the city or experiencing driving inconveniences when first-responders or law enforcement officials overwhelm emergency scenes or special event venues. While complaining, they may also admit that an excessive presence of the police may indeed keep the city safer, that a somewhat overreaction by the emergency system may have actually saved more lives or prevented more serious disruptions, and that it's better to be over- than underprepared because nobody knows what is about to happen in what scale with what calamity when it comes to crime, crisis, disaster, and terrorism.

Police officers, firefighters, and emergency personnel, on the other hand, view themselves as trained and specialized professionals in the service of the city and its residents. Overall they may have consumed more resources, secured more benefits, garnered more power, and gained more spotlight in the aftermath of the September 11 tragedy. But they more than any other public sector employee groups shoulder the risk of crime, the danger of terrorism, and the uncertainty of disasters for the sake of safety, peace, and predictability in life for all residents of the city.

As far as cost is concerned, both residents and first-responders realize that the latter live in the city as well. They pay taxes as everybody else to fund firefighting, policing, rescuing, and all other emergency operations of the city. Moreover, all first-responders and their friends or relatives are potential and real victims when individual privacy is violated, personal freedom is lost, and everyday life is inconvenienced because of the overwhelming presence of an overarching law enforcement force or the ever-frequent overreaction by an overreaching emergency response system. In other words, it's not so much about first-responders discriminating city residents. It is rather a changing era, an evolving political landscape, and a tricking security environment that hold all ordinary people hostages for fear, restlessness, and an overall compromised quality of life.

The Universal

It is necessary to maintain a police force, a fire department, and an emergency response team even though crime does not take place, fire does not break out, and emergency does not come about every so often in the city. The rule of necessity makes it inevitable that police officers burn gas in their patrol vehicles without obvious effects on crime, firefighters sit in idleness in their stations for weeks and months, and emergency personnel have nothing to do other than to engage in routine training and mock drills throughout the year. Here then comes the rule of inevitable waste, which states that taxpayers have simply to watch some of their tax contributions flush in the water like total waste because of some necessities in their collective life.

Another related issue is the margin of operation. To keep a police force in operation, sufficient resources have to be dispensed. Since there is no agreed-upon formula to determine what is minimally necessary, there is a natural likelihood to maintain a margin of sufficiency by which the police force can achieve its operational smoothness and readiness. Just as a wider road than the actual width of moving wheels has to be paved for vehicles to pass through, a battery of more sufficient than necessary materials and personnel has to be provided for a system to carry out its day-to-day operation. In other words, residents of a city have unavoidably to pay more than what they receive in worth and value over all public services delivered or administered by an operational system.

With the margin of operation and the rule of inevitable waste in the background, a police force, a fire department, or an emergency response team can be definitely blamed for manipulation, discrimination, and exploitation when it takes advantage of larger political dynamics within and outside the city to unwarrantedly expand operations, gain power and public attention, and increase salaries and benefits for rank-and-file members, all at the cost of common taxpaying residents.

SITUATION 2

In a free and open society as the United States, individuals act or take actions out of their own desire, determination, or will. With regard to consequence, however, individual actors are not always capable enough of, conscientious enough about, or responsible enough for handling what their actions have caused directly or indirectly. For example, a camper, hiker, climber, or mountaineer is so curious about an unfamiliar area that he or she decides to ignore guidebooks, posted signs, or other warnings and explore the area all by him- or herself, and the local community spends enormous manpower and rescuing resources when he or she fails to return from the wild in a few days. A homebuyer is so anxious to own a house that he or she chooses to withhold truth about employment and to secure a home loan beyond his or her financial abilities, and the government pumps one huge amount of taxpayers' money after another to assist many of these property owners in the depth of the subprime mortgage crisis. Similarly, drug users experiment with drugs in social recreation or for personal indulgence. They usurp services from publicly or privately funded treatment programs when they suffer from addiction. A considerable number of AIDS patients drain public funds or private foundations as they struggle to extend their life through expensive treatments. While they now have a compelling medical condition for public mercy, they probably would not have much sympathy for social good when they engaged in commercial sex, abused drugs, or pursued an unhealthy lifestyle to become HIV positive in the first place.

The Particular

Alibaba has close friends who work as social workers, substance abuse specialists, registered nurses, and doctors. From them, he hears countless stories about individuals who rarely make any contribution to society yet wantonly take advantage of the public welfare system for a variety of problems resultant from their own questionable lives and lifestyles. Homeless migrants count on public clinics to treat ailments caused by exposure, lack of hygiene, and irregular food intake. Low-income mothers live on food stamps and visit county hospitals for their one after another childbearing since teen pregnancy. Drug users drop in and out of treatment programs over their never-ending addiction careers. People with HIV/AIDS take expensive medications or undergo costly treatments on programs supported by taxpayers' funds. In specific cases, Alibaba has gathered enough information about Vivian, who somehow came to the United States just to avail herself of free treatment for AIDS she contracted when she prostituted in her home country on another continent.

From the mass media, Alibaba feels that he can expect to receive a few news reports each year around the country about extraordinary searches and rescues rendered to some risk-taking, careless, or outright wayward individuals. It is almost standard that teams of volunteers are gathered, contingents of firefighters are assembled, armies of emergency personnel are sent on duty, and a battery of equipment such as helicopters, speedboats, patrol vehicles, fire trucks, and ambulances are mobilized when a major search and rescue operation is under way for even one individual lost in a forest or who has disappeared from an open sea due to some individual choice of action. Behind each of these dramas, Alibaba cannot help wondering what future tax obligation the incident translates into for taxpayers within and outside the community where it takes place.

On the subprime mortgage crisis, Alibaba heard repeatedly critics blaming banks for unscrupulous lending practices and politicians pledging unconditional assistance to home owners. Out of curiosity, Alibaba took with a real estate agent a tour of a few bank-owned properties in his larger community. To his surprise, he found almost all the former owners of these properties could not afford to own a home based on their financial situations. The most irrational was that some so-called home owners lived largely on the market-created equity. In other words, they borrowed against the equity they had from the home and used the money borrowed to pay for their everyday expenses. For those home owners who took advantage of the market to own a home they should not have had by their actual financial abilities, Alibaba like many ordinary citizens has difficulty understanding why they suddenly turned into deserving victims entitled to massive public assistance orchestrated by politicians at the expense of hardworking taxpayers.

The Discriminator

All individuals who take risks, seek personal indulgences, and hence create situations of public sympathy or present needs for humanitarian assistance can become discriminators.

Discriminators in this case can be intentional or unintentional. Intentional discriminators know they will have to count on their friends, relatives, or the general public to clean and clear the mess they have created from their individual actions. There are even manipulators who plan and plot spectacular incidents to gain public attention or notoriety. For example, a few youths venture into dangerous mountain terrains or forbidden seashores just to see how parents are worried and their home community is mobilized in emergency rescues. A couple set off a balloon into the sky claiming their child was hidden in it just to obtain publicity in the media. Unintentional discriminators focus on their current act and its immediate effects. They do not seem to think or see what they later have to face or whether they can handle it on their own. For instance, a hiker may feel he or she has courage to explore an unknown area and find a unique trail to a legendary landmark before he or she is completely lost in the wilderness. A prostitute may figure that he or she has luck to stay free from sexually transmitted diseases when he or she contracts AIDS from day-to-day contacts with clients. A person who lives on equity from his or her home may calculate that he or she has acumen to wade the waves of the market before he or she suddenly realizes that he or she is deep in debt.

Whether they are intentional or unintentional, discriminators in this situation are likely to cause troubles for their partners, peers, friends, or relatives before they burden the public with costly rescue, treatment, and assistance. A falling climber may survive upon death of a fellow climber, who perished while instinctually rushing to his or her rescue. A drug abuser may have already exhausted his or her family's finances when he or she sits on a treatment program funded by the government or private donations. Who knows what colleagues, neighbors, friends, and relatives have sacrificed financially and emotionally for those individuals whose home and mortgage complications in the subprime crisis prompted massive government bailout and assistance programs at the eventual cost of all taxpayers?

The Victim

People may fall into victimization by proximity, relationship, or collective connectedness. A stranger or bystander automatically extends his or her helping hand when he or she sees a hiker, camper, motorist, or tourist hanging in grave danger or struggling for life, regardless of what careless, risk-taking, rule-breaking, warning-ignoring, or self-hurting acts the person has taken for the precarious situation. Friends may feel obliged to care for their drug-abusing peers, while a family may sense a responsibility to pay part or even the whole of debt owed by one of its members from gambling or other problematic financial dealings. By way of collective connectedness, the burden of assistance in the form of either search and rescue or treatment and bailout can shift to a community where the incident happens to occur or whose membership happens to include one or more discriminators. For example, a city can be condemned for apathy if it hesitates to mobilize its emergency response system to search and rescue a nonresident hiker cling-ing to the cliffs at one of its border areas. Most politicians have political instincts and impulses to dispense public resources just to demonstrate their resolve to tackle serious issues that reach the level of crisis, show off their spirit of care for those who are in need, or highlight their ability to unite different sides over matters of controversy. The series of promises, pledges, and actions made by the president, governors, mayors, and all other politi-cians in the subprime mortgage crisis showcase it all, how a community, city, state, or country can be abducted hostage for the care of a mess cre-ated by a few wayward players.

Victimization may come in the form of emotional stress, time lost from job or recreation, monetary payment, or a combination thereof. Over a hiker to be rescued from the wilderness or a swimmer to be found in the open water, onlookers express concern, emergency personnel show worry, and people in the general public watch news reports with anxiety. Volunteers spend hours and even risk their own lives in search and rescue. Taxpayers have to dig deeper into their coffers for payments of fees, taxes, or char-ity donations to support firefighting, policing, and emergency responses in their cities, welfare programs in their states, and general social engineering or particular bailouts in their country.

The Compromise

Life is unpredictable. Dangers happening to or troubles caused by a few reckless, irresponsible, or even mischievous individuals could occur to ordi-nary people who make common choices, take normal actions, and live reg-ular lives. Nobody dares to imagine a situation of no concern, no sympathy, or no assistance from his or her fellow human beings when he or she falls under grave danger or sheer desperation for help. Everyone then feels natu-ral to build social capital by rendering support for those who are in need.

More loftily, helping people strengthens social bonds, lifts human spir-its, and enriches life. Every time a community makes an effort to rescue an individual in danger, it secures an opportunity to rally its members, remind-ing them that they care, matter, and remain in solidarity as a whole. On an individual basis, people may learn from particular cases to reach better understandings that life is precious, that personal choice has social conse-quence, or that there are ways to make fewer mistakes and to reach higher levels of success in life. Since it is priceless to see important reasoning in or to learn from real-life examples, it is therefore no complaint to spend some time and money on a few exemplary cases every now and then.

As far as discriminating individuals are concerned, they may feel cared about or even loved through social responses to their originally senseless acts or dire situations. In the future, they may be less likely to engage in similar behaviors in which they first become involved often out of a sense of alienation. Of course, there might also be individuals who feel that they and their acts or situations give the people involved a chance to unite in collective action or offer the community impacted a case to test its emergency response system. As such, they may continue what they do, just like many drug abusers, to drain social resources or take similar risks to send another shocking wave to their surroundings.

The Universal

Human beings are gregarious. When one is at risk, under danger, or in pain, another will instinctually extend his or her helping hand. As a society, people show concern for those who are in need and take actions for those who suffer from catastrophes. In the contemporary era, there are even well-established mechanisms, such as private charities, public welfare systems, and governmental emergency responses, to systematically orchestrate rescue missions, run assistance programs, and deliver emergency services. The message is clear. That is, modern society is equipped to care for each of its members. Regardless of individual circumstances, when one is in trouble or danger, society is prepared to bring him or her back to safety, security, and peace.

Individuals are specifically experiential. When one once benefits from an overarching social assistance network, one may calculate that he or she can depend upon it for his or her various needs over and over. People are generally reflective. When they see others cared for by the system, people may figure that they sometimes can take advantage of the system as well. It is then no shock that a number of individuals become apathetically dependent on essentially sympathetic social or nonsocial assistances. Nor is it a surprise that some engage in plainly foul plays out of the particular kindness of others and the general generosity of the society as a whole.

Is there any gratitude or sorrow on the part of discriminators? Users or exploiters of social assistance may reason that it is there for people to use anyway; that if I do not use it, someone else will take advantage of it; and that I do not owe anyone when I use something from society overall. Is there any complaint or regret from the often invisible victims? Taxpayers who pay the bills for social assistance may rationalize that it is the unavoidable cost of living in a society where ordinary citizens can keep an adequate feeling of care, love, and general humanity.

SITUATION 3

In the community of life, most people think and act upon this simple assumption: if you are fair and nice, you will be treated fairly and nicely in return. While it is generally true that feelings and sentiments are contagious in social interaction, it is not uncommon that some individuals get their ways just because they are rude, discriminatory, and exploitative.

In particular, there are often times when a person is taken advantage of plainly because he or she is nice and kind. The same holds true for a group that is quiet or even a society that is content with peace.

The Particular

Alibaba seems to have countless examples from his general observation and personal experience about how kind and nice people lose while rough and rude people gain in small things as well as over fundamental interests.

A few years ago Alibaba traveled with his family in a foreign country. They hired a taxi to see a historical monument in the outskirts of a principal city. At a checkpoint where everyone was turned back, Alibaba's cabdriver came out of the car, engaging in a seemingly intense argument with the guards. Eventually the guards lifted the roadblock for Alibaba's taxi to pass by. Later at the site of the monument, Alibaba met with another family and learned that they rode through the same checkpoint without delay because their cabdriver told a lie about their connection to some important figure in the city. Although the whole case was not completely clear to Alibaba as he does not know enough about the culture and society of the country he and his family visited, he developed a general impression that people get their ways when they challenge orders, make noises, or play tricks. On the other hand, people can be only pushed out of their ways if they follow the direction, observe the rule, or take an order without any question.

Back to where he lives and works, Alibaba hears story after story, observes case after case, and experiences incidence after incidence from, among, or along with his colleagues, neighbors, friends, and relatives about kind neighbors being ignored and nice employees being put behind in promotion while the inconsiderate, the unreasonable, or the undeserving prevailing in their wants and demands. Linda complains, cries, and screams, making each and every one of her coworkers almost scared of her. As a result, she always receives lighter assignments and nobody even seems brave enough to gossip about her. Larry is quiet, does what he is assigned, and makes no complaint even when he is pushed aside for what he duly deserves. Because of his kindness, Larry becomes the one who often takes heavy loads of work yet rarely receives any public recognition or tangible benefits. In fact, Larry is asked a few times by the management to defer to his coworkers in rewards for which everyone keenly competes. At the university where Alibaba teaches part-time, Dan receives a two-year accelerated promotion because he politicks masterfully with the chair, the dean, and the provost and is able to spread a claim among his colleagues that he has secured a job offer from another institution. Jane moves to the rank of full professor, with some unspecified threats to the administration according to credible leads from the grapevine, even though she has so little in her record to meet the minimum scholarly standard anywhere in university settings to be part of an academic faculty.

The Discriminator

Human life to a large degree is a zero-sum game. When one gains a particular thing by breaking normally observed codes of conduct, people around one are likely to lose the same thing or something general.

An inconsiderate neighbor holds a boisterous party late in the night. He or she enjoys a wonderful time, whereas his or her neighbors have to postpone serious work they plan to do in their home offices, stay awake in their bedrooms, or become angry or courageous enough to make a complaint. A manipulative young mother sends her kids to an elderly lady for free care when she goes shopping, attends a party, or meets her date. She frees herself from the burden of childcare because she shifts it directly to someone who by every reasonable account has no responsibility to take care of her child at all. An aggressive worker forces his or her due share of job duty upon colleagues. He or she takes comfort of an easier assignment or lighter workload as his or her immediate coworkers have to make extra efforts to keep things going or meet specific deadlines or goals.

Besides taking unwarranted gains in practical terms, discriminators are likely to threaten cultural norms, contaminate public morale, and challenge social order through their discriminatory acts. When an unqualified candidate jumps over the bar to obtain a promotion, he or she sends a damaging message across the system. That is, rules can be bent, changed, or even put aside by individuals who know how or dare enough to do so. Social order then becomes questionable. People who ordinarily observe established rules and follow the existing order naturally wonder: what is fairness if good performance does not pay so quickly or commensurately as bad deeds? And where is justice if rule-breaking proves more effective than hard working?

The Victim

Neighbors, coworkers, or acquaintances are essentially equal. When one acts aggressively, exploitatively, or manipulatively, another will have to take some discomfort in feeling or some loss in material aspect. For example, an elderly lady who is repeatedly asked to look after kids by a neighbor in her own house would at the minimum have to take time off watching her favorite television program or participating in some entertaining activities with her age-appropriate friends. Employees who watch one of their coworkers cry over his or her assignment or act in a selfishly demanding manner would have to give assistance, offer accommodation, or at least take avoidance to bring the situation under control or keep the day going. An honest traveler who answers the plea to keep an eye on an acquaintance's belongings might have to miss a bus, a train, or a flight when the acquaintance fails to return at the time promised.

Beyond specific roles, human relations, social groupings, and system formations may suffer generally as part of victimization. A relationship can become rough and even break down when one party takes advantage of, abuses, or exploits the other consistently. A group can experience considerable upheaval and even fall apart when the membership overall is not able to absorb the negative impact left by a few rude, reckless, and self-serving individuals. A system may face constant turbulence and even collapse if the number reaches a critical level for people who ignore etiquettes or conventions, break rules or norms, and engage in corruptive, disruptive, or destructive behaviors. For example, disbelief, lack of confidence, and resentment can spread quickly across the system when some stakeholders give in to blackmails or attempt to please a minority of waywardly self-centered individuals at the expense of the rule-abiding majority.

The Compromise

Human life is like a sponge soaked with water. Squeezing water out of a sponge may change the shape of the sponge temporarily but is unlikely to cause damage to it in permanent terms.

At the time when most victims experience discomfort or material loss, they figure that it is not a big deal and that it will go away soon. Following particular incidents, victims tend to become reflectively forgiving and philosophically noble. Instead of being calculative about gains and losses, they are more likely to feel grateful with what they have learned and what they have grown to be, that is, persons of better temperament, greater tolerance, higher mannerism, and stronger character. For example, employees who accommodate an irritable low-performing coworker may only talk about the positives that have come out of their negative experience: it makes me work more effectively because I know I cannot count on him or her for that part of my job; I learn this special skill because I have to go beyond my job duty to cover him or her; and a bad example only reinforces my conviction about the importance of working with your colleagues and contributing to your team.

Discriminators, in the meanwhile, may offer such excuses: I complain, cry, scream, or act rudely, aggressively, or selfishly in front of my coworkers or neighbors because I trust them as my sympathizers and supporters. Would I behave in such an unhidden manner toward someone I don't know nor care about? Would I expose myself so nakedly to sheer strangers on the public street? Reflexively, discriminators may also feel they bring a unique yet necessary perspective to human life. Indeed, a few deviating from a rule can be as important, if not more, to normative order, group cohesion, and social solidarity as the majority observing the rule.

The Universal

Most people are conscientious, cooperative, and law-abiding. They do what they are supposed to do as diligent, competent, and self-sufficient yet contributive citizens. That is why societies hold, civilizations thrive, and human livelihoods progress.

However, there are always people from place to place and from time to time who are rude, reckless, or even ruthless in their individual behavior toward others. They jump the queue when everyone else waits for his or her turn. They shirk responsibilities, making others close the gap. They cause troubles, forcing others to clean up the mess. They take more than their due share of social benefits or seek what they do not deserve in either material resource or nonmaterial reward. They ignore social etiquettes, break rules, or violate laws. As they create inconvenience, discomfort, emotional stress, and even material loss to particular individuals in their surroundings, they eventually serve as critical social forces that push the majority of the population into higher levels of open-mindedness, tolerance, and humanistic understanding. Human connections, group interfaces, and social cohesiveness may also rise to newer latitudes of dynamic equilibriums once they pass the test, challenge, or threat posed by a minority of predatory individuals and their exploitative acts.

Of course, specific feelings of pain or loss forced by aggressive, manipulative, and exploitative individuals upon normally behaving ordinaries can never dissipate and disappear automatically. Time spent and efforts made to manage and overcome negative experiences remain real and surreal always. From individual to individual, it is essentially a matter of luck or misfortune whether one has to bear more or less in one's journey through life.

SITUATION 4

In a globalizing era, more and more large metropolitan areas around the world are becoming melting pots where locals work and live side by side with nonnatives, long-time residents with newcomers, insiders with outsiders, people of one race or ethnicity with those of another, citizens with aliens, and, more generally, members of the majority with those of the minority. From a macro point of view, this is a social mosaic of diversity, multiplicity, plurality, and coexistence in the making. In micro examination and analysis, however, almost every individual on either side of all traditional divides, racial, geographical, national, or otherwise, has some stories or feelings of misperception, misunderstanding, or ambivalence to share regarding his or her experience dealing with people of the other type.

The Particular

Alibaba has been living in the United States since age twenty-five when he came to work on his graduate degree. By identification, Alibaba is a U.S. citizen. Yet in appearance he looks still much like a non-American alien. He speaks fluent English but carries a heavy foreign accent. From time to time when he shops, dines, exercises, or talks to customer service agents in commercial or noncommercial establishments, he can clearly sense that he is treated as if he were a foreigner who has difficulty understanding English, who does not know much about the American way of life, and hence who needs to be given extra direction or not much attention by the insiders.

More substantively in the area of work, Alibaba knows for sure that he would not be treated as a jewel of his unit like some of his white colleagues even though he is one of the best-performing employees in the unit; that he would not be able to conduct himself as an insider, an old timer, an authority, or a bully like some of his white coworkers in spite of the fact that he has every credential capital to do so; and that he would not be tapped into the leadership like some of his black peers although he has the quality and qualifications to serve as a great leader. Instead, Alibaba feels he has to put up his smiling face and behave as a nice guy all the time to just keep his place at work.

A general yet deeply sentimental caveat Alibaba has learned, practiced, and kept for living in the United States as a member of the minority is this: work, contribute, and behave in full awareness and preparedness that members of the majority can make you a target of jealousy, hatred, and/or containment when you do well or better, and they look down upon, distance, and/or ignore you if you do not do well.

The Discriminator

As the force of discrimination lies generally in the context where one group dominates because it comes earlier, stays longer, or holds a larger membership than others, individual discriminators may remain unidentifiable or even invisible for the blame of their misdeeds.

In closer analysis, however, there are usually two types of discriminators. One is leading discriminators who either spearhead in public opinion about the superiority of the majority over the minority or lead in specific discriminations against particular victims. For example, a radio host uses airwaves to spread his or her personal ideology or a local business owner takes advantage of a discriminative legal or social environment to exploit a particular group of people for economic gains. The other is following discriminators who either cheer on debates, jokes, and characterizations in favor of the majority in public domains or abet in specific discriminations against the disadvantaged over their everyday work and life experiences. For example, a racist follower incorporates racial slurs as part of his or her daily language or a believer in patriarchal order exhibits considerable discomfort when he sees a female coworker progress through ranks ahead of him.

Both types of discriminators operate not only with moral apathy, but also out of practical interests. Moral apathy takes hold in the consciousness of discriminators when the discriminated are characterized as others devoid of human feelings. Practical interests, such as power and profit, can obviously reinforce moral apathy about discrimination when those interests keep discriminators feel privileged. Why do Alibaba's majority colleagues care so much about merit, meritocracy, and equality when they see a generally discriminative atmosphere against the minority serve to maintain the status quo of their majority advantages?

The Victim

Victims are real individuals who have to bear all emotional injuries and material losses at a personal level. Compared to discriminators who may shift the burden to the context or system, victims can only feel helplessly bad when they think about specific discriminators who mistreat them and the whole system that lends the contextual support for those discriminating actors.

The victimized minority breaks down interestingly into three categories. One includes pioneers, who first adventure into the majority society, who excel in mainstream activities favored by the majority, or who happen to be in a wrong place at a wrong time in their individual encounters with members of the majority. Another involves the main mass of minority members, who do not necessarily experience direct hits of discrimination from the majority, who do not always hold hostility toward domination by the majority, or who do not particularly question some discriminative restrictions faced in their everyday life. For example, slaves or servants may take it for granted that they eat after owners or sleep in makeshift shelters. Still another consists of beneficiaries, who are politically co-opted into the majority, who are tactically used as tokens of representation, or who are simply picked as lucky recipients of redemption. A story divulged by a white administrator in a professional organization is illustrative: "I am generally tough toward those smart foreign nerds regarding assignments, bonuses, salary increases, and promotions. Yet from time to time, I can always entertain one nice alien with some preferential treatments. It makes me feel better in balance."

The politics of co-optation, representation, and/or redemption by the majority can cause further victimization to the victimized minority. Explicitly, it divides members of the minority, preventing them from forming collective consciousness necessary for joint actions about their common experience. Implicitly, it may justify systematic discriminations, compartmentalize discriminative practices in specific areas, or camouflage extreme behaviors against particular individuals. As revealed by Alibaba, "My boss would court another person of my racial or ethnic background in front of me after she treated me badly on something. It seems as if she wanted to make a general statement that she is not a racial discriminator when she treats me in consistent unfairness."

The Compromise

Most victims seek comfort with their unfavorable situations by using different references. They compare to where they originate: "I come from a humble background and should feel good about my existing condition even though it is not ideal." They contrast with worse scenarios: "This is a relatively better group, culture, or society where we are after all allowed to stay and grow even though we are not recognized and promoted in the same way as members of the majority." Or they find problems with their own existence: "We indeed have accents and look like aliens; we have various minority idiosyncrasies that keep us from reaching the highs of the mainstream lifestyle; and we are not as well-rounded as members of the majority as we focus so much on our roles as technocrats."

The majority keeps discrimination at bay with legal codes on the book and public propaganda in the media. In the United States, for example, the Constitution provides equal treatment to everyone living in America. Legislations at different levels prohibit discriminations on the basis of race, gender, and other personal characteristics or prescribe punishments for hate crimes against the minority. All these keep limits on discriminatory acts by majority stakeholders: they discriminate only to the degree that discrimination cannot be documented to the reactive effect of the law. Public propaganda in the name of representation, inclusion, and diversity brings in the standards of civility, acculturation, and modernity. Members of the majority may utter derogative remarks or engage in prejudicial acts against a minority only to the extent that discrimination does not make them look rude, uneducated, or insensitive in the public.

The Universal

Living as aliens, members of a minority race or ethnicity, or just outsiders to the mainstream society can be a highly alienating experience. Collectively, there are taken-for-granted majority rules, established quotas for material appropriation or political representation, and institutionalized glass ceilings in career mobility and lifetime movement.

At the individual level, members of a minority are ignored when they follow the crowd, do what is required, and remain quiet. They are jeered at, laughed about, or looked down upon when they accidentally or mistakenly fail to meet some expectations or do not fit into some categorizations. There are so many common gossip and jokes among members of the majority about other peoples of various minorities: "He is one of those atheists from the former Soviet Union"; "She is a Third World country native. It is no strange that she does not seem to have much consciousness about her crooked teeth, messy hair, and cheap makeup while interacting with us at work"; and "He is one of those slow-witted and snail-moving members of XXX race or ethnicity. Do not ever expect him to offer any intelligent suggestion. Do not even hold any surprise if he does not finish work with acceptable quality in a timely fashion."

On the other hand, members of a minority become targets of envy, hatred, containment, restriction, or even attack when they outperform the average in the workplace, take the lead in business adventures or professional pursuits, or jump in the forefront of conspicuous leisure and consumption. There also can be simple blindness to, sheer neglect of, or quiet devaluation toward any outstanding contributions made by members of a minority to society. Some typical reactions in the minds of the majority are as follows: "They can't be this good! It's either luck or out of some strange coincidence"; "We don't accord them the same kind of recognition and rewards we normally give to our majority achievers because we have no ideas as how those people could possibly make the same deed"; and "We lay the ground, make the rules, create the order, and maintain the mainstream. There is not much unfairness if only some of those people pay a little more than due at certain times and on certain occasions."

SITUATION 5

Life involves different factors and forces. In the community of life, individuals carry their unique factors and ride on specific forces available to their peculiar circumstances. At their will and willingness, people may take advantage of certain factors or have to face unfavorable currents or discriminations from certain forces. Outside their choice and like, people may enjoy some unexpected benefits or have to deal with some surprisingly unpleasant or discriminative treatments.

The Particular

Alibaba sees himself as a smart consumer. He uses credit cards to make all purchases and pays off full balances on all credit accounts before due dates. The general benefits are clear: he uses credit card statements to keep full accounting of all his expenses on a monthly basis; he does not have to carry much cash, if any, in his wallet; he defers all payments for nearly a month; and he harvests interest on deferred cash payments that are automatically left on savings or money market accounts. Moreover, Alibaba keeps different credit cards for different rewards. He has credit cards from department stores that give him certain percentage discounts off in-store or online purchases; he has credit cards affiliated with airlines that render him complimentary tickets for travel; he has credit cards associated with major merchandise or service brands that entitle him to 5 percent rebates on brand-name purchases; and he holds a variety of other credit cards that lend him cash rebate benefits in different categories of everyday consumption: 5 percent on airlines, drugstores, hotels, home improvements, movies, restaurants, or utility bills on a seasonally rotational basis, 3 percent on gasoline, 2 percent on travels and groceries, and 1 percent on everything else. Obviously, there is a minimum of 1 percent reward for Alibaba when he uses credit cards for all his expenditures.

In contrast, Alibaba knows a few groups of people who pay most, if not all, of their purchases with cash. One group includes newly arrived immigrants or migrants who do not own any credit card accounts or even bank accounts because they do not have proper documents, credentials, or credit histories to apply for them. Another group involves small business owners, such as retailers and restaurateurs, and practicing professionals, such as lawyers and midwives, who receive much cash from clients and feel necessary to spend cash in avoidance of taxation. Still another group consists of people who don't know anything about credit cards, who don't feel safe or comfortable with credit cards, who don't like the hassles of keeping records over and making payments to credit card accounts, who fear for the induced entrapment of credit card debts, or who take cash payments as for granted due to their unique social acculturation, lifetime habituation, or ideological indoctrination.

In the spirit of commercialism, Alibaba figures that all merchants and commercial establishments that accept credit cards as payments must have incorporated credit card expenses in the pricing of their products or merchandises. As a result, cash-paying customers are virtually discriminated in comparison to those who pay by credit cards in a dynamic market that is systematically adjusted to or meticulously fine-tuned with plastic credits and all their associated incentives or disincentives.

The Discriminator

While discrimination exists unambiguously, discriminators may not so noticeably stand out for clear identification. Merchants or service providers who accept credit cards in sales transactions may say that they do not increase prices for their merchandises or services although they have to surrender certain percentages of credit card payments as fees to the banks. Some merchants or service providers may even use an extra service charge they apply to customers who pay by credit cards instead of cash as the proof that they do not universally figure credit card costs in the pricing of their products. But who knows in the commercial world of profit and greed any enterprises or corporate entities would unilaterally absorb legitimate business costs to sacrifice their profits? Who can ensure that no business would ever engage in this practice: they double their profits by charging credit-card-paying customers an extra service fee in spite of the fact that they already incorporate the cost of credit card payments in the prices of their sales?

Credit card carriers and issuers, such as Visa, MasterCard, American Express, Discover Card, and commercial banks involved in credit card businesses, are ultimate sources of discrimination. First of all, they use credit card services as prime opportunities to profit from individual manufacturers, merchants, and service providers. Reasoning from credit-card-issuing to credit-card-using companies is loud and clear: "We make customers buy your products even when customers cannot afford it at the time of purchase;

we guarantee your payments even though some customers may not be able to pay at all; and we invent incentives for and create pressures on customers to spend in the overall consumer market." And: "You may pass on our credit card service fees to customers; you may absorb our credit card service charges as market discriminations; and you may then either profit or suffer from credit card transactions."

To consumers, credit card companies seem to make each and every one pay a premium as use of credit cards becomes ubiquitous. Credit cards can be de facto double discriminators to people who do not use plastic cards for purchases because credit card costs dust over all in an indiscriminative fashion while credit card benefits fall only upon those who use credit cards. For people who allow credit cards to invade and take charge of their everyday lives, credit cards can be discriminators of various kinds: solicitors for purposeless spending, seducers for endless debt, or bloodsuckers of personal wealth. Imagine numerous consumers who struggle to pay off mountains of credit card debts. Instead of cherishing economic freedom sooner or building personal wealth faster, they offer the bulk of their hard-earned income to the banks for payments of credit card principals and interests.

The Victim

In a consumer market where use of credit cards constitutes the mainstream and the cost of credit card payments figures in most transactions, customers who pay cash for purchases automatically become victims. Victimization obviously originates from a system-wide practice which holds indiscriminate treatments for all regardless of individual needs, choices, or desires. The irony is this: discrimination takes place to some individuals just because no discrimination is assumed for all consumers. Or victimization occurs to some segments just because no victimization is intended for the whole population.

Among consumers who make regular use of credit cards, different levels of proficiency exist in terms of individual knowledge about and access to credit card benefits or avoidance of credit card shortcomings. People who use credit cards with no rewards yield benefits to people who charge their credit card accounts for the sake of collecting cash rebates or travel rewards. Credit card holders who receive smaller rewards surrender interests to those who have more rewarding credit cards in their hands. Most saliently, people who pay interest on credit card balances are likely to be the ultimate financiers for all those reward or rebate programs that credit card issuers are able to put out to the general consumer population. In other words, credit card users may actually bear various degrees of visible or invisible victimization even when they contently charge plastic cards for benefits that are so clear to their commonsensical judgment.

Finally, not every business that accepts credit cards as payment is able to apply bank-charged credit card fees entirely to the prices of its products or merchandises. Type of business, size, location, or operational style all matters. While there are merchants who might benefit from credit card transactions, there are certainly commercial establishments that have to give up various percentages of their profit in order to compete and survive in the consumer market that features dominant and omnipresent use of credit cards. The reality can be as simple as this: you take credit card payments if you do not want to lose any business; you find your profit margin lowered or narrowed when you tally final credits from the banks in the end of the month.

The Compromise

Credit card companies probably do not ever think they discriminate against some or all consumers by making credit payments a norm in the commercial market. To banks, discrimination only means that they deny credit to some customers, charge higher fees or interests on some accounts, or withhold rewards from some card users. It is not an issue of discrimination if a minority of consumers chooses to pay cash while the majority are forced or induced to use credit cards in all commercial transactions. Moreover, credit cards are revolutionary inventions and wondrous services. It is totally reasonable for banks to charge fees for credit card services they provide to businesses and consumers. It is also the essence of legitimate business when individual banks, in the name of service, make a profit from credit card offerings. As for the amount of profit banks may harvest from credit card services, obviously no moral standards other than market dynamics could stay as ultimate judgments. In fact, if banks are ever questioned about the excessive profit they garner from credit card businesses, they can handily present a list of existing programs and practices as their already made compromises to the consumer public of whom they might have taken advantage. This list includes: cash rebates, price discounts, theft protection, extension of a manufacturer's warranty, rental car insurance, special rewards such as travel and entertainment, and most important, debt forgiveness to people who cannot afford to pay their credit card balances in the end.

Merchants can seek comfort in various other aspects when they feel they are ripped off by banks over credit card transactions. These other aspects range from secured cash credits from banks, no worry over counterfeited currencies or fraudulent checks, reduced paperwork and recordkeeping, a given excuse to pass on credit card fees to customers, and a granted opportunity to raise prices to the potentiality of reaching a broader customer base of an ever-increasing buying appetite.

Customers, without thinking much about the higher prices they have to pay because of widespread credit card use in commercial dealings, may only cheer the wonders of credit cards. Smart players like Alibaba feel they do not just receive credit card benefits in default, such as noncash hence risk-free transactions and deferred payments, but also collect various extra rewards by surprise, from cash rebates, complimentary travel, and built-in warranty or insurance services to zero-interest on purchases, balance transfers, or both for a certain period of time. When they are alerted that there is no free meal and that they ultimately pay all these benefits one way or the other, they would still say that they have no complaints against credit cards as worthy services in contemporary markets. Even those cash-paying consumers would remain contentedly quiet: we receive cash from our clients or employers; we do not lose anything when we pay cash for daily purchases; we prefer cash transaction because it is instant and traceless; and rewards for credit card use are negligible compared to the reduced obligations we fulfill to tax authorities through cash transactions.

The Universal

It is an arguable point that some customers face automatic discrimination when they are not able to avail themselves of a commercial service designed for all consumers with a universal fee applied to or an indiscriminate premium built in market transactions. Credit cards are widely used. Credit card brands and banks issuing credit cards charge fees to businesses that accept plastic payments. The market must then incorporate the cost of credit card services in the general sales and purchases. On the part of consumers, whether they use credit cards or not, they have to pay higher prices reflective of credit card fees.

Another important, although subtle, point revealed in this case is that every service or product put out in the market can be both an opportunity for the corresponding provider or producer to make an unwarranted profit and an entrapment for all consumers to suffer various degrees of unnecessary discrimination. The credit card is a wondrous service product. Credit card companies garner profits. Merchants collect credit payments even from customers who otherwise cannot afford to make a purchase. For consumers, while all have to finance higher prices, some pay an exorbitant interest on balances, some fall into deep credit card debts, and only a few, if any, may feel they can get even by playing exceptionally smart as Alibaba does.

Comparable in the public sector are various taxes collected or bonds mandated by different levels of government on citizens or local residents. For example, every property owner is required to contribute to the general fund for a local school district although some of them never have opportunities to benefit from public education either by themselves or through their children. There are even cases of great irony: all city residents are taxed for a public park where only drug users, prostitutes, or rootless migrants gather for deals; all taxpayers are forced to fund a welfare program for only a small minority of undeserving people to take advantage of.

7   Within the Nation

A nation is formed or founded usually on the basis of commonality. In the constitutions of many countries in the world, there are general clauses that proclaim equal treatment or no discrimination for all citizens across all territories under one national flag.

On close examination, however, almost every nation practices differential or discriminative distributions of resources and opportunities among citizens within its boundary. It is no surprise to Vladimir Lenin because he views the nation itself as a machine of violence, where the dominant class uses the government as a dictatorship to oppress subordinate classes. In fact, even under the supposedly free and open system of democracy, a nation would still have to yield to the rule of the majority who, while making and implementing local, national, and international policies out of their invested interests, will unavoidably inflict harms to various members of the minority (Marx 1990; Lenin 1992; Sklair 1997; Chwe 1999; Edensor 2002; Abowitz and Harnish 2006; Schatz and Lavine 2007; Crompton 2008; Marx and Engels 2008; Smith 2009; Magleby, Light, and Nemacheck 2010; Skey 2010; Baecker 2011; Platt 2011; Teichova and Matis 2011; Woodard 2011; Mik-Meyer and Villadsen 2012; Sykes 2012).

SITUATION 1

Democracy seems to be the best possible political mechanism in the eyes of contemporaries. The majority rule on which democracy operates therefore becomes a golden principle or standard to judge whether a policy or practice is credible, fair, and just in modern and postmodern eras.

The Particular

Living long enough in the United States, Alibaba sees clearly not only how the United States boasts of itself as a leader of democracy around the world, but also how the country takes for granted the democratic rule of the majority across various spheres of life. In politics, the rule of the majority places whites in control of local, state, and federal governments. When whites make policies, they do not necessarily understand and consider the historical heritages of Native Americans, the shadow of slavery over blacks, and the ambivalent connections of Latino, Asian, and other first-generation immigrants with their respective motherlands. Alibaba as an average individual not so knowledgeable about racial discriminations instituted by whites and the majority government can easily make a list of openly discriminatory laws and practices from both history and reality, such as the Chinese Exclusion Act, Japanese internment, and de facto segregations between whites and blacks in school, residency, and employment.

Associated with the rule of the majority in democratic practice are the rule of participation and the rule of representation. Whereas in national politics the majority rule builds upon the fact that the majority can simply cast an overwhelming number of votes for their representatives or favorite propositions, in local affairs the majority rule often changes into a situation where whoever happens to be present decides for the rest who happen to be absent. Alibaba, as an ordinary working professional, experiences enough of what he calls the absurdity of democracy or the irony of the majority rule in local decision-making. An employee union composed of not so professionally competitive members represents all employees to decide on working conditions, standards, and benefits. Alibaba knows this saying among his coworkers: "The less productive, the less competitive, and the less successful join the union, become union leaders, and represent all." A professional association selects leaders and makes key policies at its annual conventions. One casts votes for some rules when one attends the convention. One volunteers to take charge of a position when one sits in a business meeting. Alibaba sometimes hears from fellow professionals that people who are hardworking, contributive, and meritorious end up following the rules made by people who are not so diligent, worthy, and deserving simply because the former are not able to find enough time out of their due preoccupation with professional work to participate in association democracy. And a neighborhood council votes on critical issues regarding fundamental interests of all residents with inputs from a random group of residents who show up at each meeting. Alibaba often shares this complaint with other residents in the community: "We, the quiet, busy-working, and compliant majority, seem to be always ruled by them, the noisy, comfort-living, and complaining minority."

The Discriminator

Members of the majority become discriminators against the minority when they willingly participate in political elections as voters or candidates. As voters, they are most likely to vote for majority candidates. Even when they cast protest votes for a minority candidate, they serve to highlight the critical leverage of majority voters in ultimately determining the political careers for all minority pioneers. As candidates, they are most likely to represent majority interests. Even when they speak for minority needs, they appear to showcase the subtle importance of majority figures in eventually changing the life of the minority. On nonpolitical issues, if the majority emerge from those who show up at an event, discriminators are then those who come out, make noises, or blow their trumpets loudly.

There is further distinction between the intentional and the unintentional among all the willing. Most willing participants are unintentional. Individuals follow their majority crowd, speaking their worldviews, spreading their versions of reality, and strengthening their ways of life. While conducting all these matters as businesses, they automatically consume resources, use opportunities, and take up spaces, leaving few for members of the minority just to meet basic survival needs. Intentional discriminators, on the other hand, are ideologues who spread beliefs about majority superiorities or speculate on the threat of a minority, politicians who introduce laws to limit social access by the minority or implement policies to safeguard majority privileges, and everyday-life ordinaries who shout out derogative language against specific members of the minority or take every advantage of all minority individuals within the reach of their business, profession, or practice. For example, the president of a liberal arts college, being white himself, generously promotes white members of the faculty while ignoring the needs of or downplaying the contributions by Asian, black, Hispanic, and Native American professors.

The Victim

With the majority dominating political stage and public sphere, members of the minority unavoidably experience victimization in two different forms. Universal victimization falls upon the minority as a category, making all members general victims. Major aspects of universal victimization include: a loss of ownership over societal identity, a feel of powerlessness for political assertion, and a sense of marginality in cultural expression. For instance, immigrants to the United States may never feel comfortable enough to call themselves Americans. Minority candidates can hardly succeed in general elections if they run on political platforms reflective of minority beliefs, norms, values, needs, and desires. And ethnic minorities, while observing all mainstream holidays on official calendars, can only find private time and space to mark dates important to their ethnic culture and heritage.

Specific victims are minority individuals who encounter particular discriminations in their everyday work and life. Whites move out to suburbs when blacks migrate into the city, making new owners lose property values. Asian students have to do much better in standard exams and other requirements to enroll in the best public universities than whites and other racial groups when the majority sets admission quotas for various minority groups. In Alibaba's own experience and observation, he sees whites dominate the management in private companies and the administration in public or nonprofit organizations, on the backs of many more deserving, talented, and hardworking immigrants and ethnic minorities. Indeed, numerous engineers, scientists, and otherwise highly trained technocrats from various minority groups are specific victims of discrimination, wrestling with a virtual glass ceiling from the first-track of professional success to the second-track of administrative or managerial leadership, in their career movements.

The Compromise

There is no compromise between the majority and the minority as far as the number is concerned. In democratic elections, the majority always have the larger number of votes to win for their preferred representatives, rules, and policies.

A conspicuous compromise from the majority stems from the principle of representation, which entitles the minority limited seats to sit its representatives in government or rationed spots to express its needs or perspectives over the mainstream media. The principle of representation serves to ensure a dominating position for the majority in the first place. By granting limited representation to the minority in accordance with the principle, the majority can gain some understanding of and therefore maintain better control over the minority. Another compromise on the part of the majority seems to immerse in the ideology of diversity, which recognizes the minority for its differences and uniqueness. While counteracting the majority's ethnocentrism, the ideology of diversity mainly celebrates the majority's condescendingly appreciative tolerance for minority ways of life.

An obvious way for the minority to yield to the majority is to follow the rule of participation. By participating with the majority in local and national politics, the minority gives up its rights of boycotting, objecting, and even rebelling. Another route toward compromise by the minority is to serve as a quiet audience to the propaganda of assimilation or, more substantially, to become willing subjects in the campaign of integration. Individual members of the minority, out of their specific circumstances, may feel motivated or coerced to change their names, hide their origins, court members of the majority, practice everything recognized or labeled as mainstream, and eventually turn into something the same as or similar to the majority.

The Universal

Democracy is a fashionable form of government in contemporary times. The United States as the most powerful country in the world even makes serious efforts to spread democracy across the globe. As the government of a nation adopts or mimics democratic politics, the rule of majority inherent in democracy begins to permeate various walks of life within the nation.

The rule of majority institutes clear and open discriminations against the minority. Discrimination can change and even out over time when the minority appears and disappears on religious beliefs, moral values, political positions, or cultural practices. For example, Democrats and Republicans take terms for domination in Congress and over the administration in the United States. However, a minority of race, ethnicity, language, or other permanent features may have to bear entrenched victimizations in the hands of majority discriminators from generation to generation. Blacks entered the New World as slaves, experienced economic, educational, and social segregations for centuries, and will probably have to struggle several more decades to be totally equal with whites, the majority, in America.

There are certainly logical and practical rationalities for the rule of majority to continue in various social affairs. Logically, there can never be equal numbers of peoples, forces, or materials in any possible comparison and contrast. Practically, the rule of majority makes it happen, business, game, or life, with or without conflict, discrimination, and confrontation. The good news is this: discrimination resultant from the majority rule can be compensated for to varying extents by openness, procedural correctness, the shift between the majority and the minority, the rule of representation, the vogue of diversity, and the ideal of integration. For example, in the United States where whites, Christians, heterosexuals, and born-in-Americas still dominate as the majority, both public and private institutions seem to be striving for better representation, greater diversity, and higher integration in their membership populations, with peoples of various backgrounds from race, ethnicity, religion, and sexual orientation to country of origin.

SITUATION 2

A unique creation of democracy is the phenomenon of representation. Under it, a minority of representatives takes stakeholder positions, controls media forums, brokers economic deals, and commands national stages on behalf of the majority. It is no guarantee, however, that the former would not act selfishly in the sheer name of the latter or they serve rightfully for the critical interest of all those whom they represent.

The Particular

Alibaba embraces a wide range of the mass media to stay informed with current affairs. He listens to several radio channels when he sits behind the wheel. He watches different news, talk shows, television journals, and even late-night comedies when he is in bed, at the dinner table, or around the family room. Over the weekend, he usually spends a few hours perusing major metropolitan newspapers and principal national magazines or viewing key television programs known for in-depth news analysis or dedicated to special topic presentations.

A clear and consistent impression Alibaba develops from his varied exposure to the mass media is this: across the vast land of open, free, and democratic America, it is a small minority of politicians, news reporters, celebrities, and experts who deal and manipulate in the court of public opinion. The majority, in which minds probably far brighter than those featured in the media live and through which ideas much more brilliant than those presented in the media flow, serves merely as a crowd to react to or a mass to cheer on whatever is said by the minority. The president, the governor, the mayor, and legislators command political arenas. The CEO, the CFO, the CIO, and upper-level managers monopolize economic affairs. The actor or actress, the director, the athlete, the coach, and all other entertainers dominate fashions and lifestyles. Most ironically, a popular music star who is by no means educated about public policy, health, or environment can lead and mislead a national audience by uttering his or her often biased personal views in a widely watched talk show on television. Indeed, Alibaba wonders if any media outlet would ever give the majority, hundreds of thousands of ordinary people in everyday life, any chance to speak their minds or to share their stories of life when one program after another, one show after another, and one channel after another is so entrenched to feature only famous individuals in entertainment, sport, business, and politics.

The Discriminator

The minority of discriminators in this situation include all politicians elected to represent their constituencies, all corporate and organizational stakeholders promoted to manage their offices or administer their enterprises, all experts selected to comment on issues in their fields of specialty, all journalists chosen to report news of their place, and all social celebrities featured to highlight fashions and styles of their time.

There are first inevitable discriminations. Politicians, when they serve a term, automatically prevent the majority of all non-office-holding people from directly exercising their political wills. Corporate executives and organizational administrators, when they assume office, naturally keep the large membership from making key business decisions. Experts, when they speak their view, unavoidably muffle or subdue various other perspectives. Journalists, when they take position, instantly lead the audience away from all other versions of story that take place there and then in reality. And social celebrities, when they act and utter on stage, can sentimentally swing the mass or shake up the mainstream from one sensation or extreme to another. A simple truth across all these situations is this: the majority can only listen to, react to, or follow the minority without any chance to speak, act, or lead in their actual mindsets.

Then come deliberate discriminations. Politicians do not always represent their constituents fully: they tend to manipulate political forces, pitting one segment of the constituency against another. Organizational stakeholders do not always manage their corporations or business entities professionally: they tend to follow individual idiosyncrasies, pursuing one set of priorities over another. Experts do not always speak on behalf of knowledge: they tend to spread ideologies, prompting people to make not necessarily best choices over various matters. Journalists do not always report news faithfully: they tend to engage in event dramatizations, captivating the audience with a desirable rate of viewership or readership. And social celebrities do not always act in genuine identity: they tend to manage public impressions, making people believe what appears to be unbelievable or even impossible. A common thread through all these characters is this: they each do everything they can to command their field, to control their audience, and to stay as career or lifetime politicians, executives, knowledge authorities, newsmen or newswomen, and luminaries.

The Victim

Beginning with a basic clause in any typical constitution, all men and women are created equal in origin and therefore ought to be treated equal before the law. In other words, everyone is entitled to exercise his or her political will, speak his or her inner mind, and pursue his or her favored ways of life, without coercion, distortion, false representation, or unwarranted influence.

In reality, the majority of people yield their individual political rights and powers to a minority of politicians under modern democracy. They make monetary contributions to elect their political representatives into public offices. They spend time and efforts to answer calls from politicians. They rally behind the policy initiatives put forth by government officials. In the end of the game, however, most people are likely to find that they are not represented fully or correctly, that they are completely misrepresented, or that they are just betrayed. Political victimization is now a universally shared syndrome for all ordinaries of the mass who count on a few privileged others for representation in the governmental machinery.

Over the court of public opinion, while a mass of readers remain quiet to read books, magazines, journals, and newspapers written by a limited count of knowledge producers, experts, commentators, and reporters, a crowd of viewers stay silent to watch news, movies, shows, and other programs produced by a selected number of writers, directors, newsmen and newswomen, actors and actresses, and other media players. The majority forgo their chances and opportunities to create stories, utter words, and spread opinions over the phenomenally free and open media to a minority in the so-called information age. They pay to send their favored albums, books, films, or programs to the top of the best-selling list. They attend to create continuing shows, lasting series, or enduing personalities. They cheer on to entertain and sustain big networks, mega-studios, and global media empires. But the irony is this: most people feel they are brainwashed, lost in soul, disturbed in taste, addicted to a twisted portrayal of life, or blindly dependent on the media. For example, with a lost soul and disturbance in taste, individuals are not able to distinguish holy from unholy, noble from disgraceful, right from wrong, or good from bad. Indeed, media victimization is like an epidemic that threatens not only the spirit of all contemporaries, but also the meaning of human civilizations.

The Compromise

People in the majority know that it is impractical and impossible for every individual to take public stage to directly exercise his or her political will, speak his or her worldview, and showcase his or her lifestyle. There has to be a minority of representatives, spokespersons, models, and celebrities in political arenas, behind public forums, over the court of mass opinions, and across various open domains to act on behalf of, demonstrate to, and entertain for the sake of the majority. Representatives, spokespersons, models, and celebrities are individuals with their own beliefs, values, ideologies, desires, likes, and dislikes. It is natural and perhaps reasonable that they reveal or realize some of their personal ideas or ideals while serving the large interests of an audience or constituency. Misrepresentation, misuse of privilege, and even abuse of power can happen when these individuals are given the charge to control powerful positions, make critical decisions, and wield widespread influences. Incompetence, incapacitation, and total failure may occur even though these individuals oftentimes have passed keen competition and close scrutiny. Indeed, it takes high intellectual and physical calibers to perform on public stages. In one's private circle, one may feel one clearly possesses tons of brilliant ideas and talents. But who knows if one is capable of translating one's personal intelligence and potentiality into viewable and testable deeds in public spheres?

Individuals in the selected minority understand that they have to represent constituencies well to ensure reelections, to report news honestly and produce programs professionally to keep reception rates, and to stay in fashion and style to attract public interests. Some might even lament that they just act as puppets of the general populace and would rather live a private life, like every ordinary person in the mass. Of course, there are also individuals who take the mass as ignorant, opinionated, shifting, and unpredictable and think they have the wisdom, experience, and capital to manipulate, exploit, and mislead the mass with their individual ideals, ideologies, and idiosyncrasies. However, in the end of or during some reflective moments of their own public plays, these self-prized elites are likely to feel they actually act upon the impulses of the majority of their time and place. To historians from time to time, it is a universal truth that extraordinaries only rise from, shine over, and fall into ordinaries. There are even historical lamentations that a legend becomes the ultimate victim of his people, empire, or era.

The Universal

Some street jokes characterize entertainment celebrities and sport stars as exotic pets that people raise and keep for sensational enjoyment in their society. People watch athletes play in sports, betting how far humans may stretch over their own physical limits. People see actors and actresses perform onstage, figuring how crazy fellow beings may go beyond their own psychological, moral, or spiritual norms.

It is generally fair that people in the majority remain fed with much-needed news, entertainments, and games while paying a minority of representatives and stars a premium for some doses of misrepresentation, manipulation, and exploitation over a range of substantive or trivial matters. There is not much discrimination under way when a few stakeholders and celebrities exercise power, enjoy luxury, and wield influence over the populace because they at the same time have to endure scrutiny, stress, and criticism for optimal performances in public arenas. Victimization overall is not an issue as it is logically impossible for every single individual to have a turn on public stage and it is through relatively open and competitive social dynamics that a minority of representatives and superstars emerge to lead or mislead, to manage or manipulate, and to use or abuse the majority in social spheres.

In the meantime, the game of democracy is basically unfair as often the rich, the privileged, and the educated become political representatives in almost all seemingly open elections. The court of public opinion is essentially discriminative when a few control sources as well as outlets of information to influence what people in the majority think, choose, and act in everyday life. Victimization is inevitably part of each and every social operation where the majority serves as the mass to be manipulated and the means to be utilized by the minority to fulfill the latter's ideal, ideology, or superego.

SITUATION 3

Most nation-states in the contemporary era have some welfare features. A number of developed countries in the West contain so many welfare characteristics that they are even called welfare states. Under a generic system of state welfare, all working and well-off citizens contribute part of their income and wealth in the form of taxes to local and national governments. The state then has resources to provide basic citizen services, such as national defense, public safety, and communal recreations, as well as to administer various social assistance programs, from affordable housing for low-income residents, complimentary medical treatments to the poor, free care for the unattended elderly, and living wages to the unemployed to other accommodations for those who are one way or the other in need.

The Particular

As working professionals, Alibaba and his wife shoulder an array of taxes and taxations by all different levels of government. They pay income taxes to the state and the federal government on earnings for which they work diligently from jobs and investments. They pay real estate taxes to the county for the house that they own as a family residence. They pay personal property taxes to the state for the cars that they drive for everyday work and life. They pay sales taxes to the city, the county, and/or the state whenever they purchase daily life necessities, from food, clothes, and transportation to household items.

With care and compassion, Alibaba and his wife make regular donations to established charities. From season to season, they send used and unused furniture, clothes, shoes, consumer electronics, toys or games, and various household items to thrift stores or truck stops operated by major charitable organizations. They volunteer in a few donation drives or rescue missions each year. They respond to general calls for assistance in the aftermath of major catastrophes around the world. One time for a major earthquake that took place on another continent, Alibaba and his wife even persuaded their then eight-year-old son to empty his piggybank for an extra fifty dollars so that the whole family could send a bigger check to an official relief fund pooled by a reputable charity. Alibaba likes travel across the country and around the world. From place to place, he leaves countless coins and bills to those who beg for help on public streets.

Alibaba and his wife worked hard and saved smart to have built and maintained self-sufficiency for the whole family. They raise their two children with respectable education, ethics, and habits so that both in all likelihood will follow the path of a well-off middle-class lifestyle. They themselves do not expect to become a public charge when they retire from work and age to the senior stage. In other words, they do not ever imagine that they will someday in their own life or in their children's lives take a penny of benefit from the social welfare machinery to which they have contributed through years of taxes, donations, and other offerings.

As a side note, Alibaba has story after story in his recollection that he and his family seem to opt for more frugal choices in everyday life than some of those who take advantage of the welfare system. He is in awe and amazed when he sees some low-income housing residents purchase pounds of Maine lobsters, Alaskan king crab legs, and New Zealand lamb steaks in neighborhood supermarkets. Alibaba most of time chooses to only look at those pricy items. He used to feel sorry for his kids when they were little playing in public parks where they could only envy other kids, even those whose parents live on food stamps, over some of the ice cream bars bought from a walk-along vendor. Alibaba rarely allowed his kids to enjoy what he considered a nonnecessity in life. He had many after-the-moment regrets for his kids when they were young eating at fast-food restaurants where they could only look jealously at other kids, even those whose parents receive monthly welfare checks, over some of the foods favored by all kids. Alibaba usually bought his kids only those items that were on sale or allowed by coupons. He and his wife sigh every time when one of their close friends, who works at a county hospital, tells them stories about her patients, who use county health care without payments, play fashionable high-tech devices, or spend generously on foods for visiting relatives in the cafeteria. Alibaba does not own any trendy electronic gadgets, and he knows his wife, like himself, always carries a lunch bag to work.

The Discriminator

A nation is built upon contributions from individual citizens. One may draw resources from one's country at some stages while contributing to it during other periods over one's life course. Some individuals may give more than they take, whereas others may use more than they add to the national wealth in their whole life. Technically, however, a nation will fall in debt or ruin if it offers more than it receives in total from its constituents. And anybody who consumes more than he or she creates is a discriminator against his or her fellow citizens, eventually his or her nation.

The modern welfare system obviously produces a variety of discriminators by frequency, duration, and gravity. There are seasonal, cyclical, and chronic discriminators who utilize public assistance only during periods of immaturity, disability, or unemployment, who live between government subsidy and self-support, and who take social welfare as a way of life. There are partial versus full, onetime versus lifetime, and marginal versus hardcore discriminators. The range in all these dimensions can be as wide as from a minimum wage worker living with his or her family in government-subsidized housing to a rootless AIDS patient bleeding taxpayer-funded medical care until death. The contrast through all these categories can be as sharp as between a single mother raising her children with food stamps and a heinous murderer serving his lifetime sentence in a federal prison.

Discrimination in welfare can be an inevitable feature for any nation-state. The state organizes people into a social hierarchy, forcing a segment of the population into a situation where survival becomes a mercy of public assistance. Who wants to live on social welfare if one occupies an advantageous position in society with ready access to resources and opportunities for legitimate profit, success, fame, and status? In other words, it is not welfare recipients who discriminate against the state and its contributing citizens. Instead it is the state and all its profiting citizens who push welfare recipients into the corner for a life of dependence and discrimination.

The Victim

On the surface, all contributing citizens who have to pay higher taxes for the social welfare system are victims. The state that has to balance welfare spending with various other demands can be considered a bearer of victimization as well.

In close analysis, not every contributing citizen takes the same degree of victimization with the same level of public sympathy or social appreciation. The rich may have to contribute a relatively higher proportion of their wealth or an absolutely larger share of the whole welfare expenditure according to the size of their subpopulation. However, in the eyes of social critics, the rich possess so much wealth that they would have wasted a considerable part of it by way of luxury and extravagancy had they not made any contribution to social welfare. In other words, it is through welfare that part of unfairly concentrated wealth is put into nonwasteful use. More critically, some may charge that much of the wealth in the hands of the rich is ill gotten and ought to be redistributed to other segments of the population anyway. Social welfare, therefore, is just an institutional mechanism through which part of social justice is restored.

Middle-class citizens, in comparison, are most likely to receive recognition and commendation for their contributions to the welfare system. First, they do not seem to hold any added advantage over other social groups in economic competition or wealth acquisition. Second, they work hard and save smart in achieving success and building self-sufficiency. Third, they are more likely to contribute to than to benefit from social welfare. Fourth, when individuals take advantage of the welfare system, middle-class citizens become real victims. Unlike people of the rich who may just give up some of their luxury, middle-class citizens are likely to either stretch their muscles or squeeze from their necessities. Indeed, they have to work harder, save smarter, or do both for the net result of a compromised quality of life when they pay higher and higher taxes for a welfare system that is exploited by more and more people as a simple source of dependence or a convenient way of life.

The Compromise

Taxpayers who shoulder the welfare system may find some comfort in their contributions or sacrifices through one of these rationalizations. Generally, a social welfare system puts a positive face on the country or presents a caring image of the state in the world community of nations. It reflects an admirable attainment of humanity or signifies a remarkable progress in civilization over the course of social evolution. In specific terms, feeding the poor, protecting the weak, and aiding the needy unites the nation, defuses social tension, and creates peace. A social environment of minimal hostility, optimal harmony, and enduing stability benefits each and every member of society in his or her pursuit of career success, personal expression, and a desirable quality of life. Further down to individual levels, welfare recipients and their partial or whole dependence serve as fresh and clear reminders for all contributing citizens that anyone could fall into poverty, misery, and neediness in the unpredictable dynamics of life. Interpersonally, if some welfare dependents live without human shames, motives, or purposes, they may virtually teach people in the larger community that it is important to keep one's dignity, direction, and diligence as one strives to live a meaningful life.

The minority of people who tap into social welfare as a source of support may take on a number of thoughts and acts to keep the system in perspective. In terms of act, they could only use public assistance to meet their basic survival needs. Use of a welfare check for a binge of drinks, an indulgence in drugs, or a family feast may happen once in a while but usually at the cost of a month-long hunger. Some welfare recipients may commit fraud and take an unwarranted advantage of the system. But in doing so, they are less likely to engage in high-profile rebellions against established social order. With respect to thought, while many welfare recipients hold some degree of gratitude toward specific sources from which they receive assistance, some may even help spread a sentiment of admiration and appreciation for individual success and social progress. Parents who live in public housing projects may tell far more mainstream success stories to their children than those who reside in affluent neighborhoods. Excitement can be no less among homeless vagrants, drug addicts, and street beggars when a breakthrough takes place in science or medicine, a new technology device makes its debut on the market, or the country wins in a major game of sport.

The Universal

It is natural for middle-class citizens to develop a sense of unfairness when they work hard and save smart to fund a social welfare system that shelters not only good people in real need, but also not-so-good people who only exploit society in their life. A critical question is this: is it fair to allow a minority of nonproductive citizens to discriminate against the majority of hardworking people by way of taxation and welfare?

Specifically, are productive citizens overtaxed to a degree that they have to work harder, save more, and take a higher level of compromise in the quality of life? Among all contributing citizens, do the rich pay enough taxes in proportion to the wealth they hold in their hands? Are self-sufficient working people forced to take an excessive share of social contributions beyond their financial capacities? Of course, taxation is driven by a wide variety of government expenditures. To what extent is severe taxation solely or primarily caused by an outgrowth of social welfare?

On the part of welfare beneficiaries, how much blame can they assign to society, social stratification, and human hierarchy for their experiences of misfortune, misery, and hence partial or complete dependence on public assistance? How much problem should they find with self-choice, personal effort, and individual lifestyle for their downfalls into lack of productivity, poverty, and further a half or full state of neediness for welfare support? It is no doubt that a minority of people who choose to abuse drugs, commit crimes, exploit the social system, and live a nonproductive life can be out-and-out discriminators against the majority of conscientious citizens, a whole society, and even the general humanity.

SITUATION 4

An interesting phenomenon in modern population dynamics is that the rate of birth or the reproductive contribution to the population changes inversely with socioeconomic status. The richer, the more powerful, and/or the higher educated one becomes, the more likely one focuses on one's own life through a line of business, a fulfilling profession, an expressive adventure, a recreational way of leisure, or a combination thereof, rather than giving birth to an offspring, raising children, and cultivating dreams and hopes in their descendants. The poor segment of the population, on the other hand, is seen from place to place to have offered proportionally higher additions to the grand total of the citizenry. The question is then this: does a population suffer from discrimination when people in lower social echelons give more births than their fair share or when people in the higher social hierarchy do not make enough of their due contributions to the population growth?

The Particular

As working professionals, Alibaba and his wife have only two children. They would like to have more if they could find more time and energy for kids beyond their respectively demanding careers. There is not much regret, however, as Alibaba sometimes teasingly says to his wife, "With the perfect combination of a daughter and a son, we are making a due contribution to the continuation of the population in our country and the survival of human race in the universe."

In his middle-class neighborhood, Alibaba notices that most families have one to two children. Whereas a few couples are childless, only a small number of families raise three or more children. Among his professional colleagues and friends, Alibaba observes that many stay late to get married and rarely raise more than two children upon marriage. By number, it seems to be an absolute decline from older to newer generations. Looking higher up into more wealthy neighborhoods as well as people of higher status in economic, political, and social terms, Alibaba only finds the situation of population decline become more and more acute.

To his relief, Alibaba also sees many what he calls population-multiplying scenes in various places. These scenes include: a pregnant mother with one or two of her older kids pushing a cart carrying her sleeping baby pays with food stamps at a grocery store checkout; a jobless father with a bunch of his kids searches for movies and storybooks in a public library; a young couple dig deeply into their pockets for enough change to order food for an army of their children in a fast-food restaurant; and many immigrants who speak their native languages watch a mass of their kids or grandkids play in community parks. Besides his delight for population growth, Alibaba wonders whether all those children from disadvantageous social backgrounds will grow into productive, self-sufficient, and even successful citizens.

The Discriminator

Against the population of a country and further the human species as a whole, who can be the discriminator?

The rich, the powerful, and the educated enjoy their own lives with bounty resources and ample opportunities. They are reluctant to spend time on, they hesitate to put their wealth, power, and knowledge into best use for, and they are unwilling to make efforts at giving birth to children, raising them with care, and preparing them for entry to the productive labor force. As they fail to fulfill a fair share of additions to the population with their distinctive genes, personalities, and characters, they throw discriminations against the population, especially on its sufficiency of diversity.

The poor, the powerless, and the uneducated struggle in everyday work and life under a myriad of constraints and difficulties. They give birth to children because they have no control over natural reproduction, take advantage of social welfare, count on the future generation for hope and support, or simply do not have any better things to do between day and night. They raise children with limited resources and restricted opportunities. They spread descendants in the bottom of the social hierarchy, where grown-ups either replicate what parents do or have to make extraordinary efforts for the basics of survival or toward the rarity of success. Insomuch as they overfill the population with their unique biological properties, psychological propensities, and sociological traits, they hold discriminations against the population, particularly over its necessity of vitality.

The Victim

Children cannot choose what parents they have, what families they grow up with, and what resources and opportunities they avail of in their drive toward life and success. Fewer children can benefit from existing wealth, power, and knowledge as the rich, the powerful, and the educated opt to shun their due responsibility for human reproduction. More children have to suffer from lack of wealth, power, and knowledge as the poor, the powerless, and the uneducated take the natural path of unplanned, uncontrolled, and unwarranted childbirths. As a whole, the future generation bears net victimization when the distribution of its members skews toward less wealth, power, and knowledge than the past generation. In other words, the future generation drops its due entitlement to or loses its fair share of social resources and opportunities when either fewer are reproduced of the rich, the powerful, and the educated or more are replicated of the poor, the powerless, or the educated. The situation becomes worse as both go hand in hand oftentimes.

The population may grow out of balance when one segment shrinks unexpectedly only to the advantage of an irrational outgrowth of another. In terms of sustainability, competition and conflict inevitably increase in the swelling subpopulation, while waste and idleness unavoidably take place in the contracting subgroup. With regard to character development and social morality, people who barely succeed upon hard work tend to develop a feeling of injustice and unfairness, whereas people who own without much effort are likely to lose their sensitivity about virtue and rectitude.

The human race can miss an evolutionary gradation as individual traits acquired by people who have made it to the higher social hierarchy are not proportionately preserved and passed along. An evolutionary degradation, on the other hand, may occur when individual traits kept by people who are entrenched in the lower social hierarchy are overly represented and reproduced from generation to generation.

The Compromise

There is obviously neither face-to-face negotiation nor direct compromise between or among different parties or sides involved in human reproduction. Mutual adjustments can nonetheless be achieved through self-moderation on each part.

The rich, the powerful, and the educated make financial contributions to social welfare, health care, and the educational system so that children from unprivileged family backgrounds can climb the social ladder after reasonable efforts. They may also adopt, sponsor, and foster-care disadvantaged children to give the latter a family environment or a source of support by which to grow into adulthood.

The poor, the powerless, and the uneducated endure hard labor to bear and rear children. While they are not always able to provide all necessary material resources and social opportunities, they commit time, deliver care, show concern, offer companionship, and set an example for their children. As it is proved from time to time, spiritual guidance, love, and modeling are far more important than mere material support in a young person's growth.

The future generation may become stronger when individuals develop and mature in relative material deprivation. A national population may turn more dynamic as people of higher social echelons are not mechanically reproduced by the natural process of birth and death but rather are organically created through a social procedure of screening, testing, and stratification. The human race can only attain higher vitality and vibrancy as competitive traits and adaptive mechanisms are constantly customized at each generation among individuals who make it to the higher social hierarchy, not conveniently from the top but painstakingly from the bottom.

The Universal

On the surface it seems to be one of the greatest irrationalities in the contemporary world. That is, people who have resources choose to raise no or fewer kids, whereas people who suffer from lack of social capabilities tend to give birth to more children, oftentimes far more than their collective share of all offspring in a population.

An immediate result is this: more children of the future generation have to struggle in poverty, illness, inadequate education, lack of opportunity, and even problematic biosocial traits such as those inherited by children born to alcoholics, drug addicts, or people infected with HIV/AIDS. Theoretically, it is possible that disadvantage breeds advantage, tough environments make strong people, or pressure for survival gives rise to competitive personality. If this holds true, there then stand two derivative generalizations. One is that human competition is maintained at the expense of individual sufferings and sacrifices. The other is that life is a ruthless strive toward survival and success. One succeeds after one beats one's competitors. One fails on one's way to survival when one is beaten in social competition.

Also in each generation, as more individuals start from scratch and fewer people begin with inherited advantages, social competition overall takes a general outlook of fairness and justice. People who have made it to the top of the social hierarchy can legitimately say they are proved to be the fittest of all, whereas those who drop out of competition or struggle in the bottom of society for a lifetime can only blame their own bad luck, maladjustment, or lack of adaptation. With regard to the logic of human evolution, apparent irrationality appears to exist for the sheer sake of essential rationality. Indeed, only when more individuals are born to lower socioeconomic status with relative material deprivation, can the majority of the population live and relive the spirit of competition, the triumph of the fittest or the misery of the unfit, the blessings of fairness or the givens of justice, and, ultimately, the vibrancy of humankind.

SITUATION 5

The age of information and mass media seems to render talkers and onstage performers, such as politicians, entertainers, celebrities, news reporters, and broadcasters, an unwarranted advantage in gaining power, wealth, fame, and influence over doers and backstage practitioners, including writers, scientists, engineers, healthcare professionals, and all different kinds of workers who labor diligently on either blue-collar or white-collar jobs. However, as it has been since the beginning of human civilizations, it is always the doers who produce goods, provide services, and make substantive contributions to society, social life, and social progress.

The Particular

Like every other ordinary contemporary, Alibaba surfs the World Wide Web, listens to radios, watches televisions, scans newspapers, and flip pages of magazines. Across all these channels of information or outlets of the media, he either hears politicians propagandize partisan ideologies, journalists report dramatic events, and program hosts advocate different ideas and practices or sees entertainers perform in scripted roles, athletes play games, and celebrities expose themselves like exotic pets or public puppets. Although he rarely gives much thought over how much he is influenced by what he hears and what he sees in the mass media, Alibaba has to admit that he is left with a general impression by his day-to-day exposure that the whole world seems to be all about talkers in public spheres. Doers and their deeds are simply submerged, neglected, or made irrelevant in the media-featured flow of contemporary life.

In material terms, politicians give orders while speaking, broadcasters command visibility while reporting, and entertainers gather fans or followers while performing. Besides fame, stars in sports and entertainments collect huge payments for acts in one dimension or another, diminishing the value of all-out endeavors in science, health, education, engineering, and every other professional field. In addition to influence, politicians, experts, and program personalities gain enormous power for words of one extreme or another, casting a shadow over the worth of multifaceted deeds in agriculture, industry, commerce, and every other sector of human production. To Alibaba, the world turns upside down when public stages are set up for a few superficial stars to lead or mislead real-life movers with mere words or just some dimensional acts.

The Discriminator

Talkers become discriminators simply because they steal a far greater share of fame, wealth, power, and social status than they deserve by their acts of talking, presenting, and acting.

Most noticeably, talkers commandeer public stages, creating a general impression that they are the guardians, stakeholders, spokespersons, or representatives of a whole population, society, or nation. Foreign dignitaries first speak to preaching politicians, from whom they obtain information about current affairs of the country. Outside visitors first approach report-ing media staff through whom they communicate to peoples of the terri-tory. Inside the nation, ordinary citizens listen to radios, attend theatres, watch television programs, see onstage shows, and read printed materials, relating to all hosts, anchorpersons, actors, or performers throughout the mass media as if those acting and presenting personnel were the sources of life or the manifestations of human creation in their time.

In more specific terms, talkers discriminate against doers when the for-mer mislead, misreport, misrepresent, misinterpret, or midjudge the latter. For example, journalists can make inaccurate reports about a line of busi-ness while commentators may unfairly vent criticisms over a series of con-sumer goods. Indirectly, talkers hold inherent discriminations against doers when talking seems to generate faster and more rewards than doing or as the value of doing diminishes in light of cheap and easy talks. Since social progress builds essentially upon the concrete contributions by the mass of doers, talkers may even leave an incalculable harm to society as a whole when socially manufactured and maintained spurious correlations between talking and fame, wealth, power, influence, or a combination thereof bal-loon to threaten the morality or virtue of diligence, doing, and deed.

The Victim

Doers can face a variety of victimizations when talkers rule. First, doers may be persuaded or forced by talkers, who often do not have any experi-ential feel of the detail and difficulty of doing things, to engage in actions that appear to be doable conceptually yet in reality essentially undoable or extremely difficult to do. For example, numerous people may have to labor unnecessarily or even lose lives in vein under an action plan of war, political reform, economic takeoff, or cultural renewal devised and implemented by politicians. Second, doers may be led or misled by talkers to deviate from the rightful course of certain action or even defy the logic of doing some-thing. As a result, they have to struggle extra hard or face needless harms in the process. Third, doers may be given unfair comments and reviews by talkers for what they do and have done. Public pressure and hostility may hence build and spread, tarnishing the reputation of a practice or threaten-ing the prestige of a profession.

In the dimension of morale and morality, doers can easily develop a sense of alienation when they see doing and deeds degraded and devalued relative to the words of talkers. What is fairness when thousands of workers who do hard labor at McDonald's make only minimum wage while a celebrity can harvest a million for a few seconds of talking and acting in one of the restaurant chain's commercials? Where is justice when talkers wield power and privileges to comment and criticize doers, but not vice versa?

A society or country as a whole may suffer in both productivity and spirituality when a general impression or atmosphere looms large and pervasive in the minds of people that talking is more rewarding than doing, words hold more worth than deeds, and talkers have power to lead doers. What motivates people to create, produce, and build material things when superficiality of talking and acting reigns high in public spheres? How can people place their beliefs in diligence and put their minds on specific crafts and craftsmanship when opportunism runs wild in the ample emptiness of words throughout the mass media?

The Compromise

There are a few common rationalizations on the part of victims. First, most doers know that only a small elite of talkers exist in comparison to the huge mass they make in society. It does not cost or hurt each individual much when all doers stand together to shoulder the burden of supporting a limited number of talkers for some extravagance. Second, many doers may believe that they are born and reared to be doers. As doers, they can only do what they do and be who they are. They can neither act out of character nor make sense out of nonsense. Third, some doers may even think that talkers are special people with blessed gifts, endowed talents, or bestowed opportunities. They dream to be a talker but cannot really become a talking celebrity because they are essentially doers.

Talkers, in the meantime, often realize that they act and perform to entertain the mass of doers. They lose public attention if they fail to keep doers interested and paying. Talkers sometimes recognize that they sing and speak to the pleasure of doers. They fade from public spheres when they fail to keep doers impressed and attending. More generally, talkers always understand that they appeal to doers as listeners, readers, viewers, or general audiences. They may have fans, followers, and well-wishers. They may also have criticizers, haters, and saboteurs. As they strive to achieve and maintain ratings and public blessings from doers, talkers may feel no shame, no apology, and no regret for taking what they gain in wealth, power, fame, and social status.

The Universal

It has been a long-established bias in human civilizations that manual labor holds less worth than mental work and laborers who produce with body command lower prestige than intellectuals, artists, and policymakers who create by brain. In everyday life, it is a common observation that a farmer tilling land for crops from dawn to dust struggles to make ends meet while a priest presiding over a local church enjoys sufficiency and even affluence in material sustenance. Or it is a normal practice that hundreds of fine products handmade by numerous laborers are not worth a piece of drawing, a moment of preaching, or a few lines of poetry and prose made by one single mind-mining person.

The devaluation of body, manual labor, and blue-collar workers reaches the level of the surreal in modern and postmodern times. In any typical business conglomerate, thousands of mass production line workers earn minimum wages so that a few top executives can harvest millions in their annual compensation packages. Under every standard democracy, millions of ordinary citizens exercise rights to vote so that a small group of career politicians can muster and keep enormous power in their day-to-day political maneuverings. Over all regular social transactions, doers set up stages, perform acts, make products, offer services, and clean up scenes so that talkers can conjure up ideas, write scripts, give orders, render judgments, and decide on distribution of rewards and penalties.

An interesting exception is in sports and entertainments. Over sport arenas, athletes can gain far greater fame and wealth by going beyond and above body limits in competitive games than scientists who study bodies or devise games, engineers who invent equipment and design facilities, and coaches who select talents and train candidates. Around entertainment fields, actors and actresses usually take much more publicity and compensation by exposing body parts, manipulating body skills, or acting out with body movements than directors who plot acting scenes, playwrights who make stage scripts, and authors who create original stories. Ironically, physical performances embodied by acting celebrities are all faked, resulting in few practical utilities to everyday survivals in natural environments. Bodily skills demonstrated by competing athletes are essentially nonproductive, leading to little substantive contributions to human creations on the face of the earth. In other words, overvaluation of bodies and bodily acts in entertainment and sports only serves to highlight the surreal irrationality of degrading physiques, devaluing manual labor, and downplaying virtual contributions of massy yet particular doers in the modern and postmodern eras.

8 Around the World

The world is not a flat collection of nation-states or territorial sovereignties in equal status. Countries differ in size, manpower, resource, development, and overall income and output, such as gross domestic product, gross national product, and net national income. Larger, advanced, or generally more powerful nations can hold a variety of advantages over smaller, yet-to-be-developed, or by and large weaker countries in trade, diplomatic relation, geopolitical dealing, military interface, border-to-border transaction, and people-to-people interaction.

In the current world system, a few powerful countries even join hands to form international entities, such as the United Nations, the World Trade Organization, and the World Health Organization. These worldwide bodies make rules reflective more of the values from some countries than others, implement policies representative more of the interests of some nations than others, and coordinate actions indicative more of the intentions of some states than others.

With historical versus existent forces and natural versus manmade practices playing out in the world, it is no surprise that discriminations take place conspicuously and inconspicuously over many different international dealings (Wallerstein 1984, 1997; Simon 1997; Schultz 1998; Kerbo 2005; Therborn 2006; Ray 2007; McDonough 2009; Chen and Ravallion 2010; Griffiths 2010; Beck 2011; Edwards 2011; Keating 2011; Todaro and Smith 2011; World Bank 2011; Boeri et al. 2012; Yap 2012).

SITUATION 1

Human capital is essential to scientific discovery, technological invention, economic development, and general social progress. It is often the human capital that determines the level of development a country can attain and maintain.

Around the world, while most developed countries benefit from an educated population and a trained labor force within their boundaries, many developing nations struggle with a lack of technical and managerial talents in almost every area of work and life. The great irony, however, is that talents educated and trained with limited resources in developing countries where they are most needed flee, flock, and flow to developed nations to make substantive contributions over there. The so-called brain drain from poor to rich economies, from backward to advanced societies, and from developing to developed environments is indeed one of the most hurtful discriminations the latter can possibly hold against the former.

The Particular

Alibaba knows well about the brain drain across national borders himself. He came to the United States when he already had a master's degree in science. In the country of his birth, he attended free elementary, middle, and high schools. As the best-performing student in all his classes from grades one to twelve, he went on to an elite university, where he obtained his bachelor's degree and later his master's degree upon successful completion of a four-year undergraduate study and then a three-year graduate school, with full funding of tuitions, fees, rooms, and boards for seven years from the state. He worked for only a short period of three years on his native land, and he spent most of his time on learning English and applying for admission to doctoral programs across the United States. He landed a job right after he defended his dissertation. He now has worked and lived in America for more than two decades. To his country of origin, where he received most of his education, he only made a few visits over the years. Alibaba holds a deep feeling of gratitude and regret because he draws so much from yet hardly returns any to the land of his birth, which lags far behind the highly developed Unites States and critically needs talents in its drive toward socioeconomic development and modernization.

Among his classmates, colleagues, neighbors, and friends, Alibaba knows many scientists, engineers, and other specialists who work in hospitals, universities, governmental agencies, high-tech firms, and various manufacturing or business corporations from automobiles, chemicals, and pharmaceuticals to semiconductors. Some land in America with a doctoral degree to work immediately in the forefront of their fields as postdoctoral scholars or full-fledged researchers, and some arrive to continue their college education or undertake graduate study, but all have more than half of their educational careers to thank for the country that they forever call home or place of origin. Some migrate from poor societies where resources to educate youths are scarce, and some come from developing economies where needs for talents are acute, yet all choose to stay in America to make contributions to developed capitalism while forgoing much of the educational indebtedness they owe to their undeveloped, underdeveloped, or just developing birthplaces and homelands in Africa, Asia, South America, or elsewhere in the world.

The Discriminator

Developed economies and advanced societies are principal discriminators in the global competition for talents and productive labors. Taking advantage of the gap in income and standards of living they have over poor nations, rich countries attract able-bodied and smart-minded aliens to their labor force without spending a penny on the rearing of those individuals as they grow up in their homelands. Boasting of the stability in government and social order they have in comparison with weak polities, powerful states draw work-age foreigners to their production army without investing much in the training of those people when they attend schools in their native territories. More actively, using economic incentives, touting cultural amenities, and applying legal leverages they conveniently have at their disposal in contrast to undeveloped or underdeveloped economies, advanced societies pull creative and productive immigrants across all possible professional fields into their human capital pool without bearing much cost in caring, educating, socializing, and entertaining those contributors when they are young, old, sick, or simply burnt out. It is not uncommon that immigrant workers return to their home countries to recuperate from fatigue, recover from illness, rejuvenate for a new round of productivity, or retire for the senility of life because they cannot afford to pay for those needs in advanced societies where they create, produce, and contribute.

With talents and productive labors from around the world, advanced countries produce name-brand consumer goods, manufacture high-tech equipment or machineries, maintain first-rate universities, and operate state-of-the art medical facilities. They charge poor, weak, and yet-to-be developed nations with high premiums when the latter buy consumer goods, purchase technical devices or tools, or use educational, research, or medical facilities from them, even though the latter offer their talents and productive labors for free in the creation, production, and maintenance of those pricy products or facilities. It is interesting to observe that Japan, the United States, or a European Union membership state employs scientists, engineers, and skilled workers originally born, raised, educated, and trained with limited resources in China, India, Mexico, Russia, or any other underdeveloped or developing country to invent high-tech products for a high-profit export, to man advanced research laboratories for a high-fee lease, and to manufacture ordinary consumer goods for a high-price sale to those countries.

The Victim

Developing countries, underdeveloped economies, and undeveloped societies are principal victims in cross-border brain drain around the world. The victimization they bear is multilayered or multistaged. First, they invest in childbearing, childbirth, childcare, K–12 schooling, and even college education before would-be emigrants become capable enough of leaving the homeland. Second, they suffer from a lack of talents and skilled labor in various areas of production and life. For example, when a homegrown talent leaves for a foreign destination, a neighborhood program, a business project, a community plan, or even a national initiative has to slow down, scale back, or close up. Third, they have to pay for a large number of value-added products or sell at a low price a wide variety of raw materials they would otherwise be able to produce or process if they could keep their own skilled labor. Fourth, they are forced to import technology or hire foreign advisors or experts in areas of critical needs, such as military operation, national security, and civil aviation. Finally, they spend resources to care for expatriates as some expatriates tend to return home when they become sick or old.

Besides all these visible and invisible victimizations in material aspect, countries or societies bearing brain drain experience critical alienations in spiritual dimension. Scientists, engineers, and other intellectuals who work in different areas of production and life tend to lose confidence and motivation to create and innovate as they feel they are not talented or fortunate enough to flee like those who have left in the wave of brain drain. Politicians and businesspeople struggle in serious doubts that they can ever do anything significant with their domestic skills and talents, whereas the general populace wrestles with a widespread suspicion that they can ever trust their homegrown nurses, doctors, professors, technicians, technologists, scientists, and other professionals with all the domestic products and services they use in everyday life. A phenomenal lack of self-trust and self-direction can typically permeate the whole society, keeping idle even innate human imagination, innovation, and productivity.

The Compromise

Countries losing talents in brain drain do not usually think far and deep enough by imagining what they would have accomplished had they kept their intellectual resources. Instead, some of them even take pride that they are able to send their native sons and daughters to the forefront of art, science, and technology in developed economies to make significant contributions to human civilizations. They feel rewarded when emigrants thank motherlands for rearing and training, send money to parents and siblings within family networks, offer consultation and assistance on projects and programs in hometowns, or invest in businesses and services on native lands. Even on reflection, they seem only to hold a sense of luck and gratitude that they had not kept their native talents idle and wasted at home, that they have produced valuable human capitals for active use to social progress, and that they are able to benefit in various spheres of life through emigrants and emigrant connections to the larger world.

Countries drawing talents in brain drain, on the other hand, can conveniently take their advances to developing, underdeveloped, and undeveloped societies as returns or paybacks for use of intellectual resources from the latter. Following immigrants back home, they sell consumer goods and may reason that they do a favor to immigrants' homelands by bringing the latter high-tech or first-class products, entertainments, or services. For example, a Hollywood moviemaker can expect huge box office sales in one of the movie characters' homeland. Deploying immigrants as scientific, technical, managerial, legal, or other specialty advisors, consultants, or operatives in international dealings, advanced countries maintain business, trade, or technology advantages and may rationalize that they offer a service to immigrants' homelands by training workers, improving productions, and modernizing economies to the benefit of the latter. For instance, a multi-national corporation from the United States can smooth its operation in Brazil, China, or India by using naturalized Americans who were originally born and raised as native Brazilians, Chinese, or Indians. The arrangement makes the multinational corporation and even the United States look gracious: training Brazilians, Chinese, or Indians with advanced science, technology, or managerial skills for them to work for and contribute to economic development and social modernization on native lands.

The Universal

An old Chinese saying goes, "Up people move while down water flows." Brain drain is a collective outcome of individual choices. People migrate from rural areas to urban centers, from developing societies to developed economies, or from poor countries to affluent nations, according to their individual abilities, resources, and networks. There is no solid base to assign blame to a city, a society, or a state for attracting talents simply because they are industrialized, urbanized, and overall advanced.

Brain drain is a macro phenomenon rooted in micro actions. Cities, developed economies, or rich countries may actively apply incentives to draw trained and skilled labor from the countryside, developing or undeveloped contexts, or poor nations. While the former can be condemned for stealing talents, the latter may also be blamed for failing to provide proper platforms for native talents to play and exhaust potentiality. After all, human talents should not be confined to any particular locales. They are treasures of human civilizations and ought to be fully employed to the benefit of social progress. In other words, advanced environments can only be praised for their facilitation of individual development and their utilization of talented manpower in the process of human evolution.

Oppositely on behalf of the disadvantaged, a universal observation is this: it suffers multiple victimizations in social exchange. For example, between a poor nation "A" and a rich country "B", "A" takes first victimization when it loses to "B" a considerable number of the talents it has raised and trained. "A" bears second, third, or fourth victimization when it has to abandon projects, seek advice on programs, or import products or services because of a loss of critical talents to "B." Lastly, "A" endures victimization when it becomes a caretaker for sick and retired expatriates from "B."

SITUATION 2

Under the media limelight, people hear that entertainment celebrities, sports stars, and business philanthropists make donations to disaster relief, disease prevention or treatment, victim assistance, human development, and other specific programs in impoverished countries or territories around the world. In the headline news, people learn that advanced societies send funds, deliver foods, equipment, and other material goods, dispatch volunteers, or provide peacekeeping forces to backward or otherwise needy nations on the face of the earth.

However, it is totally unknown or little known to the general public in the international community that state officials, business owners, and aristocratic families in poor countries transfer personal assets of large worth to and hold secret accounts of huge balance in rich nations. It is completely unmentioned or rarely mentioned to the overall audience in the world that cross-border investments, international banks, and multinational corporations from developed economies make millions of profit and extract billions of raw materials and consumer goods produced with cheap labor from developing, underdeveloped, or undeveloped contexts.

The Particular

Alibaba does not maintain an extensive network with people in his homeland or seek any active involvement in the local immigrant community. However, in his routine contact as an average immigrant, he hears about and even meets with a few persons who came to the United States with considerable fortunes.

One is a former business executive from the same city where Alibaba studied as an undergraduate student. At the time when Alibaba underwent his college education, the person was a citywide sensation who led one of the largest enterprises in the city with phenomenal success. Suddenly he disappeared with an undisclosed amount of company funds from an overseas trip. A public uproar of anger, betrayal, and distrust ensued across the city. Then about twenty years later, to his great surprise, Alibaba came across the person in an affluent community of greater Los Angeles where he met with the father of his wife's classmate. According to the latter, the former business executive lives a high-class life although he does not take any formal job in the United States.

Another is a high-ranking official from Alibaba's home province. Although he never sees him in person, Alibaba hears enough about the official and his life among fellow townsmen from the native land. The official first sent his child to study in an Ivy League institution when he was in office back home. He transferred funds continuously to America over the years of his child's study. By the time he left office and his child was able to sponsor him and his wife to the United States, he already had sufficient assets to support a luxury lifestyle for the rest of his life. A moderately luxurious life can easily cost millions, although it is quite difficult to imagine how even one million could ever be saved from his official salaries.

Besides these two, Alibaba knows directly and indirectly a number of similar cases. Sometimes, Alibaba wonders how much cash could be transferred this way from his developing land of birth to his developed country of citizenship. Around the world, there are so many business executives of so many large-scale enterprises in a middle-sized economy. There are so many high-ranking officials in so many provinces and ministries in a large country. If only one out of a thousand business executives or ranking officials find opportunities or become corrupt to transfer assets or funds overseas, each year millions could drain from Peru, the Philippines, or Thailand, and billions could leave China, India, or Russia.

The Discriminator

In an ideal world of fairness and rationality, developing, underdeveloped, or undeveloped regions would keep their limited capitals and resources to build infrastructure, train manpower, and grow economy. Developed areas would provide capital investment, financial aid, and technological know-how to the less developed in their drive toward industrialization and modernization.

In reality, however, developed states conspire to make rules so that the rich can easily exploit the poor, the powerful can handily influence the powerless, and the advanced can conveniently transfer profit from the backward around the world. As they build wealth, expand prosperity, and maintain affluence, rich nations become natural magnets for handfuls of elites from poor countries to come to live and enjoy with funds from home. In the sense that they sit in default to normally attract funds to their economies, all developed countries are natural or unintentional discriminators against their less developed counterparts in the world capital market.

Moreover, a number of advanced states pointedly change their immigrant policies with knowledge that elites of poor nations often bring with them considerable assets. For example, when Australia, Canada, or the United States welcomes immigrants who can bring in one million, it actually makes an open declaration of discrimination against all less developed countries on the face of the earth. Imagine how many business executives of public enterprises in socialist China or how many private entrepreneurs in capitalist South Korea would become motivationally innovative in wrenching money from their employees, businesses, and eventually national economy for immigrant visas to America. Besides natural or unintentional discrimination, some developed economies are indeed premeditated or intentional perpetrators in the irrational transfer of wealth across the globe.

The Victim

The cross-border transfer of funds and assets from poor to rich countries causes victimization on multiple levels. At the individual level, employees, taxpayers, and all common citizens in poor nations have to bear direct or indirect costs of the transfer. Employees take less pay, work longer hours, or face layoffs when independent entrepreneurs or corporate executives save for amounts of money required for immigrant visas, close down businesses for emigration, or just want to hold sufficient balances in foreign bank accounts. Taxpayers pay higher taxes and receive fewer or no public services when corrupt government officials send funds overseas to support their children on education, to pay for their own sightseeing trips, leisure, or luxury, or to buy properties on foreign lands. And all common citizens suffer both materially and mentally when they wrestle with poverty, lack of opportunities, despair, and demoralization in everyday life.

At the organizational level, small businesses are likely to put off maintenance, hiring, or routine upgrades when owners strive for relocation to more developed economies. Corporations tend to neglect working conditions, community obligations, or environmental protection when they manage to pay high salaries to some of their managers, consultants, or executives, who then can send money to support middle-class or upper-class lifestyles for their families in advanced societies. Governmental agencies can fail to attend public needs in various areas from education, health, and welfare to even emergency response when officials in some critical positions abuse power to primarily entertain their overseas economic interests, secret bank accounts, or private estates in developed countries.

In the system level, a whole national economy suffers from lack of funds and resources for investment, reinvestment, and growth when profit is ruthlessly circulated out to foreign destinations. Years of exploitation in the form of "making money domestically and spending money overseas" can easily put a society in a miserable shape: dilapidated warehouses, abandoned factories, mountains of trash, polluted waters, exposed hillsides, rural slums, urban ghettos, flocks of displaced migrants, and all other scenes so typically witnessed in developing and underdeveloped countries around the world. Spiritually, an entire population can be left in deep alienation, apathy, or cynicism. People hate the society because it is chaotic, offering neither much comfort nor much hope. People condemn people because the average stay to squeeze a problematic life here and the fortunate or the opportunistic leave quickly for a better world elsewhere as soon as they wrench enough wealth from this place.

The Compromise

The outward transfer of wealth could cause serious public outcries if it is widely known by the general populace in poor countries. It keeps going without much notice mainly because it to a large extent is a secret shared among social elites who know where to transfer assets, how to expend transferred funds, and what to do to remain hidden from scrutiny. Ironically, as they are major stakeholders in economic, political, and social arenas, social elites can even represent their nations to see the benefits of the transfer and therefore fashion some national compromise to it. For example, they may reason that the transfer motivates people to work hard, save smart, and hence spur economic productivity while promoting the ethics of frugality. They may figure that the transfer keeps the country connected to advanced markets, modern consumer goods, and contemporary lifestyles, all of which serve positively as a goal to attain, a model to follow, or a success to dream about. They may even rationalize that the transfer makes more developed states take notice of the country, which could naturally lend the national government a better chance of being provided with development aid, relief funds, philanthropic handouts, humanitarian projects, and/or various assistance programs from the international community.

Countries that attract assets and funds from less developed regions around the world do not necessarily feel they commit moral wrongs in serving as a kind of hideout or safe haven for ill-gotten wealth by corrupt officials, greedy businesspeople, or socially irresponsible elites from other places. Instead, they boast of themselves as open and free societies for anyone who can afford to come to play and enjoy. If they ever have any moment of a moral upset, advanced nations and politicians, intellectuals, the mass media, and public opinions within can easily override that upset with investments, donations, relief materials, volunteers, missionaries, peacekeeping forces, and even tourists they send to various poor countries or troubled spots to the benefit of many ordinary people there.

The Universal

An old saying goes, "Beautiful flowers blossom only on a few trees in the orchard while only a couple of branches of the tree bear tasty fruits." The saying epitomizes the timeless phenomenon of the rich getting richer, better, and more attractive from place to place.

In the contemporary world, advanced economies or developed countries obviously have more stable governments, more secure financial systems, better infrastructures, better amenities, and more diverse lifestyles for common citizens to rely on, choose, utilize, and enjoy than developing, underdeveloped, or undeveloped societies. They gradually become world stages or international playgrounds for people of different origins, races, cultures, or nationalities to play, display, or engage in what Veblen calls conspicuous consumption and leisure. In a sense, New York is not merely an American metropolis, London not a British city, or Paris not a French capital, and all these urban centers are now gathering places for the rich, the powerful, and the knowledgeable from around the globe.

A more general learning or rule is this: a place, whether it is a country, a city, a community, or a zone, such as the zone of transition identified by social ecologists from Chicago School, declines and falls when people who live within are not able to develop proper identification with it as home or homeland; it rises and thrives when people who call themselves residents or citizens embrace, invest in, and take care of it as their ultimate destination. This general rule explains why a considerable number of countries are mired in economic difficulty while a few nations enjoy material affluence on the face of the earth.

SITUATION 3

Tourism is now an important part of economy. Neutral by itself, though, tourism is not a fair game for every country in the world. Countries in the North attract more visitors than their counterparts in the South with better advertisements about cultural heritages and social achievements. Nations in the West draw more tourists than their competitors in the East by commercials on material amenities and physical infrastructures.

At an individual level, it is quite natural that well-to-do citizens in poor countries would be willing to save hard and smart through much of their lives for once-in-a-lifetime trips to Europe or North America, while commoners in rich nations might not even bother to travel to some developing, underdeveloped, or undeveloped territories with just what they would normally spend on a few meals at local restaurants.

The Particular

Living in the Unites States, Alibaba has the opportunity to receive and entertain a considerable number of visitors year after year from his land of birth, which by measure of development remains far behind America.

The visitors Alibaba sees from his homeland range from officials, businesspeople, and intellectuals to young students. Whether they are on business trips or for individual leisure, they take time to visit major sites across America. They spend on lodging, airfare, ground transportation, and other tourist services typically more than any average American traveler would pay for the same or similar expenditures because they are not familiar with local markets. They purchase name-brand consumer goods often with extravagance even by American standards because they figure they can only buy those luxuries once in the United States. They pay colleges, universities, and other training programs for workshops and classes even though they already know what they can actually learn from those assumedly knowledge-centered exercises. Some of them even pay hefty fines for traffic tickets as they mistake the Unites States as a land of freedom on freeways. When asked why they feel seemingly so easy with their expenses in America, they almost say the same: "It's only once in our lifetime; we've saved hard for this trip; and we'll figure out how much more we have to squeeze from our everyday life when we get home." Indeed, Alibaba knows too well that the considerable amount of money lavishly pumped into the American economy by visitors from his homeland uniformly costs a great deal of hardship not only to those lucky visitors themselves, but also to many more people around them for quite long time.

As an enthusiastic traveler, Alibaba also has numerous observations of how tourists from advanced economies spend in poor countries. First, youths and students stay in hostels, drink Coca-Colas, eat at Western fast-food chains, and use public transportation. They spend minimally, with some of their expenditures even channeling back to their home economy through multinational corporations or other avenues. In Africa and South America, Alibaba meet many European tourists who stay in hostels and budget lodgings owned by people from Britain, France, Holland, and Spain. Second, expatriates from advanced societies enjoy hospitalities provided by their relatives and friends when they visit their hometowns. Alibaba knows for himself that he does not spend much out of his own pocket every time he meets his classmates and family members in the land of his birth. Third, middle-class vacationers make smart plans and tend to stay with name-brand establishments for lodging, eating, and entertainment operated by multinational corporations. For example, Alibaba arranges to eat lunch at McDonald's, Subway, or Kentucky Fried Chicken, stay overnight at Holiday Inn, Hilton, or Sheraton, join tours with Gray Line, and rent cars from Hertz, Avis, or Budget when he vacations with his family in Chile, Egypt, India, Malaysia, Mexico, and Thailand. Finally, business travelers, such as engineers, technicians, lawyers, scholars, consultants, managers, and executives from advanced countries, conduct business often at the cost of enterprises, universities, or governmental agencies in poor nations. While they may make money handsomely, they rarely have any category to spend it like a typical tourist.

The Discriminator

It is not immediately clear who discriminators are in the unfair flow of visitors, visits, and spending in tourism. In general terms, the market may be called the perpetrator because it favors the developed, the commercialized, and the advanced to the disadvantage of the undeveloped, the un-marketed, and the lagged-behind. Or the world system may be assigned blame because it benefits the rich, the powerful, and the knowledgeable at the cost or suffering of the poor, the powerless, and the illiterate. As part of the system, mass media serve as major mouthpieces in spreading positive images about rich nations while presenting negative portrayals about poor countries. For example, some signs and warnings on destination guidebooks or over travel channels can scare off interested tourists from ever planning vacations to a broadly perceived poor or troublesome society, whereas a few words and pictures in world almanacs or on television programs may motivate inspired individuals to spend their life-time savings on trips to an assumedly advanced or sophisticated culture.

Individuals can reasonably be named discriminators to some extent as well. First, most travelers follow their commonsensical knowledge and comfort fed and nurtured by the mass media to choose developed over undeveloped destinations even though they know they could help or hurt local economies by visiting or avoiding particular places with or without tourist expenditures. Second, tourists from advanced countries use infor-mation and other built-in advantages to find bargains and minimize spend-ing while traveling in backward territories, leaving minimal income to local merchants and service providers. Third, travel agents, merchants, and well-off everyday residents in advanced societies may make travelers from poor nations spend beyond capacity either because they set prices for travel and leisure naturally high amid their affluent standards of living or because the latter do not want to look miserable and shabby in front of the former. Finally, travelers from poor countries have to find savings or wrench profits from people around them in their native land, from friends, relatives, and employees to merchants, in order to support their trips, sometimes once in a lifetime, to an advanced destination.

The Victim

The uneven and unequal flow of tourists and tourist spending has imme-diate impacts upon developing, underdeveloped, and undeveloped econo-mies. On the one hand, they have to sell cheap and save hard to earn and muster foreign currencies to support their diplomatic missions and pay for international trips made by a minority of their social elites. On the other hand, they find it difficult to collect revenues from tourism to build infra-structures, establish services, and improve advertisements. Major natural and cultural sites struggle in dire conditions. The whole tourist industry remains undeveloped or in a weak shape. The situation opens the door for either avoidance by international visitors or takeover by foreign corporate interests. Ironically, some lodgings, transportations, and even food services surrounding some significant travel sites in some poor countries are actu-ally in the hands of some enterprises and entrepreneurs from rich nations.

The ultimate victims are individuals who labor in poor societies. Around tourist sites and travel services, craftspeople make souvenirs in days for little credit, merchants attend shops in hours without much income, porters carry loads through thousands of stairs up to some mountainous sites for a meager salary, and taxicab drivers plow through a whole city for a whole night without a decent earning. Alibaba hired drivers with their taxicabs in Bulgaria, Ecuador, Egypt, India, Indonesia, and the Philippines. At the time of each car hiring, he could not literally comprehend how a taxicab driver makes ends meet with so little earned from a long day of numerous trips spent with a foreign customer. Close to people who travel to affluent countries, parents sacrifice lifetime savings to send children to study in the West, employees work long hours and take minimal pays to support owners or management executives to vacation in foreign resorts or make business trips to advanced societies, and even friends and relatives may have to pool funds and resources so that one can fulfill one's dreamed visit to a developed destination.

The Compromise

From a third party's point of view, developed societies indeed provide more advanced tourist infrastructures, better consumer goods, higher traveler services, and a broader variety of visitor attractions. Travelers from poor countries pay for similar services and treatments like everyone else. Some of them pay a little more on certain occasions often because they do not know enough about the occasion, not because they face any intentional discrimination under the circumstance.

Developing, underdeveloped, and undeveloped countries, in contrast, do often not offer much more than some natural landscapes and cultural sites that happen to sit on their territories. Travelers from rich nations may not need to dig much into their pockets for expenditures. However, given what they are so accustomed to in their everyday living at home, they are likely to have to bear a considerable amount of inconvenience, discomfort, trouble, worry, and even fear when they travel in poor countries.

For those who labor around travel sites in poor economies, they at least have opportunities to make a living. Without foreign tourists, they might have to struggle even harder in their life. For those who save for a few privileged individuals to travel to advanced societies, they may learn or benefit from the stories related to them, pictures shown to them, and, most important, new perspectives, approaches, or attitudes taken toward them by their business owners, managerial executives, family members, or close friends upon completion of the trip.

The Universal

Good places attract people. Advanced societies evoke awe, mystery, and sensation among people around the world. Citizens of poor nations dream to see them as models, sources of inspiration, or wonderlands, whereas residents of rich countries want to visit them as competitions, references, or playgrounds. Developed economies hold wealth, information, technology, and other resources to invest in tourism, promote travel attractions, and deliver hospitality services. Visitors spend in the system, enjoy the process, and leave with memorable experiences. An overall positive public impression makes all developed or advanced countries or territories taken-for-granted places or attractions for leisure, business gathering, and luxury living.

Negative images scare off travelers. Stereotypes take deep roots in the minds of people about political instability, economic poverty, or civil disorderliness in many countries in the developing world. Diplomats, missionaries, technocrats, and managers take assignments to those places as dangerous challenges. Travelers include those destinations in their map of adventure only if they hold some unique perspectives for, special connections to, or unfathomable passions toward them. However, when news breaks out over tourist kidnapping, infectious disease, or civil disturbance, all business and leisure travels can halt to an indefinite standstill in any one of the poor nations on the face of the earth.

It takes time and effort for a place to be found and visited as a site of cultural significance or natural uniqueness. Lacking resources, small, poor, or otherwise marginalized countries will need to invest a lot more than normal to put any of their deserving attractions on the list for world tourists. On the other hand, once a place is established as a renowned travel attraction either by convention, timing, or luck, it tends to stay so for a long time. Leading in development, large, rich, or otherwise center-positioned nations will not need to do much to benefit from series of visits by throngs of visitors to some of their worthy sites in the global market of tourism.

SITUATION 4

The global labor market is not a level field amenable to the rule of merit and meritocracy. There are inherent discriminations against certain nation-states as known exporters of maids, nannies, gardeners, waiters or waitresses, farming workers, and other manual laborers. So are there established preferential treatments for some groups of individuals as trustworthy practitioners in consultancy, engineering, foreign language, health, science, technology, and management. For example, emigrants from Mexico are likely to work as housekeepers, yardmen, or fruit or vegetable pickers in the United States even if they hold college degrees, whereas whites from Western Europe or North America may teach Dutch, English, or French in private homes or public schools in many parts of the world even if they have yet to complete their own schooling in higher education.

The Particular

Living in the United States and traveling extensively around the world, Alibaba makes casual yet impressive observations of who does what across professions and job categories in a seemingly related world labor market. In Hong Kong, Alibaba hears about babysitters, housekeepers, and maids from Indonesia, the Philippines, and Thailand working in middle- and upper-class Chinese families. In Los Angeles, he sees yardmen from Mexico mowing lawns, garment workers from Thailand sewing clothes, nurses and medical technicians from the Philippines attending patients, and engineers from India designing products and maintaining production lines in factories. In Dubai, he finds a whole international labor force differentiated by nationalities, with blue-collar workers distinctively represented by citizens of some countries while white-collar professionals are uniquely dominated by expatriates of other nations.

Over the conventional divide between rich and poor, developed and developing, modern and traditional countries or societies, Alibaba seems to have a generally clear impression about labor movements or transfers across borders. While poor, traditional, and developing, underdeveloped, or undeveloped countries are mined for cheap manual labor, rich, modern, and developed nations are positioned to send trained personnel as high-profit exports. At an individual level, regardless of one's educational and occupational background, one may have to work as a manual laborer overseas if one's country is known as an exporter of manual labor or as a white-collar professional on foreign soil if one's homeland is perceived as a place of high talents.

The Discriminator

Who is the discriminator when certain countries can only export cheap labor for the import of highly paid consultants, engineers, scientists, and managers? There are discriminating factors in history. Colonizers, conquerors, and imperialists subject colonies, tributaries, and vassal states to subordinate positions. From the former to the latter missionaries are dispatched to preside over churches, scholars to teach in schools, officials to operate government agencies, and trained personnel to run factories, farms, and production facilities. From the latter to the former, there are only inexpensive supplies of foot soldiers, household workers, and manual laborers. Forces of discrimination built in history continue in the existing world system. Leading economic powers export capitals and send high-floating labor forces to the rest of the world. As core countries demand high return from investment, nations in the periphery have to squeeze their own citizens as a whole body of cheap labor to keep the few advantages they have in the world economy.

Who does the discrimination when people of certain nationalities, races, or ethnicities can only work as domestic workers, yardmen, handymen, janitors, and other types of manual laborers in the global labor market? There are geopolitical, national, and racial influences. Geopolitically, Europeans colonized much of the world, grooming peoples of occupied lands as fearless soldiers, honest guards, or hearty maids. Racially, whites took blacks as slaves, creating images of blacks as plantation workers, housekeepers, or janitors. Nationally, when a dependent state had to give much of its upper labor space to citizens of its colonizer, from civil service to research, education, and medicine to business management, it naturally lost its ability to nurture a full spectrum of its own people for various professional or occupational needs. There are also individual and collective endeavors. For instance, new immigrants seem to follow older immigrants of similar backgrounds in finding and fashioning ways of survival, growth, and expansion in a new society. Typical businesses or characteristic professions for different ethnic groups or nationalities therefore rise to prominence, especially in a few countries of immigrant labor. Overall in the global labor market, as epitomized by employee profiles or distributions in world organizations and multinational corporations, whites, peoples of European origin, and citizens of developed nations dominate the upper echelon, discriminating all other peoples into roles of hard labor, minimal compensation, and negligible social prestige.

The Victim

It is sad that individuals, regardless of their own talents, skills, aspirations, dreams, efforts, and accomplishments, can only work in certain job categories, occupations, or professions due to their ethnicity, race, nationality, or a combination thereof in the global labor market. Filipinos make impressive representations in childcare, nursing, and medical laboratory testing even though many of them may aspire to medicine and have the potential to become doctors. Indians maintain a noticeable presence in telemarketing, engineering, and industrial technology even though many of them may dream of management and have the talents to serve as business executives. In comparison, Americans, Britons, or the French keep a proportionally high existence, if no longer dominance, in leadership across international organizations, over management through multinational corporations, and at the higher echelon of the whole world job market even though some of them are not necessarily capable or competent leaders, managers, or specialists. Individuals, as they are collectively funneled into one job category, tend to become blindfolded from other choices, increase competitions among themselves within the category, and take less material compensation and social prestige for the job. For example, when many Filipinos follow the invisible hands of discrimination to become nannies and nurses in Hong Kong or across the United States, they forgo the opportunity to turn into other professionals of perhaps much higher socioeconomic status.

Institutionally, an ethnic group, a race, and a country can be victimized with negative public images, spiritual deprivations, and unfair treatments in material dimension. In terms of image, some ethnic groups are portrayed as nannies carrying babies, maids washing dishes, or nurses attending clinics, whereas others are stereotyped as illegal immigrants picking fruits, processing vegetables, mowing yards, and running errands. Spiritually, an ethnic group may be deprived of a fine tradition or cultural practice to imagine, explore, and prepare for various jobs and careers among its members, while a country may be taken away its right and obligation to educate, train, and socialize all citizens for the full gamut of occupational and professional needs in society, especially when much of the higher layer of the job market is filled by foreigners from colonizers as it used to be in the past or multinational corporations as it is in the present. In material dimension, a race may be groomed for jobbing in some fields or cornered to work over one area. However, even in the place it is known for representation or overrepresentation, it may not receive the same economic and social benefits as other races. In policing and military services, for example, whites can move up much faster through the rank and file, and may overall keep control over a whole organization even though blacks fill much of the security or military force.

The Compromise

Institutional discriminators and victims may reach common understanding or compromise on the basis of material and nonmaterial necessities for talents, such as research base, educational infrastructure, and training facility. Countries that have to import talents or send their students for higher education overseas realize that they are too small, not advanced enough in science and technology, not bountiful enough in economic resources, or too lacking in human capitals to build research capacities, educational institutions, and training grounds necessary for producing and nurturing talents. Nations that export experts or expertise and receive foreign students know that they invest billions in science, medicine, and technology in the form of endowment, foundation, and grant, millions in education and educational infrastructure, especially colleges and universities, through tax exemptions or direct appropriations, and hundreds of thousands in individual development and growth by way of public assistance, social welfare, or scholarship. It might not be so outrageous as first seen when colleges and universities in the West charge high tuitions and fees each year on a foreign student to an amount that could feed scores of families for the same period of time back in that student's homeland.

At the individual level, people who can only attempt lower-level jobs may find comfort with their circumstances. As housekeepers or yardmen, they may feel they have landed a retreat from school and schooling where they had to solve head-aching math problems or write mind-bugging essays. As nurses or medical technicians, they may feel they have found a short-cut to health care for relatively adequate income after spending only two years in nursing school or even just a few months on training with medical techniques. On the other hand, people who dominate the higher echelon of the job market may have all the justifications for why they deserve to be holding more power, entitled to higher salaries and benefits, and receiving better social treatment. Becoming managers or leaders in professional organizations goes far beyond professional training and work as doctors, lawyers, researchers, or professors. Working as consultants in science and technology calls for tremendous educational preparation and intellectual intensity. It might not be so unfair as generally perceived when only certain groups of people are able to keep their presence in certain fields of professional practice or some parts of the job market because it takes generational rearing and adaptation as well as individual choice and effort to excel in those professions or job roles.

The Universal

The labor market becomes global. However, it is far from a level field for people of different origins, in terms of gender, ethnicity, race, nationality, mother tongue, or birthplace, to enter upon aspiration, to compete on the basis of merit, and to excel with effort.

There are outer barriers to keep people of certain backgrounds from practicing in certain areas. Institutionally, small, poor, colonized, or undeveloped countries are deprived of rights, abilities, or opportunities to prepare their citizens for entry into high-tech fields when large, rich, and advanced nations dominate multinational corporations and world organizations with trained talents from their free-floating labor force. The former can only export manual laborers at a discount while the latter may sell talents by a premium. The grave consequence is entrenchment: the former falls in permanent disability to rear talents as the latter takes ever-unchallengeable dominance over the higher end of the labor market. For example, the Philippines in its approximately lower-middle position in the world labor market may open many professional schools to train nurses or medical technicians for work at home or overseas. But in all likelihood it will have to depend, wholly or partially, upon larger, more advanced countries for training or importing of scientists and engineers who design, produce, and service high-precision instruments in commercial or military use.

There are also inner ceilings to prevent people of certain characteristics from reaching the higher echelon of the job hierarchy. Individually, European settlers use native peoples and black slaves to perform manual labor in colonies. The latter, as they work in lower-level jobs for generations, are historically disabled from developing a family tradition, a communal custom, or an ethnic culture to nurture their children for higher-level job roles. It takes time to catch up with the former, who hold all the advantages in social, economic, and cultural aspects. Another factor is stereotyping: Asians are perceived to be smart, good at working as scientists, engineers, or technical staff; African Americans are portrayed to be physically strong, suitable for jobs in public safety, private security, or military service; and whites are propagandized to be fair-minded, fit for power-holding positions in administration or management. The associated self-fulfilling prophecy results in interesting racial distributions of employees in both corporate and professional organizations. Across America, visitors can almost expect to see janitors, security guards, technical staff, and executive managers line up clearly by race or ethnicity when they visit colleges, hospitals, governmental agencies, or business enterprises.

SITUATION 5

Conspicuous and inconspicuous discriminations can be viewed live nowhere better than international trade. Powerful nations maintain controls over worldwide organizations that host negotiations, set policies, make rules, and settle disputes. Rich countries hold capitals, produce consumer goods, harbor multinational corporations, and dominate currency markets. Gems, rare metals, raw materials, and other natural resources from small, poor, or undeveloped places are priced to the minimum to the benefit of large, affluent, and developed destinations. Brands, trademarks, designer goods, high-tech devices, and other value-added products from core industrial centers are marketed at the maximum to the disadvantage of societies in the periphery of the world system.

The Particular

As a traveler from America, Alibaba knows too well how much he can buy with U.S. dollars in many economically less fortunate places around the world. He bought nicely handmade souvenirs with rare wood for a few dimes in Africa. He spent just several quarters on meticulously crafted belts and handbags with genuine leather in Central and South America. He purchased marvelously decorated porcelain cookware and utensils plated with silver for a dozen green bucks in Asia. Reflecting upon his own experience of bargain in mini-purchases through different parts of the Third World, Alibaba wonders how little Britain, France, Japan, the United States, and other industrial countries might pay for gems, rare metals, and various other raw materials from many small, poor, or undeveloped nations on the face of the earth.

As a consumer in the United States, Alibaba sees too well how Walmarts, discount chain retailers, traditional department stores, and even factory outlets amass Chinese-made consumer goods for sales from season to season and all through the year. The prices are set so low that even Chinese tourists madly buy Chinese-made consumer goods while traveling in the United States. Asking some Chinese tourists, Alibaba is shocked to learn that they have to pay much more, a few times more on certain name-brand products, when they purchase them in China, where they are made. Alibaba then wonders how much the United States cuts on prices when it imports consumer goods from China to the benefit of its common citizens as everyday life consumers. China is a large country with a considerable power of bargaining in international trade. If the United States can still force significant discounts upon imported goods from China, how much more bargain could it wrest from many smaller, less developing countries by way of exploitative pricing over their supplies of various natural resources, raw materials, and low value-added products?

The Discriminator

All developed countries are positioned to discriminate in international trade. They exploit developing, underdeveloped, and undeveloped societies when they franchise brands, export high-tech products, and sell value-added consumer goods. They take advantage of small, poor, and disorganized territories when they import natural resources, raw materials, and labor-intensive products. Typical ways of discrimination range from pricing in favor of tech-intensive and value-added products or services, making a few national monies superior as hard currencies over a great many soft currencies, dominating world trade organizations, controlling international policymaking, rule enforcement, and dispute resolution, and building business monopolies to threatening with economic embargoes.

Partly yet to a considerable extent in some instances, with economic gains made from trade and other cross-border dealings, advanced countries find resources to support their ways of doing business, maintain social prosperity, and spread an affluent lifestyle across the common citizenry. For example, democracy as a form of government can cause millions and millions spent on political campaigns, wasted in partisan bickering, or lost in policy balancing, indecision, inaction, or change. Infrastructure amenable for conspicuous leisure and conspicuous consumption demands billions and billions put in construction and maintenance for roads, waterways, airways, parks, cultural sites, shopping malls, restaurant rows, entertainment complexes, communication lines, and various other facilities. And a typical middle-class lifestyle in the ordinary form of a single-family home, cars for adults, schools for children, health care, vacations, spending on everyday needs, and retirement savings requires hundreds of thousands in salaries and fringe benefits paid to individual workers employed in blue-collar and white-collar settings.

The Victim

Any country that has to buy expensive products and sell inexpensive materials in international trade is a qualified victim. The pressure on less developed nations to import goods from advanced societies can be multifaceted. First, there are basic needs to import high-tech equipment and devices in defense, communication, transportation, and various other aspects just to follow ways of life dictated by modernity. Second, there are innate drives and urges on the part of the populace to mimic lifestyles led by citizens of affluent societies. Third, there are explicit or implicit threats from powerful nations to open domestic markets for foreign consumer goods. Fourth, there are inescapable bombardments of commercial advertisements upon common citizens by multinational corporations. Finally, there are abundant supplies of goods and services from advanced economies to make, nurture, and keep people addicted consumers.

With both inner pushes and outer pulls to import high-tech devices and luxury consumer goods from core industrial nations, developing, underdeveloped, and undeveloped countries have no other choice than to export natural resources, raw materials, and products with minimal added value. The irony of victimization is this: while advanced economies, the discriminator, can make a claim on quality for a high price with their goods or services, less developed societies, the victim, can only bid on quantity toward a huge discount for their products. Imagine how many shiploads of wood products a country in Africa has to deliver for a battery of machineries from China, how many shiploads of shoes and apparels China has to send for a fleet of automobiles from Japan, or how many shiploads of consumer electronics Taiwan has to sell for an F-16 jet fighter from the United States.

The Compromise

How do countries forced to sell inexpensive materials in exchange for expensive goods find balance in their minds? On the one hand, they have to admit that they need high-tech devices just to exist as part of the modern world, that they cannot manufacture many precision products on their own, and that goods or services imported from advanced economies are often in undisputable quality, durability, and dependability. On the other hand, these countries realize that they have no other ways to earn hard currencies than selling natural resources, that they often lack adequate technical capacities to add values to raw materials available on their lands, and that exporting unprocessed resources or minimally processed products can still benefit many individuals in their essentially low-skill labor force. Indeed, by working long hours with low pay and minimal benefits, workers can at least earn a living. Without cheap exports, many able-bodied laborers would have to live an even more difficult life.

Do nations positioned to profit from international trade find reasons to keep the advantage they hold over all their less developed partners? Domestically, they understand that it is expensive to fund scientific research and technological innovation, that it is costly to conduct business in an open society featuring free media, public votes, fair market, and participant consumers, and that it is capital-heavy to dwell on a labor force accustomed to middle-class lifestyles. Internationally, these countries figure that they create opportunities, present new standards, raise expectations, and expand horizons of life for various peoples on other lands. For example, the United States often sees the connection between foreign visitors coming to tour America or foreign students coming to study in American universities and U.S. imports of inexpensive products from specific foreign countries.

The Universal

The world is connected. Cross-border exchange is a way of life for all nations on the face of the earth. Unfortunately, international exchange, especially trade, is not completely equal, fair, and free from manipulation. Large, rich, and powerful countries tend to hold advantages over small, poor, and powerless nations. The advantages, over time and through the multiplicity of transaction, can translate into enormous gains to the discriminators and devastating, decapitating, or disabling losses on the part of victims.

In the grapevines around the globe, people talk about China feeding the whole world with its cheap products, the United States consuming two-thirds of the earth's resources by its fewer than 5 percent of the world population, and advanced economies living on the shoulders of less developed societies as both their sources of material supply and markets of product consumption. A general yet serious question then is this: to what extent is prosperity of a country self-created, self-kept, or self-sustained? Historically, a few developed countries used to be imperialist colonizers who pillaged other lands as part of their primitive accumulation of capitals for industrialization, development, and modernization. At present, developed countries dominate world organizations, control global markets, and hold power as how to set prices, make rules, and settle disputes for international trade. For example, the United States can literally print money and use green papers to buy properties, energies, raw industrial materials, and consumer goods around the world, especially from countries hungry for hard currencies, as the American dollar reigns in the global market as a de facto world currency.

Focusing on price and pricing in international trade, people around the world seem to know, understand, or simply take for granted that developed countries sell their high-tech devices and consumer goods for high profits because they produce with a labor force accustomed to middle-class lifestyles, whereas less developed nations can export their raw materials and labor-intensive products at low prices as they do not have to pay much for workers who are used to frugality, hardship, and even suffering. The reality leaves any thoughtful person wondering to what degree middle-class lifestyles in a few developed countries are supported by hard work, harsh life, or sheer poverty for various peoples in many developing, underdeveloped, and undeveloped nations of the world.

9 Throughout the Life

How does life treat each individual? One may respond to the question with a partial answer based on what one feels at the present or what one has experienced through one's life course so far. Typical answers vary: "life is fair" if one sees people receive rewards or face punishments as they deserve in terms of law or religion; "life is tricky" when one does not necessarily harvest what one expects out of one's commonsense wishes and everyday efforts; and "life is good" where one achieves measurable success in both material and nonmaterial dimensions.

A complete answer, of course, has to wait until one serves out one's entire life at the point of death. Indeed, a religious person would not know until the last moment of life where he or she enters, the heaven or the hell, with all his or her lifetime deeds. Also, there are subjective versus objective sides as well as personal versus societal levels to the question. On the subjective side and at the personal level, an individual may feel he or she is misunderstood by peers, discriminated at work, and ill-treated by fate throughout the life. The feelings are real in his or her everyday experience, affecting how he or she thinks about and acts upon the world. On the objective side and at the societal level, differences among people are first made at the time of birth. One born into a poor family is set far apart from one born as part of a resource-bounty kin. From then on, individuals can differentiate in achievement regardless of intelligence, choice, or effort. Talents struggle in frustration and failure, while mediocrities may shine with success and honor. Upon death, some leave behind considerable wealth, whereas others may make many in their surroundings pay a huge debt (Adler, Adler, and Fontana 1987; Hawke 1988; Larkin 1988; O'Rand and Krecker 1990; Moore 1992; Sampson and Laub 1992; George 1993; Friedman 1996; Csikszentmihalyi 1997; Green 2000; Sutherland 2000; Certeau 2002; Hirschl, Altobelli, and Rank 2003; Caproni 2004; Meyer 2006; Schlitz, Vieten, and Amorok 2007; Hardie 2008; Reich 2008; Mauk and Metz 2009; Felson and Santos 2010; Dalai Lama 2011; Highmore 2011; Morgan and Kunkel 2011; Templar 2011; Vaneigem 2011; Christensen, Allworth, and Dillon 2012; Hutchinson 2012; Sommers and Sommers 2013).

What lies under all these conspicuous or inconspicuous comparisons and contrasts among individuals throughout the life? Is it the fate of humanity, the hidden hand of God, or the irrationality of contemporary society?

SITUATION 1

Life is lived by an individual. But it cannot be wholly chosen by the individual who lives it. Conception, pregnancy, and birth, which are solely at the will of parents, determine an individual's genetic features, physical characteristics, and mental faculties. Development and growth from infancy to childhood to adolescence, which are mainly up to parents according to their finances, status, and heart, affect an individual's personality, intelligence, endurance, and social adaptability. From a sociological point of view, individuals born to caring, supportive, or law-abiding versus abusive, irresponsible, or deviant parents can grow into principally incomparable persons in terms of character, success, and consummation, whereas people raised in rich, powerful, or educated versus poor, powerless, or uneducated families may take drastically different occupational careers, living standards, and life courses.

The Particular

As an everyday life person, Alibaba sees enough among relatives, friends, neighbors, and colleagues about their children going to different schools, opting for different careers, and living different lives. Relative "A" pulls her son from high school to help with the petty family shop, and he now struggles to make ends meet in a small township, whereas Relative "B" saves hard to send his daughter to college, and she now works on a high-tech team at a major multinational corporation. Friend "A" takes efforts to care for her only child due to a birth complication, while Friend "B" enjoys time with all his five kids, each of whom appears to be healthy, smart, and promising for a wonderful life. Neighbor "A" sees his daughter become a physician after an unyielding support for her from private K–12 schooling to an Ivy League undergraduate study to a prestigious medical education, whereas Neighbor "B" watches her son change from job to job upon spotty supervision over and little investment in him through public schools, community colleges, and nontraditional universities. Finally, Colleague "A" takes pride that all his three kids follow his footsteps to become educated working professionals, while Colleague "B" bears shame that he could hardly trace his only child, who lives on the street with addiction to illicit drugs.

In the literate world, Alibaba reads enough about alcoholic families, cocaine babies, business empires, professional kinships, and political dynasties where children build upon family assets, heritages, or influences to continue a pattern of behavior, a line of practice, or a mode of dominance from their parents, grandparents, or even great-grandparents. Children of alcoholics tend to abuse alcohol in their lives, while cocaine babies whose mothers use cocaine and other drugs during pregnancy are likely to show defects in cognitive development. A college dropout takes the helms of a corporate conglomerate because he or she is the taken-for-granted heir or heiress of a family business empire. The son or daughter of a powerful political family successfully runs for the office of mayor, governor, senator, or even president although he or she does not necessarily possess any personal charisma, barely makes any professional achievements, or as a matter of fact might have abused alcohol or drugs during youth, scored horrible grades in school, or messed up important issues in various spheres of life. Similarly, it is not uncommon that parents apprentice, coach, groom, and prepare children for professional practice from fortunetelling to religious preaching to craftsmanship to medicine to science even in the contemporary era of standard education.

The Discriminator

It is not immediately clear who qualifies as a discriminator as to when, where, what, and how children are born, reared, and prepared for a life of comfort or difficulty, success or failure, consummation or unhappiness.

Parents who become pregnant knowing they carry inheritable defects, who abuse substances during pregnancy, who abandon, neglect, or mistreat children, and who use children as ploys, pawns, or shields for self-interests can all be considered as discriminators. However, it is not without dispute that parents from the poor, the powerless, and the illiterate who make the best efforts to raise children are called discriminators simply because they are not able to provide necessary and sufficient resources and opportunities for children and hence put the latter in disadvantageous positions in social competition. For example, to what extent can a single mother who lives on welfare yet takes care of each of her children be fairly blamed as a discriminator to her children, who later become welfare recipients themselves because of a lack of education or job skills?

The system is undoubtedly a discriminator since it favors the strong over the weak, especially the rich over the poor, the powerful over the powerless, and the educated over the uneducated. The system of health care renders treatment and prevention upon payment. The system of education delivers hope and promise in terms of qualification. The system of mass media grants access and exposure according to status. The system of culture accords privilege and esteem by custom. The system of politics builds upon family influence and personal connection. The system of economy correlates with capital and profit. And the whole system of society features classification, differentiation, and hierarchical placement, sorting people into different levels or positions with different accesses to resources and opportunities for different achievements and enjoyments in life.

The Victim

Children are unambiguously victims. With defects and deficiencies from birth, they may never be able to experience the world as any other normal human being. Instead of moving around, some remain confined in beds, wheelchairs, or other devices most of the time. Instead of dreaming freely, some stayed mentally disturbed, polarized, or numbed for a lifetime. After birth, naturally healthy children without adequate nutrition, care, and support by parents may die prematurely, develop chronic or contagious diseases, or take on a nonproductive lifestyle as drug addicts or homeless vagrants. Children with negative examples and role models from family, on the other hand, may turn into radicals, deviants, criminals, or rebels even though by nature they have all the potentials to become law-abiding citizens or successful professionals. Most commonly, children growing up in environments lacking adequate resources and opportunities have to struggle hard and smart for limited success or for sheer survival all their life.

Parents may claim victimization by the system as well. For example, people who follow God, popular culture, or political propaganda to give birth to children even though they know they are likely to pass on certain defects or diseases to offspring can be legitimately seen as victims of religion, morality, or ideology. The effect of such victimization can be no less for parents than for children as parents take care of their born-to-be infirm sons or daughters day and night for the entirety of the latter's life. More generally, people of the poor, the powerless, and the uneducated can be fairly considered as victims of capitalism, socialism, or any other existing political economy as they bear the same hardship or pain as their sons and daughters when the latter strive for a better life in the bottom of the social hierarchy.

The Compromise

Not a great many children living under parents of irresponsibility, neglect, mistreatment, or abuse accuse parents of such a wrongdoing. Some may run away, some may fight back, but most take their life as a matter of fate. Intriguingly, almost everyone may still feel grateful to parents for the gift of life, specifically for bringing him or her into this world, regardless of whether it entails misfortune, suffering, or misery.

Not a great many children growing up in families of poverty, deprivation, or illiteracy blame families for the lack of resources and opportunities they face in social competition for upward mobility. Some may wonder what if they finished school, some may wish they lived in an affluent community, but the majority approach their life as a thing of reality. Interestingly, almost everyone may still feel thankful to families for the care of life, particularly for anchoring him or her to this society, no matter whether it involves hardship, endless effort for little success, or hopelessness.

On the part of parents, they can cite pregnancy, childbirth, and childrearing as painstaking processes especially when they give birth to children with disabilities, when they raise children by negative approaches, or when they care for children without adequate resources.

The Universal

From a system point of view, individual uniqueness makes population diversity, personal differences fuel social dynamics, and people-to-people contrasts and competitions provide ultimate forces for human vitality and vibrancy.

Generation-wise, parents serve as primary agents to keep and pass on individual differences to offspring. In every possible circumstance, parents choose or do not choose whether, when, where, and how to give birth to and raise children, with or without consideration of their own physical, mental, and financial health or their children's prospects for survival, success, and happiness. As a result, children arrive in the world in every possible scenario by every possible character with every possible potentiality for life.

In terms of social institution, families are principal agencies to preserve and perpetuate gaps and inequalities among people. Wealth transfers within the family from older to younger generations in the form of inheritance. Power and status continue within the family from kings, queens, the appointed, or the elected to princes, princesses, or otherwise legitimated heirs through a royal rule of succession or an open game of democracy. Knowledge, craftsmanship, and professional practice persist within the family from parents to children by way of apprenticeship or role-modeling.

As differences continue, it is inevitable that some individuals will live an easier, more successful, and happier life, while others have to struggle in difficulty or misery just for survival. In a sense, society stays as a dynamic system with necessity of sufferings for some, whereas human civilizations progress at the expense of sacrifices on the part of others.

SITUATION 2

For many individuals, class in high school or college serves as a lifetime reference or network. In high school or college, classmates compete and compare with one another in areas from academic subjects, extracurricular activities, and personal characters to individual relationships. While class performance to a large degree determines where a particular graduate goes for college, graduate school, or job placement, class image or impression about individual personality, ability, and potentiality usually predicts whom one keeps contact with, what one chooses for a professional career, or how far or high one reaches in life.

The Particular

Alibaba maintains regular communications with many of his high school and college classmates. The high school class gathers partially or wholly almost every year when classmates return to the hometown to celebrate the major holiday of the year. Besides face-to-face gatherings, the class shares an email list for individual members to post news and photos. The college class happens to have an enthusiastic convener who keeps contact information for all classmates and has successfully organized class-wide get-togethers once every five years since 2000.

With frequent contacts, Alibaba knows well what and how most of his high school and college classmates do in their professional as well as personal pursuits. Back in high school, as Alibaba clearly remembers, the class differentiated distinctively into the smart half, who prevailed in natural sciences, and the not-so-smart half, who could only dwell on the humanities and social sciences. The college class was no less divided by academic performance and personal ability either. Those who excelled in the major went to graduate school for advanced studies, whereas those who struggled throughout the undergraduate years had no choice but to take jobs in practical fields.

Now as everyone is basically settled into his or her career and life without much possibility for significant change, Alibaba observes that his high school classmates in the humanities and social sciences overall score higher levels of success and satisfaction than those in natural sciences and engineering, and that his college classmates in practice on average command more wealth, power, and social status than those in academia. This general finding makes Alibaba wonder why his seemingly more intelligent classmates do not do better now than his less intelligent classmates in their careers and lives as he and everyone else expected in high school and college years.

The Discriminator

God is the discriminator if there is an almighty god who watches the whole world, ensuring that each individual receives what he or she deserves by physique, intelligence, and effort. God acts erroneously when he lets those who work harder to take the higher rigor of training not to achieve more professional success for a better life. God is unfair when he allows those who have difficulty meeting the challenge of higher learning to gain unwarrantedly in material and nonmaterial possessions from the secular world.

No solid discriminators can be apparently identified at the individual level. People who happen to do well in the humanities and social sciences could not possibly make trouble in natural sciences and engineering to prevent individuals therein from achieving their due success. Similarly, people who happen to shine in business, industry, or practice could not possibly set up barriers in academic fields to keep individuals thereof from reaching their scholarly potentials.

At the societal level, however, there seem to be obvious discriminating forces. First, competition turns keen, ruthlessly killing talents when people flock to a field. Second, vacancy becomes considerable, producing stars out of scarcity or "making a monkey the king of a tiger-less mountain" when people shun an area. Third, reform, revolution, and other forms of social change bring about opportunities for growth and expansion for some professions or categories of activities while forcing other practices or domains of affairs into decline and demise. Alibaba can relate to all these three factors well as he attempts to understand the differentiations and differences he sees among his high school and college classmates.

The Victim

Victims are clear when Alibaba and his high school or college class communicate or meet one another. High school classmates in natural sciences and engineering think they are smarter and have worked harder, but have not reached comparable levels of success attained by those in the humanities and social sciences. Given the nature of their work, some of them even face the challenge of knowledge antiquation and the danger of layoff. Likewise, college classmates in academia feel they are brighter and have put more effort into their professional careers, yet have not commanded similar latitudes of power, wealth, or influence enjoyed by those in business and practice. Indeed, most of them live in solitude, frugality, or invisibility for much of their lives. Certainly, neither group would consider themselves or be viewed as clear victims if there were no references from the time of high school or undergraduate study.

Victimization is real when Alibaba and his high school or college classmates hear from or watch over each other. Classmates in natural sciences and engineering spend days and nights in laboratories doing experiments, building models, and filling project details, while those in the humanities and social sciences read books in the comfort of home, write articles out of imagination, and take speaking tours from place to place. Oftentimes, the former have to answer tough questions by supervisors over data and calculations as the latter get the opportunity to appear on the mass media, pouring out personal opinions on current affairs and national policies. Similarly, classmates in academic fields spare no talents and efforts for graduate study and advanced research, whereas those in business and practice apply textbook knowledge with ease, forge business relationships at the dinner table, and strike moneymaking deals over the golf course. From occasion to occasion, the former have to save over a long period of time for money to attend an academic conference as the latter take the liberty to use business profits for upper-class luxury, aristocratic-style extravagancy, or ultimate indulgence in personal gratification. Of course, neither cohort would feel the pain of victimization if no referents remained in sight from the past high school or college class.

The Compromise

No compromise can be fashioned directly between parties in comparison and referencing since one group of the class that do well is by no means involved in causing the other group not to reach what it deserves by talent and effort. Out of individual sensitivity, however, high school classmates in the humanities and social sciences would normally avoid boasting about their own fortunes or mentioning a comparably less successful situation for their once enviable peers in natural sciences and engineering. In fact, when the class meets with considerable turnout, attendants would primarily talk about what the whole group used to be in the time of high school. The memory of the popularity of those in natural sciences and engineering then surfaces, making the now less successful part of the class feel better to join the fun in the gathering. The same holds true for the college class. Indeed, it is individual sensitivity or indirect compromise that keeps both high school and college cohorts stay in touch from year to year.

In their respective minds, those who have achieved less than anticipated find peace by looking into larger social processes. First, science demands intelligence while it does not necessarily produce immediate rewards in secular terms. Similarly, scholarship requires intellectual rigor while it does not always deliver tangible results for mundane enjoyments. Second, science is an arena for fierce competition. It takes a mass of scientists to maintain a few giants. Likewise, scholarship is a field of intense comparison for omission or elimination. It takes a collection of scholars to showcase a few stars. Third, regardless of what one gains or loses in science or scholarship, one can take credit and pride in being just part of science, scholarship, and the knowledge enterprise as it is science, scholarship, and the knowledge enterprise that provide the ultimate driving force for social progress and human evolution.

In contrast, those who have obtained more than expected seek comfort by focusing on smaller individual factors. First, they are not conscientious choice makers. As a matter of fact, they were forced into their current path because they had no other track to take due to their then personal circumstance. Second, they are not opportunists. Indeed, they chose the humanities, social sciences, industry, or practice neither because they knew there would be less competition nor because they took a gamble on more opportunities out of a possible political or economic change. Third, they are not reap-without-sowing idlers. They work hard and spare no intellectual capabilities in pursuit of their professional or business success.

The Universal

People follow their dreams, hopes, and expectations when they take actions and steps in life. Individuals with physical assets, whether the asset is handsomeness for men or beauty for women, normally look for partners or spouses of similar or matching characteristics. Persons with intellectual talents, whether the talent is the gift to create arts, music, or crafts or the genius to excel in science, engineering, or general scholarship, usually expect to achieve professional success and social recognition over career pathways. To a large degree, the world operates fairly and justly in accordance with individual assets, talents, efforts, and expectations.

Life is essentially unpredictable, however. It is not uncommon that students who look pretty, seem popular, and attract each other as fairy-tale sweethearts in high school have difficulty finding love, establishing intimate relationships, or cementing marriages through adulthood. It is not unheard of that college graduates who appear to be brightest, most promising, and best privileged to have valuable resources and enviable opportunities at their disposal do not perform on a par with peers who do not show much potentiality at the time of higher education. To the shock and awe of commonsense wisdom, people fail in professional careers from time to time because of individually owned assets or become victims of no success in life from place to place due to socially bestowed advantages. Here is a warning to keep like a saying: "you could become the slave of your own circumstance."

SITUATION 3

Leaders are partly born from nature and partly made through social dynamics. On the one hand, people who own a systematic frame of mind, operate with a reasonable understanding of human process, or by nature possess all essential leadership qualities may not necessarily become leaders in the real world. On the other hand, people who think without much rationality, act in frequent error, or by every sensible measure do not have any leadership skills can be surprisingly pushed into leadership positions in groups, organizations, and even nation-states. It is not just an intellectual insult to, but most critically a day-to-day suffering for members of a collective when the collective is in the hands of incompetent leaders. From an individual point of view, life can be ironically discriminatory when it favors ineptitude, mediocrity, or stupidity over competency, excellence, or wisdom in different areas in general and over leadership in particular as leadership symbolizes personal success.

The Particular

Having lived in different political systems and worked for various organizations, Alibaba commands a wealth of observation and experience about how leadership is decided, what kind of people become leaders, and whether people in leadership positions live up to the basic expectations of their duty.

One thing Alibaba feels seeing clearly across groups and systems is that leaders of a collective are not necessarily most talented, experienced, or qualified members of the collective they lead and represent. In nondemocratic systems, emperors, kings, and dictators pass power onto their children or confidants with no regard to the latter's capabilities. Under democracy, political candidates may gain popularity and win election through conspicuous or inconspicuous consumption, manipulation, or misrepresentation. In organizational settings, open recruitment, inline appointment, or mini-election is often subject to a collective fear of the extreme and a mass preference for the mean. Leaders emerged or selected are average people at best and can be less than the average in some circumstances.

Coinciding with his macro observation, Alibaba notices in the micro level that some of his friends, peers, schoolmates, neighbors, colleagues, and acquaintances who do not seem to own any leadership qualities surprisingly ascend to leadership positions in their respective workplaces, communities, or professional associations. When folks in a related cohort gather or chat over the phone, they naturally exchange these utterances: "Can you believe that Joe is now the dean of his college?" or "It is beyond our common imagination that Jennifer would ever be able to take charge of a corporate business like hers!"

The Discriminator

It is debatable whether or not people who do not possess leadership qualities but nevertheless occupy leadership positions are discriminators. They are discriminators because when they take leaders' roles, they automatically push aside those who have better credentials and abilities to lead in their organizations. They steal power, honor, and prestige inherent in leadership, which they do not deserve either by natural gift or social experience. Lacking adequate leadership talents and skills, they likely place a collective under danger, create misery for the membership of an organization, or take a whole society to a difficult journey with ill-conceived policies and disorganized action programs.

These fortunate individuals are not discriminators because they become leaders out of the work of the principle of the mean. People abhor the worst, fear the best, and tend to follow the average in collective representation. Similarly, these lucky individuals are not discriminators because they emerge in leadership roles from interpersonal or group dynamics. People divide into cliques, extremes, or factions, and are likely to seek middle grounds to keep contrast and balance. Indeed, it is the invisible hand of human life that determines who leads or represents in any particular time and at any particular place. An individual can only say "life treats me well" when he or she is blessed with the opportunity to lead or represent an organization irrespective of his or her talent, qualification, experience, or deservedness.

The Victim

Victims are relatively clear and valid. Individuals can feel victimized when they think they are more qualified, experienced, or deserving to be leaders in their groups, organizations, or social systems. People may bear a variety of losses or sufferings when incompetent leaders make erroneous policies and take serious missteps. Members of an organization or citizens of a country may face embarrassment, disgrace, or dishonor when leaders representing it fail to deliver or demonstrate the level of diplomacy, elegance, intelligence, or wisdom it normally holds among competitions.

From a life course perspective, people who have instincts and motives to become leaders may see themselves victims if they never grasp the opportunity to take leadership roles and responsibilities in the real world. Although they could feel quite negative about the fact that they are led and represented by individuals whom they consider having less qualification, experience, and ability than themselves in leadership positions, they might still not be able to pinpoint specifically who or what causes their perceived victimization. Instead, they could only mention "fate of life," "God," or "randomness of society" as possible mischief for being pushed aside or living under the shadow in their personal journeys.

The Compromise

Regardless of ability, frame of mind, intentionality, vision, judgment, and circumstance, most people in leaders' positions feel they do the best they can to fulfill headship duties for the good of their constituencies. They may make conciliatory gestures or take expedient actions to comfort some of their constituents who suffer under certain policies or programs. Internally, they can refer to the inconspicuous part of leadership responsibilities, such as long hours of labor, delicate human maneuvering, and intense brainwork for the power, honor, luxury, glory, and various other privileges they enjoy in public eyes.

People who are not in office sooner or later understand that actors make mistakes because they act, that observers find problems because they are not in action, and that individuals tend to think they could act smarter or do better when they observe someone else acting or doing things. More directly, people who think they could be better leaders must at some point of time admit that they are not chosen due to some of their shortcomings and that people who are selected as leaders own specific advantages over competitions. Finally, there should be no complaint at all if selection is done by God, time, the fate of life, or the invisible hand of social law for what a group, an organization, a nation, a society, or an era is meant to be during a particular period of time.

The Universal

Individuals are born with certain dispositions and traits. They demonstrate their potentialities or show their promises as they grow up. However, it is a combination of individual asset, personal effort, lifetime opportunity, and social selection that determine whether individual potentials or promises translate into specific achievements or deeds in reality.

Children born with artistic gifts may not necessarily become artists. Kids blessed with intellectual faculties may not necessarily grow into scholars. Boys or girls perceived of having a leadership mind and talent may not necessarily end up leading any collective as adults. Instead, an occupational career, a professional field, or a political landscape can from time to time feature surprising success, unbelievable fortune, or even undeserving entitlement for some individuals.

Would a field, a profession, a collective, or life and society as a whole be better off if it always had the right people in place, in charge, or in domination? Only God knows. From a life course point of view, though, an individual needs to know that he or she may not become what he or she perceives to be on his or her own. Be prepared for surprise, the unbelievable, the unthinkable, or the unimaginable in the real-life world.

SITUATION 4

Over the normal progression of human civilization, older generations leave burdens or heritages, make rules and policies, as well as set expectations, standards, and the evolutionary course for newer generations although the world belongs to the latter. In cases when older generations refuse to relinquish control beyond their legitimate term, a whole new generation may have to live under shadow, without ever fulfilling the substance of the world in their due possession and realizing the meaning of the life under their rightful ownership.

The Particular

Working in organizational settings through his occupational career, Alibaba notices that members of the old guard sit in the higher echelon of most organizations. They make policies, enforce rules, and control accesses to opportunities and resources even though younger members constitute main productive forces, make fundamental contributions, embody what is right and fashionable at the present, and represent what is promising and likely in the future.

As a casual observer of politics, Alibaba can cite a number of historical and current cases where an emperor, a king, a queen, or simply a ruler stays long beyond his or her due term, ruling out any possibility that the next generation makes its rightful claim to the throne or power in a timely manner. The most known example is from the existing British monarch: Prince Charles may never have the opportunity to become the king as Queen Elizabeth enjoys her longevity in life and royal highness.

The Discriminator

On average, each generation has its rightful window of time to serve and shine. Members of a generation become discriminators when they cling to power beyond their term of service or when they fail to take charge for their turn of duty. Beginning with the family, parents discriminate against children if they make the latter labor at an early age or if they still refuse to pass the torch of family management to the latter in a late time.

In secondary institutions such as schools, businesses, professional organizations, and public agencies, leaders are usually much order than the mean age of the membership. They hold discriminations against the membership when they make and implement policies reflective more of the perspective of their own age group. They turn into blatant discriminators when they hold on to power in the name of benefiting the organization with their age-old wisdom. The situation is more conspicuous in state politics, where leaders may even change constitutions to lengthen or perpetuate their stay in office.

With advances in medicine, people live longer and can function adequately in various business affairs to a considerably old age. Discriminations across generations in terms of service and control can become ever more common and intense. How much longer and more difficult for members of the old guard to retreat from control and power into rest and retirement in contemporary times?

The Victim

Victimization can take place in various arenas and among different categories of people. Adult children are victims when they have to live by the will of parents in terms of school, job, marriage, finance, and lifestyle. In traditional society, some adult children may have to forever forgo the chance, due to their generation, to take charge of family affairs if their parents happen to be long-living, strong-minded, and unwilling to surrender control.

In organizational arenas, younger members become victims when they perform hard labor without due recognition, when they offer ideas for little or no credit, or when they make contributions without taking rightful honors or rewards. They follow rules to support the order favored by members of the old guard. They produce products or deliver services to sustain an organization, a business, or a profession in the hands of senior leading elites of the membership. At the level of nation-state, adolescent soldiers die in the battlefield, youthful talents perform on stage or experiment in laboratories, and middle-age citizens sacrifice hard-earned income so that a small group of career politicians, a senior leadership, or an old dictator can keep playing their favorite political games and gambles.

From a life course point of view, adolescence now extends to age twenty-four while early adulthood already reaches forty in social definition. How much more time do members of the younger generation have to wait, idle, and waste over the labor market, in organizational leadership, and across political landscape for their turn to take charge or just to be independent, full adults in the modern and postmodern era?

The Compromise

Directly, members of the old guard may invite younger constituents to participate in the policymaking process, allowing the latter to voice their opinions, co-opting the latter in the leadership team, or using the latter to implement rules. In specific terms, parents may assign adult children to take care of individual areas of family affairs. Corporate executives may tap youthful talents as advisors or assistants or avail younger members of the opportunity to obtain material benefits or seek upward mobility. Professional power holders may incorporate feedback from younger members and offer the latter training and other tangible resources for expansion and progress in career. Similarly, national leaders may grant amnesties, use think tanks, or create forums for different population groups to grow, express, and entertain themselves.

Ideologically, members of the old guard may cite the need to keep heritage, the momentum to continue history, the difficulty to rear, prepare, or groom the newer generation, or the necessity to ensure certainty, stability, or durability as reasons for them to stay in power. They may even justify their domination as an unselfish effort for setting the stage or paving the way for the next generation to shine.

Victims may take the discrimination as part of human evolution. Nothing seems wrong when parents make rules, organizational seniors impose standards, and national leaders keep controls. With a little bit of cynicism, some members of the newer generation may even feel a sense of fortune, luck, or relief when the older generation dominates the world to make them free from leadership responsibility, human maneuvering, and political manipulation through much of their lives.

The Universal

In absolute terms, each generation has the opportunity to take charge, shine, and leave its mark. The opportunity may come sooner or later. When the opportunity comes sooner, a generation may then grasp a longer window of time to make contributions or cause damages to human civilizations.

This logically leads to the relative aspect of the issue. That is, a generation may take the historical stage longer than its fair share of time. It may even overshadow later generations in control and influence. Especially, when it stays in power long overdue, it likely creates a tradition or adds to historical inertia that older people rule, dominate, and enjoy the world at the expense of the younger majority of the population.

That points back to the absolute side of the matter. Namely, it is always the old who control the young. Individuals serve and sacrifice for most of their lifetime in the wish or at the will of their elderly parents, mentors, protectors, and leaders. When they live long and endure hard enough to take the turn, they do the same to their younger children, advisees, protégés, and followers. Isn't it absurd and insane that individual humans can only act in otherness, either live for the wishes of the old or exercise their will at the sacrifice of the young? Unfortunately, the situation seems more and more severe as medicine advances and society progresses.

SITUATION 5

In relation to society, history, and human civilizations, individuals may add nothing, cause damages, or offer contributions over the course of their life. There are obviously people who work hard, save smart, and live a life of productivity, simplicity, and frugality. There are people who meddle through work, spend freely, and live a life of hedonism, luxury, or extravagance. There are even people whose life features only nonproductivity, waste, or profligacy. In net terms, for society to grow, history to advance, and human civilizations to progress, people who contribute more than take must outnumber and outshine people who take more than contribute as well as people whose contributions are totally nullified by their misdeeds or misfortunes.

The Particular

In his middle-class life, Alibaba witnesses countless live cases of pure individual contributions to society. Adam, one of Alibaba's senior colleagues at work, started his professional career and personal life from scratch, with neither any inheritance from his parents nor any assistance from the public. He worked diligently, paid taxes, and spent little for his own enjoyment throughout his entire life. When he passed away, he left behind a considerable estate for the government to take over as he did not have any children or deserving relatives upon whom to bestow his assets. Darleen is one of Alibaba's neighbors. She and her late husband raised four children, watching all their children graduate from college into professional careers with full financial support. She and her husband did not spend much on their own. When she died, she followed her late husband's will to have passed all their wealth to their children, giving each of them a strong boost in their individual pursuits, which eventually will to some extent benefit society as a whole.

Besides individual cases, Alibaba observes that most of his middle-class colleagues, friends, and neighbors resort to hard work, rational planning, and delay of gratification to accumulate wealth for their children or their late life. As they are likely to live a healthy late life without much need for costly medical care, they will surely leave considerable assets for others to benefit in society.

On the other hand, Alibaba sees no lack of individuals who need assistance, who exploit welfare without any shame, and who assault society with no sense of guilt. Every morning in his neighborhood park, Alibaba watches minivans bussing in dozens of mentally handicapped people to play. Occasionally, Alibaba notices people using food stamps and WIC coupons to buy expensive items he himself is hesitant to purchase for family consumption out of his normal conscience of saving. From time to time, Alibaba hears and views from the news repeat criminals exhausting law enforcement resources and prison convicts draining public funding. Whereas it is disputable as to what extent people in all these categories might contribute to society, it is crystal clear that society needs to spend here and now to care for, help, or contain them.

The Discriminator

In strict terms, any individual who takes more from than he or she contributes to society in his or her lifetime is a discriminator.

Discriminators can be either intentional or unintentional. Intentional discriminators are those who choose to inflict injuries to fellow human beings or cause damages to recognized social establishments. Criminals are condemned discriminators to particular groups, communities, and social systems against which they perpetrate. Adolf Hitler, Joseph Stalin, and other historical evil figures are known discriminators to the overall humanity against which they sinned. Unintentional discriminators, in contrast, are those who depend upon society for care and support because of born defects, acquired disabilities, or forced social circumstances. A deformed infant passes away after an intensive period of costly medical care. A retarded person lives a fifty-year-long life under the wholesome supervision of his or her relatives. A college student suffers from total disability following a traffic accident during his or her senior year. And a used-to-be-productive citizen becomes a beggar, a vagrant, or a junkie after some life-changing experience.

Discriminations can be both specific and general. Specific discriminations involve tangible economic interests, such as time spent, efforts made, funds dispensed, or resources utilized by individual persons, groups, or organizations over particular periods of time. For example, care has to be rendered for mentally retarded or accidentally disabled members of the society. Taxes have to be levied to fund social welfare, the police, and correctional institutions. General discriminations figure in communal atmosphere, human morality, and social progress. For instance, crime creates public fear, genocide spreads moral decadence, and Adolf Hitler might arguably have pushed the world back decades.

The Victim

Overall, human civilizations suffer with smaller progresses or even setbacks when significant numbers of people take more from than contribute to society from era to era.

Down to particulars, many countries have to offer substantial contributions to make up damages inflicted by several nations if the world in an era is not blamed for human regression. Multiple families, organizations, and communities have to make serious efforts to compensate for losses caused by numbered social units if a country in the world is not condemned for global misery. A majority of individuals have to offer time, spend money, perform labor, forgo opportunities, or contribute material supplies to care, cure, contain, or control a minority of people who are in need, at risk, or committed to do harm if any collective remains as a whole contributive to social progress.

It is obvious that just as original discriminators are real individuals, ultimate victims are actual humans. Indeed, given the inevitability of social progress, taking from society excessively by some members, if it does not inherently trigger automatic altruism, it necessitates extra contributions, victimization in a sense, by many more members.

The Compromise

People who can give more to than take from society owe to a multitude of factors or forces for their fortunes. First, they are blessed by nature with adequate physical and mental health. Second, they are equipped by society with proper rearing, education, and employment. Third, they are awarded by the world with opportunities or resources for growth, enrichment, and actualization. Fourth, they are likely to live their life in independence and dignity, to its full potential and meaning, and with a sense of satisfaction and fulfillment. Most relevant, they can keep a feel of social responsibility, world ownership, pride, superiority, and nobleness when they give to society in general and help the needy in particular. It is common to hear donors, caregivers, and guardians saying their life has reached a new level of depth, meaningfulness, or richness by giving or just caring for someone else.

From a critical point of view, society may owe people who apparently live in social indebtedness. For example, people born with physical defects or mental handicaps take sufferings in their whole life because parents made some unwise choices in some socially created hazardous environments. People forced into deviancy and criminality live under shadows while affording society the opportunity to develop and fine-tune an indispensable mechanism to manage conflict, keep order, and maintain balance. It is forever an unsettling debate as to whether human civilizations suffered or benefited from Adolf Hitler, Joseph Stalin, or other historical Satans and their evildoings.

The Universal

Life is an experience. It does not always boil down to the take or give in purely material terms. People who take materialistically may give spiritually. The handicapped, the disabled, the addicted, the sinner, and all others who are in need of material takings can offer valuable teachings about nature versus nurture, body versus mind, pain versus joy, gain versus loss, life versus death, medicine versus miracle, and society versus individuals.

Society is a dynamic process. Just as demand stimulates supply, taking motivates giving. Had there been no taking by the needy, there would have been no philanthropy, no sympathetic care, and no social welfare. Society would not have developed many of its dimensions in empathetic understanding, counseling, health care, human protection, and social control. Indeed, society expands and advances only when it has the opportunity to open every possible area of life and activate every possible line of events for all its members in an overall equilibrium between giving and taking in particular and between consumption and production in general.

More abstractly, human civilizations progress with time, not necessarily by measure of material accumulation. One society or era may add a collection of artifacts or a bounty of wealth, whereas the other can present a scene of massive deficits of taking over giving, material damages, or individual sufferings to human history. Either way, human civilizations would still have to build upon it, bid farewell to it, and move forward to a new stage of the future.

10 Theoretical Significance

Studying everyday life calls for observation, reflection, and analysis. While observation remains a methodological issue, reflection and analysis involve use of theories, not only application to explain individuals and their day-to-day living experiences, but also generalization to expand theories and their scientific utilities.

This chapter assesses the relevance as well as the significance of the three major social theories, symbolic interactionism, conflict theory, and functionalism, in the study of everyday life. Since it is in the back of the book, it also attempts to frame all the learning from this study about everyday life in the perspective of each one of the three theoretical paradigms in social sciences.

SYMBOLIC INTERACTIONISM

Everyday life is about assuming different roles, carrying out different activities, and dealing with different parties in various settings associated with living. Study of everyday life can both draw from and add to symbolic interactionism (Mead 1934; Goffman 1959; Blumer 1969; Droit 2003; Lefebvre 2008; Stryker 2008; Burke and Stets 2009; Charon 2009; Sandstrom, Martin, and Fine 2009; Collins 2011; Gordon and Tanaka 2011; Perinbanayagam 2012; Turner 2012; Gorski 2013).

The Original

The main thrust of symbolic interactionism is to focus on individuals and their interactions in societies. First, symbolic interactionism examines how people use symbols to denote things in the material and social world, how meanings and symbols allow people to carry on their actions and interactions, and how language as a system of symbols improves the human capacity for thought. Use of concepts and logics, for example, allows actors to transcend space, time, and even their own persons and imagine a metaphysical reality, such as the heaven and the hell. As a result, people are able to better perceive the world, more effectively solve problems, and less likely be enslaved by their environment.

Second, symbolic interactionism explores how individuals develop the self, engage in self-evaluation, form self-identity, and maintain self-image in social interactions. According to Mead (1934), the self develops through three stages, from play to game to generalized other stages. A developed self divides into two phases, an emissive "I" and a reflective "me." As far as evaluation, identity, and image are concerned, Mead emphasizes "taking the role of the other" in gathering critical information about oneself while Goffman (1959) stresses staging or dramatization on stages to achieve the goal of impression management.

Third, symbolic interactionism inquires how people engage in social interactions as actors, role-players, and exchangers or traders. For instance, individuals assess their relative advantages and disadvantages, weigh different courses of action, and make the most appropriate choices. There are initial calculations and projections in terms of reward, need, and chance of success. There are also final accounting and auditing of gains or losses by measure of economic interest, political power, and social status.

Fourth, symbolic interactionism researches how belief affects action, how perception feeds back on behavior, how intentionality relates to consequence, and essentially how mind connects to body or individual world links to social existence. Beginning with Cooley (1922), a looking-glass self can imagine, judge, and feel its own appearance to the outside. According to W.I. Thomas (1928), if men define situations as real, they are real in their consequences. In the eyes of Merton (1968), a false definition of a situation may even evoke new behaviors that make the original false conception come true, in what he pointedly characterizes as a self-fulfilling prophecy.

Finally, symbolic interactionism studies how individual actions and interactions make up groups and societies. At the abstract level, symbolic interactionists proclaim that social structure is created, maintained, and changed by individual interaction. In the concrete, they have made efforts to show how individual, specific, and micro factors or forces turn into social, general, and macro existences or realities. For example, Blau (1975) presents a four-stage sequence from the former to the latter. According to him, personal exchange transactions among people (stage one) give rise to differentiation of status and power (stage two), which leads to legitimization and organization (stage three), which sow the seeds of opposition and change (stage four).

The Applicable

Everyday life features individuals who take roles, assume responsibilities, and perform duties under specific social situations. Symbolic interactionism can be applied to inform and inspire everyday life in various aspects.

Focusing on use of symbols, for instance, people can better understand how an everyday life person grows and matures as he or she learns vocabularies and accumulates effective ways of verbal and nonverbal expression. Description of an event originates in interactive experience. It can in turn clarify thought, improve planning, shape behavior, and enhance performance. Similarly, explanation of an incident derives from experiential interaction. It may then enlighten reflection, stimulate imagination, motivate prediction, and boost confidence, which in combination will lead to a heightened capacity for thought and an emboldened mind for action.

Paying attention to definition of situations, on the other hand, people can better appreciate not only how an everyday life individual serves as his or her own agent in a lifelong journey, but also how he or she demonstrates his or her agency in the dynamics of social structuration. Personal satisfaction or dissatisfaction is subjective. However, when it is perceived by someone it becomes an objective behavior-shaping force in his or her everyday life. Social justice or injustice is in the eyes of a beholder because when one sees injustice one is likely to act on it, either by way of personal revenge to balance one's inner world or by way of social reform to change one's outer environment. Likewise, if one does not see injustice, one can still feel one's life with peace and comfort even though in reality one has taken considerable unfairness, mistreatment, or victimization.

The Generalizable

Symbolic interactionism investigates individual actors and their day-to-day interactions in social settings. Everyday life provides fertile soils for symbolic interactionism to grow and expand in different ways.

At the outset, everyday life acts and activities create and maintain social structures and processes. Families arise as men and women mate, marry, and reproduce. Groups and organizations come into being when people gather, work, and recreate by belief, interest, and trade. Communities appear where families and organizations develop and expand. Cities emerge as communities thrive. Nations form when cities compound and consolidate. It is seemingly natural, perhaps inevitable, that individual acts and actions converge in broader group dynamics and processes. So is that smaller groups and groupings combine into larger social structuring and structures.

Specifically, everyday life subjects grow and mature through social interactions. From parents, individuals learn to acquire beliefs, develop personalities, and mold characters. With teachers, individuals study to accumulate knowledge, master skills, and understand social mores. Along peers, individuals explore to build friendship, maintain networking, and obtain social support. It is widely, if not universally, salient that family, school, workplace, and community serve as focal points where people locate opportunities and resources, find comparisons and references, set goals and standards, and engage in actions and interactions in their everyday life.

The Known

There is no question that symbolic interactionism can shed light on everyday life with inspirational ideas. Nor is there any doubt that everyday life may enrich symbolic interactionism through insightful generalizations.

In definite terms, learning about everyday life in light of symbolic inter-actionism can be put into five propositions. First, everyday life provides the interactive environment where each and every individual acquires language, takes roles, develops self, establishes self-identity, and tackles self-actualization. Second, everyday life involves each and every individual in settings from home to workplace to community to nation-state to the world. Third, everyday life engages each and every individual in task performances from daily chores on the backstage to professional pursuits in the front theatre, from interest fulfillments over the personal space to assignment completions in public or supervisory eyes, and from thinking in the mind to acting out of bodily conditions. Fourth, people in everyday life compare and contrast among themselves, between past and present, and between part and system, at any time and all the time. Finally, people in everyday life perceive and act on discrimination and victimization concerning themselves, groups, and the system, at any place and all over the place.

Similarly, learning about symbolic interactionism by way of everyday life can be made in five statements. Statement one affirms that symbolic interactionism offers a unique theoretical paradigm where everyday life and hence human behavior can be better informed, understood, and shaped. Statement two claims that symbolic interactionism explains not only small groups, but also large social institutions as individuals connect and criss-cross both settings in everyday life. Statement three declares that symbolic interactionism applies to specific person-to-person interactions as well as general social processes because people take part in or switch back and forth both levels of acts, activities, and dynamics in everyday life. Statement four holds that symbolic interactionism is correct about role-taking, referencing, and impression management as evidenced by everyday life actors and agents from time to time. Lastly, statement five says that symbolic interactionism is right on point regarding looking-glass self, definition of situations, and self-fulfilling prophecy as demonstrated by everyday life actions and agencies from place to place.

The Unknown

Everyday life is an evolving process. There are facts and connections to be constantly found, observed, and explained. Symbolic interactionism is an encompassing theoretical paradigm. There are hypotheses and points of view to be continuously explored, tested, and confirmed or rejected.

Looking forward, what major things are yet to be learned about everyday life in the perspective of symbolic interactionism? First, symbolic inter-actionism needs to explore how tracks of everyday life are chosen for and by individuals, inside and outside social interactions, before and after birth, with and without the will of a subject. Second, symbolic interactionism has yet to determine what common references individuals use in everyday life contrasts and comparisons. Constant references are likely to be structured in a relatively stable hierarchy for the ease of day-to-day referencing. Third, symbolic interactionism is theoretically obliged to identify what blind spots individuals face in everyday life due to their lifestyles, social positioning, and cultural practices. A blind spot for a subject is where things remain inconspicuous, unobservable, and invisible to him or her. Fourth, symbolic interactionism holds a logical obligation to examine what different courses of action individuals would have taken had they known those important things they could not see in their blind spots. Finally, symbolic interactionism is due to investigate how equity, fairness, and justice figure in everyday life, affecting individual actors in their approaches to mistreatment, discrimination, and victimization amid day-to-day social interactions.

Contrastingly, what major things remain to be learned about symbolic interactionism from everyday life? One thing is that everyday life can make symbolic interactionism a theory of the past, the present, the future, and their interconnections. At present, symbolic interactionism seems to focus only on interactions that take place here and now. Following everyday life, questions as to how patterns of interaction transmit from generation to generation and how parental choices influence children's acts and actions can nevertheless be answered. Another thing is that everyday life can make symbolic interactionism a theory of parts, the system, and part-to-system connections. Parts and the system are basically conceptual characterizations. It is people and their day-to-day actions that make parts, connect parts into a system, and keep the system in realistic existence. By studying people-to-people interactions, symbolic interactionism holds the key to understanding human structuring and social structuration. Still another thing is that everyday life can make symbolic interactionism a theory of processes, the evolution, and process-to-progress connections. Process is ongoing while progress measures changes between any two points in process. Informing the process of everyday life, symbolic interactionism may also reveal social progress and foretell human destiny. Fourth, everyday life can make symbolic interactionism not only an embedded or immersed study of the mundane world, but also a lifted or even transcended research into the essence of human civilizations. And fifth, everyday life can make symbolic interactionism both an inventory of situational rules and a repository of general principles for interacting, grouping, structuring, systemizing, and globalizing across the human universe.

CONFLICT THEORY

Conflict is part of life. People create, intensify, deescalate, and resolve conflict as they go about everyday life. With regard to conflict theory, what inspiring and enlightening power does it hold for everyday life? Contrariwise, to what degree can everyday life inform and enrich conflict theory (Coser 1956; Mills 1956; Dahrendorf 1959; Berger and Luckmann 1966;

Horkheimer 1972; Collins 1975; Habermas 1975; Smith 1987; Marx 1990; Bourdieu and Wacquant 1992; Lenin 1992; Marx and Engels 2008; O'Brien 2009; Kliman 2010; O'Connor 2010; Walby and Spencer 2010; Bartos and Wehr 2012; Turner 2012)?

The Original

Conflict theory views society as composed of people with different economic interests, cultural values, political goals, and social agendas. Interest groups form, subcultures develop, political parties appear, and social classes emerge as people act, congregate, and disperse. Economic monopolization, cultural normalization, political domination, class confrontation, and social stratification ensue, intensify, and sustain when groups, parties, and institutions coalesce, consolidate, and expand. In one view, society is a hierarchy, placing people in differential access to power, resources, and opportunities. From another perspective, society is a division, featuring exploitation of the poor by the rich, oppression of the powerless by the powerful, and manipulation of the uneducated by the educated.

Individuals are active social agents according to conflict theory. Society is essentially a human product. It is after all individual human beings who create society. In the sense that humans translate their ideas into social reality, society is an externalization of human mind. However, society is an objective reality. In other words, once human ideas pass through the process of objectification, they become realistic facts and forces bound to shape and reshape future human thoughts and conducts. As a matter of fact, each and every individual is born and reared in a particular social environment. He or she internalizes social norms and values as he or she matures into the social mainstream. Indeed, internalization tells it all about individual development and adaptation in society.

Between present and future, conflict theory characterizes conflict as the driving force for social change and human evolution. In a typical event of change, the exploited, the oppressed, and the manipulated overcome their false consciousness, organize themselves, and rebel against reality to establish a new social order. Generally, change is constant as conflict is omnipresent. Change can be gradual when conflict appears in manageable forms. However, a drastic change, such as revolution, may break out when conflict takes place explosively. Similarly, a transformational change, such as social evolution from mechanic to organic solidarities, may occur when conflict prompts change and change feeds back on conflict accumulatively over a historical period of time.

In methodological dimension, conflict theory urges researchers to be critical, holistic, and reflective. Holistically, researchers should focus on the totality of social reality so that they can relate parts to the whole or attend to the whole while analyzing parts. Reflectively, researchers should place emphasis on the formation of ideology, the spread of propaganda, or just the use of language so that they can see how reality is socially constructed. Being critical, researchers would examine how people are constrained to act and to identify themselves by particular social institutions so that they can challenge not only the way by which authority is maintained, but also the manner in which tradition is sustained.

Lastly, conflict theory takes a reformative approach to social reality under study. It is only halfway traversed when information is gathered for the sake of information, not to be used to change and improve social conditions. There is little worth achieved when knowledge is sought for the sake of knowledge, not to be applied to reform and better human life. In the mind of a conflict theorist, a recurrent and overwhelming concern is this: once the causality of fate is uncovered, what better social form can be designed for the future generation?

The Applicable

Conflict theory eyes differences and resultant conflicts among people in everyday life. It can shed critical light on the way life is lived by individuals through contrast, comparison, and competition.

One application of conflict theory, for instance, is to recognize the inevitability of conflict in everyday life. Individuals are born to be different. The tall may bully the short. People are reared to be different. The educated may manipulate the uneducated. Acts are performed for different purposes. Some acts are selfish while others are altruistic. Actions are taken to reach different goals. There are individual and organizational goals for self-actualization, group solidarity, and social betterment. There are also individuals and organizations who aim at inflicting personal sufferings, instilling public fear, or causing social destruction. Besides actors and actions, conflict is immersed in process, reflected in consequence, and fermented in structure. Regarding process, conflict is unavoidable because there are different ways of thinking, doing things, and living life. With respect to consequence, conflict is inevitable when one's gain is made at another's loss. Structurally, groups, organizations, and societies are set up in hierarchical order, differentiating people and hence pitting one against another in access to power, benefits, and status.

Another application of conflict theory is to realize the manageability of conflict in everyday life. People stay together in groups regardless of conflict. Society sustains from generation to generation in spite of tension. The reason is simple: people solve problems, settle disputes, and manage conflicts in everyday life. From birth, individuals are rendered an instinct to share. In the process of socialization, people cultivate a spirit to agree. Over group living, members are taught a habit to conform. With instinctual and habitual forces in place, people tend to make efforts to prevent conflict. When conflict happens, people are likely to resort to accommodation, avoidance, cooperation, and compromise to avert, eliminate, or minimize its immediate impacts. Even when they take an approach of confrontation, people aim at pushing conflict out of their current sight. In the spirit of conflict theory, preventing and managing conflicts show vividly how conflict serves as a constantly active force for people to change, for institutions and societies to evolve, and for human civilizations to progress.

The Generalizable

Everyday life is about ordinary individuals who work to meet the day-to-day challenges of survival in their specific environments. Lessons can be learned from everyday life struggles to enrich or expand conflict theory.

Regarding people in everyday life, for example, are there any general propositions that can be drawn to the benefit of conflict theory? First, are people sources of conflict? Is it safe to say that where there are people, there is conflict? Second, are people agents of conflict? Is it true that conflict appears, spreads, escalates, or disappears when people perceive, create, or make conflict the way it is? Third, do people necessarily bear the bruises and wounds of conflict? To what degree is it general that conflict delivers specific consequences for people once it takes place? Fourth, do people change sufficiently in the aftermath of conflict? To what extent is it common that people alter their thoughts and acts whether they have a positive or negative experience with conflict?

With respect to society, what universal observations or statements can be made for the perspective of conflict? Is society an inevitable stage for conflict? Conflict involves people in groups. When it occurs, it unavoidably falls in a social situation. Does society amplify conflict? In typical group settings, there are doers, bystanders, and spectators. The spectator effect alone can alter the way conflict develops. Does society constrain or contain conflict? It is obvious that conflict or the wave of conflict will not disperse freely in all directions given the structure of society or the configuration of people in society. In what sense does everyday life society change because of conflict? Conflict provides force for change when it prompts people to act. Conflict supplies substance for change as it involves people and people's actions in overall social dynamics.

The Known

What is clearly known about everyday life in the perspective of conflict and conflict theory can be crystallized in five propositions. One proposition is that everyday life produces conflict. Conflict is bound to happen when people of different interests compete for limited social resources and opportunities in everyday life. Another proposition is that everyday life settles conflict. Conflict brings people together to fight for winning, to negotiate for an agreeable solution, or to settle for peaceful coexistence. Still another proposition is that everyday life builds upon conflict. Conflict is an experience for individuals to grow and mature, for groups to move forward, and for society to make progress. The fourth proposition claims that everyday life informs conflict theory. Eyeing everyday life, conflict theory broadens its view of individuals, groups, and human dynamics. The fifth proposition states that everyday life enriches conflict theory. Embracing everyday life, conflict theory deepens its analysis of grouping, structuring, and social hierarchies.

On the other hand, there are five major pieces of learning about conflict and conflict theory from everyday life. First, conflict emerges from contrast and comparison in everyday life. People find differences and grounds for grievance by comparing with one another, against the system, and between past and present. Second, conflict takes the form of discrimination and victimization in everyday life. Problems arise or a situation turns problematic when one discriminates and another becomes a victim on the matter of interest, power, or status. Third, conflict drives everyday life. Issues appear, actions follow, things materialize, and everyday life unfolds before, after, and around conflict. Fourth, conflict theory inspires everyday life. Knowing the omnipresence of conflict, people take conflict as an opportunity to create things or a means to reach goals. Lastly, conflict theory directs everyday life. Understanding the inevitability of conflict, people follow conflict to find ways toward personal success and to some degree even roads toward social progress and human consummation.

The Unknown

What main things are yet to be learned about everyday life in the perspective of conflict theory? First, everyday life invites people. To what degree do people create conflict because of their physical, psychological, and socioeconomic differences? Second, everyday life invokes actions. By what standard are actions categorically opposed to one another? Third, everyday life is a process. Is conflict in everyday life processual in nature? In other words, does conflict come and go as part of an inevitable process? Fourth, everyday life takes place within a social structure. Is conflict structural in the sense that it takes a new structure to solve conflict derived from an old structure? Finally, everyday life stalls, falls in turmoil, declines or accelerates, climbs to a higher latitude, prospers upon conflict. Is there an attainable and maintainable homeostasis of everyday life amid conflict?

In contrast, five major things can be further learned about conflict theory from everyday life. For one thing, conflict theory can offer an academic explanation for cause and effect in everyday life. Following conflict as an unbreakable thread through life, conflict theory has the potential to illuminate the logical chain of human actions. For another thing, conflict theory can supply everyday life people with an intellectual motivation for reflection and contemplation. By cultivating a critical attitude toward reality, conflict theory holds the promise for making people think deeply and holistically about the meaning of what they face and do in everyday life. For still another thing, conflict theory can serve as an action guide for individuals in everyday life. By calling for action, conflict theory has the obligation not only to inform people as to what effort to make, but also to guide people as to how action to be taken effectively and efficiently. Fourth, conflict theory can be a natural connection from micro issues, small groupings to macro forces, large structures. Seeing everyday life subjects in action and conflict, conflict theory holds the key for understanding how individual actors and actions converge to form population masses, produce social consequences, and charter human destiny. Lastly, conflict theory can become a golden mine for both specific rules in everyday life and general principles over human civilizations. Studying everyday life dynamics, conflict theory keeps the best hope for unraveling the myths and mysteries about the duality of human thinking and reasoning, between the concrete, the specific, the particular and the abstract, the general, the universal.

FUNCTIONALISM

Individuals and their day-to-day living activities make society and social dynamics. Society sustains as people go about everyday life. Insomuch as functionalism is concerned, it draws valuable inputs from everyday life, on the one hand, while offering critical outputs for everyday living individuals on the other (Parsons 1951, 1954; Coser 1956; Merton 1968; Luhmann 1982; Dickman 1990; Demerath 1996; Alexander 1998; Smelser 1998; Isaac 2010; Marsh 2010; Maher 2011; Wan 2011; Inglis and Thorpe 2012; Turner 2012).

The Original

Functionalism examines how a social system integrates individual parts and their respective contributions to meet overall system needs and challenges for existence and sustentation. First, a social system has four salient features. From within, it comprises parts, integrating parts and keeping their interrelations. From without, it sits in an environment, maintaining boundaries and stabilizing relationships with the outside. Over time, it remains static or engages in an ordered process of change. As a whole, it tends toward equilibrium by way of allocation and integration.

Second, function is a complex of activities directed toward meeting a need or needs of the system. There are four fundamental functions. Adaptation is to deal with situational exigencies, transform external conditions, and adapt to the environment. Goal attainment is to define goals and mobilize resources to attain goals. Integration is to regulate system components and their interrelations in coordination with adaptation and goal attainment. Pattern and latency maintenance is to motivate members, pass on knowledge, and keep tradition or heritage.

Third, the four fundamental functions are fulfilled by four corresponding subsystems. The behavioral organism handles adaptation. The personality subsystem performs goal-attainment. The social subsystem copes with integration. The cultural subsystem takes charge of pattern and latency maintenance. For example, through the cultural subsystem, people learn appropriate social norms and cultural values that motivate them for action.

Fourth, functions can be manifest or latent. Manifest functions are the consequences people observe and expect, whereas latent functions are the consequences that are neither recognized nor intended. In a similar line, subsystems can be functional or dysfunctional. A subsystem is dysfunctional when it performs activities or generates consequences that lessen the adaptation or adjustment of the system. Also, no given institution or subsystem is sacrosanct for any particular function. In fact, a wide range of functional alternatives or substitutes can become available to perform the same task.

Finally, functionalism stretches from grand scheme to middle range in theorizing, from positivism to interpretive approach in methodology, and from order or status quo to action or change in social agenda. Through inquiry made into the function of conflict, functionalism makes a natural connection to conflict theory. With attention paid to self-referencing by interaction, organization, and societal systems, functionalism in its neo form reaches out instantly yet logically to symbolic interactionism.

The Applicable

Functionalism draws attention to function and functionality of acts to the actor, means or activities to the goal, and parts to the system. Applications can be made in all these aspects to everyday life.

At the macro level, functionalism can examine everyday life as a routine, a practice, or a mode of survival and sustention to see how it keeps the volume of production, the intensity of interaction, and the scale of society. For example, tourism develops as individuals rest and recreate through travel, vacation, and leisure; the economy booms when people stay in the labor force, work efficiently, and spend with considerable financial ease; and society prospers where everyday life ordinaries feel free to express ideas, find opportunities to pursue occupational careers, and gain access to resources to keep preferred lifestyles.

In the micro dimension, functionalism may follow specific acts, activities, and experiences to figure out whether they facilitate or hinder personal pursuits and fulfillments for particular individuals in everyday life. For instance, comparing with peers, perceiving discrimination, and acting on mistreatment sometimes motivate people to do better things. Similar acts sometimes demoralize people, pushing them into a situation where they do things harmful to others or themselves. Also, it is important for everyday life individuals to know and understand that not every act or action leads to its intended consequence; effects of certain efforts may remain latent for a considerable span of time; and different things can be done or one thing can be done in different ways to achieve the same outcome.

The Generalizable

Everyday life engages individuals in mundane activities ranging from attending school, working on jobs, and maintaining relationships to taking care of families. As individuals embrace everyday life, society finds original materials and forces to keep the scale, expand the operation, and continue the progress. Learning from everyday life in the perspective of functionalism can be generalized in similar dimensions as well.

Individually, it is interesting to follow everyday life subjects to gain knowledge of how day-to-day activities, efforts, or experiences translate into success, crystallize in personality, or take shape in the form of a life course. Are there general rules or principles to be discovered as to what facilitates, what hinders, and what neutralizes toward the equilibrium of a wholesome character, career, or identity? Further down to specific acts and actions taken by everyday life subjects here and now, it is fascinating to investigate what serves the purpose, what brings about the opposite, and what messes up a whole situation. Are there general patterns or sequences of action to be identified for the purpose of minimizing cost, saving time, and attaining goals? For example, rebellion amid consistent conformity may work effectively in dealing with the authority just as one conforming act out of a series of rebellious activities can bring about surprising welcome and acceptance.

Socially, it is enlightening to study how individual ideas add up to form national ideology, how individual lifestyles converge to constitute fashions or vogues, and how individual conformities align with one another to generate social mainstreams. Are there clear watersheds or thresholds above which micro acts and actions are bound to turn into macro effects and phenomena? Further up to social stability, order, and progress, it is insightful to know and understand why society tends to hold up as an upward-moving equilibrium while seeing individual members contributing and taking, stabilizing and sabotaging, or pushing and pulling at the same time. Are there critical percentages or ratios of individual deviance, lawbreaking, or infighting to be avoided or contained to prevent society from falling apart structurally or from lagging behind in human evolution?

The Known

What is known about everyday life in the perspective of functionalism can be summarized in five propositions. Concerning the functionality of everyday life to individuals, proposition one points out that everyday life presents people with a natural sequence of activities to exercise mind, entertain body, and live a life. Proposition two finds that everyday life provides people with a platform to demonstrate talents, create things, and build careers. Proposition three emphasizes that everyday life provides people with a track or a roadway to develop personalities, mold characters, and acquire identities. With regard to the contribution of everyday life to society, proposition four claims that everyday life engages people in the mundane acts and activities of living, producing and maintaining mass consumptions, public fashions, cultural vogues, and social mainstreams. Proposition five declares that everyday life serves society as the ultimate material forces for prosperity and progress.

Likewise, existing learning about function, functionality, functionalism from everyday life can be put in five statements. First, function exists as a common variable because people constantly experiment what works and what does not work in everyday life. Second, functionality turns into a general measurement when individuals explore how effectively and efficiently means advances goals, input facilitates output, and cost justifies benefit. Third, functionalism becomes a useful perspective as contemporaries learn to be instrumental or goal-rational in day-to-day dealings. Fourth, social equilibrium expands as everyday life rises. It contracts when everyday life declines. Lastly, functionalism works well in the middle range when it explains everyday life with such concepts as manifest function, latent function, dysfunction, and functional alternative. It shines in the grand scale when it connects individuals and their everyday life actions to larger social structures and processes.

The Unknown

There are obviously more things to be learned about everyday life in the perspective of functionalism. One thing is how negative events or incidents in self-experience contribute to individual growth, maturation, and success. Another thing, on the other hand, is how positive happenings or results in self-feeling or evaluation might end up being disruptive or detrimental to goal attainment or self-actualization. Still another thing is to what extent individual efforts dissipate in time and space, leaving no measurable effect on the quality of life or the quantity of success. Fourth, are individual contributions or takings socially conditioned, structured, and determined? In other words, individuals located in the bottom of society can be automatically forced into the role of takers or dependents, whereas people sitting on top of the world may naturally take pride as contributors or guardians. Finally, is there a critical ratio of total contributions over total takings by all members of a society below which the society as a whole would decline or regress and above which it would prosper or progress?

Similarly, more knowledge can be gained about functionalism from everyday life. First, an everyday life person is a dynamic system. An everyday life course is a moving process. To what degree can functionalism rooted in macro tradition apply to everyday life individuals and their life-long journeys grounded in micro social phenomena? Second, everyday life involves interpersonal comparison, referencing, and exchange, each of which is either functional or dysfunctional to individual actors and their respective life pursuits. In what sense can functionalism combine with symbolic interactionism to offer integrated insights over day-to-day living? Third, everyday life creates competition, conflict, and confrontation, all of which cause upheavals or add fuels to individual growth and actual-ization. To what extent may functionalism reconcile with conflict theory to generate higher explanations for everyday life? Fourth, functionalism is known to favor historical analysis, system-to-system comparison, and overall positivistic methodology. With everyday life under the radar of its inquiry, will functionalism soon demonstrate its potential to benefit from case study, intra-versus-interpersonal referencing, and generally interpre-tative approach? Lastly, functionalism tends to side with the system, the goal, or the equilibrium to make judgments about parts, means, and mov-ing processes. Following everyday life in the agenda of its research, will functionalism eventually prove its promise to become a balanced school of thought so that it not only evaluates individuals and individual inputs in terms of social prosperity and progress, but also judges society and social outputs in terms of individual health and happiness?

Conclusion

Everyday life comes and goes. People take it, follow it, and live it. However, only when they embrace it with passion, entertain it with patience, and reflect upon it with heart, can people know, understand, and appreciate their everyday life and its meaningfulness. Everyday life pours in and flushes out. Scholars watch it, measure it, and comment on it. Nevertheless, only when they observe it with instrument, analyze it with science, and contemplate it with imagination, can scholars see the unfamiliar from the familiar, extraordinary from the ordinary, and the significant from the trivial in the incessant flow of everyday life.

In everyday life, people compare, contrast, and make distinctions with reference to different sources, standards, and contexts. Sources can be selves, others, and the system. Within oneself, one may feel better or worse off over time. Compared to peers, one may consider oneself privileged, disvalued, or mistreated in certain aspects. In contrast to the system, one may see oneself below, on, or above the average in effort, performance, or reward. Standards concern equity, justice, rationality, or reasonableness. A sense of unfairness develops when recognition is not commensurate with contribution. A feeling of injustice spreads if violation of norms goes undetected, unchecked, and unpunished. Or on the opposite, the spirit of logic, reason, and order may run high and bright when education is respected, science is honored, and law is observed in the everyday lifeworld. Finally, contexts may involve an organization, a community, a nation, or the whole world. Inside an organization, there can be member-to-member, member-to-group, or group-to-group referencing. Within a nation, there may be citizen-to-citizen, citizen-to-institution, and institution-to-institution comparisons. Across the world, contrasts can take place among people, countries, systems of political economy, and tracks of civilizations.

Through comparisons and contrasts, people find, face, and feel differences, discrepancies, and discriminations. From this study, ten major dimensions can be generalized about social discriminations in particular or human distinctions in general. First is the perceptual versus actual aspect. Discriminations in existence may be recognized or unrecognized, whereas a nonexistent discrimination can be actively perceived.

For example, dedicated wives, devoted parents, or committed teachers rarely feel any discriminations by husbands, children, or students even when in actuality the former could offer far more than they take through these bilateral relationships. With regard to perceived discriminations, the Thomas theorem holds: "If men define situations as real, they are real in their consequences." Second is the intentional versus unintentional dimension. Intentional discriminations are acts by active perpetrators such as women batterers, alien haters, and celebrity stalkers. Unintentional discriminators, on the other hand, may never realize that they put other people in disadvantage. For instance, a driver who carelessly or incompetently disrupts traffic during rush hour does not usually think far about how he or she makes many fellow drivers and their passengers late for school, work, or appointment. The third contrast is role-related versus status-dictated. Role-related discriminations stem from specific social roles people assume in everyday life. A student may suffer discriminations by a teacher while a child may face abuse or neglect in the hands of his or her caretaker. Status-dictated discriminations go hand in hand with the status one is ascribed, assigned, or achieved. A girl is put behind her male siblings for schooling in a poor family. A newcomer is looked down upon when he or she does not do well. And an alien is hated when he or she does better than the homegrown or the local.

The fourth dimension is situational versus contextual. Situational discriminations occur over specific events in a particular time and location. For example, a sold-out exhibition or performance is canceled at the last minute; a hand-raising participant is repeatedly ignored for a chance to voice his or her opinion in a focus group; and a sales clerk becomes an innocent target for a junior engineer, who is reprimanded by a senior supervisor in his or her office, to release anger at a supermarket when the latter activates his or her defense mechanism of displacement. Contextual discriminations, by comparison, unfold against a group, organizational, or communal background or in a local, national, or international environment. Workers are not rewarded for their exceptional job performance in reference to a particular organization; welfare recipients take advantage of public assistance with regard to a specific social system; and developed nations steal talents, resources, and treasures from less developed countries in relation to a unique state of the world system. Fifth is victim-specific versus victim-general. Victim-specific discriminations often involve one-on-one interactions between discriminators and victims, whereas in victim-general discriminations a discriminator may never directly deal with his or her multiple victims. Specific victims can be a hardworking husband facing a jobless yet shopping-crazy wife, an organization having a liability-causing employee on staff, or a country exporting raw materials or labor-intensive products for import of high-tech equipment. General victims may, in contrast, include taxpayers who pay for an overblown police force, a community of professionals whose image is tarnished by a few wayward practitioners, or even mankind when the impoverished under-class contributes far more than its fair share to the future population. The sixth comparison is explicit versus implicit. Explicit discriminations are apparent, conspicuous, and widely known, such as majority versus minor-ity discriminations and discriminations against the poor, the powerless, or the uneducated by the rich, the powerful, or the educated. Implicit discriminations, on the other hand, may remain hidden, uncovered, and unnoticed. For example, one is denied early promotion even though fulfill-ment of requirements for promotion in a shorter period of time logically makes one a stronger candidate for consideration; A complaining employee is automatically suspected of incompetence or maladaptation regardless of any defects the employer may have in its organizational setup; or an alien professor, while being a member of a privileged profession, may never enjoy the same level of visibility, respect, and fame accorded to his or her native counterpart for the same amount of work and contribution.

The seventh facet is combination versus separation. By combination, discriminations in two or more categories converge to form a larger, more harmful discrimination. For example, one is a foreign alien, a woman, and a member of an ethnic minority; one could then face a kind of discrimina-tion due to a combination of all three factors at one time, in one occasion, or over one thing. Through separation, an overall discrimination breaks down into two or more subtypes, with varying yet not necessarily less or more detrimental effects. For instance, colonialism boils down to political subordination, economic dependence, and cultural nihilism, each of which serves as a canvas to record part of the general discrimination against many indigenous societies by a few imperialist colonizers. Eighth is a related yet distinctively different dimension of reinforcement versus mitigation. With reinforcement, one type of discrimination escalates in intensity, frequency, duration, or effect when it co-presents with another. An alien as an excep-tional job performer is more likely to face rejection for early promotion than a native candidate of the same profile. By way of mitigation, in compari-son, one kind of discrimination becomes lesser in impact or consequence as it meets with another. Although a black entertainer, sportsman, or even politician may be treated differently than his or her white counterpart, he or she can still enjoy much of the fame, celebrity, or privilege accorded to entertainment, sports, or politics by the larger society. In other words, even though professional or economic discrimination might have pushed members of the minority into certain fields, it can mitigate racial, ethnic, or gender discrimination when members of the minority become established in those arenas.

Ninth is the structure versus process aspect. Structural discriminations inhere in the way a group, an organization, a community, or a nation is built. In class societies, stratification is meant to place people in different levels and positions for differential access to resources and opportunities. More critically, the rich, the powerful, and the educated are privileged in the social hierarchy to discriminate against the poor, the powerless, and the uneducated. Processual discriminations, in contrast, take place in social interactions, during organizational processes, or amid social dynamics. For instance, a black mayor is searched as part of racial profiling by a police officer who does not know the former's identity as mayor; a more qualified majority candidate is bypassed for promotion to a leadership position in an organization because of some quotas reserved for the minority; and voices for the other side are silenced or ignored through the prohibition era, in the war against terrorism, and even at the time when gays, lesbians, and their nontraditional marriages gain currency in the media. The tenth dimension is random versus cumulative. Random discriminations occur with no specific connection to demographics or socio-structural conditions. An individual becomes a victim when he or she is at a wrong time. An organization turns into a discriminator when it happens to be in the place. Over time, most individuals or organization are likely to get even with random discrimination, either as victim or perpetrator. However, a few individuals or organizations may consistently remain on the side of victimization and therefore systematically take on the impact of discrimination because of their pattern of behavior, fate, or social positioning. In other words, random discriminations can cumulate into systematic conditions which may hold victims in constant or permanent disadvantage or subordination. The same holds true for all other types of discriminations: discriminations in different categories and occasions can add up to an overall unfavorable, depressing, or even devastating condition for some victims. On the other hand, discriminations of various sorts or in various situations may also cancel out each other for both individuals and organizations, leaving no one with any obvious sense of discrimination throughout the course of life.

With discriminations identified, felt, and verified, people take actions. They may avoid, accept, or fight discriminations or work with discriminators through collaboration or compromise. By avoidance, people simply walk out of a relationship or circumstance in which they face tangible discriminations. In acceptance, people are likely to change inner perceptions, outer references, or the comparison itself in an attempt to rationalize their experience of discriminations. For example, an aged billionaire may see his love for a young beauty as invaluable when he spends millions on numbered days or months with her. Third, fighting discriminations may take place in the form of oral argument, administrative review, legal challenge, social movement, and even war. In the United States, it took generations of civil rights protests and activisms to put a legal end to racial segregation. Fourth, collaboration involves discriminators and victims to join hands to create a win-win situation where they coexist, co-grow, and co-prosper without mutual harm. Finally, compromise requires that each side of the discrimination change its view, expectation, and position to develop a practically workable solution to a thorny issue in reality.

Besides people-to-people discriminations, all these five major approaches hold true to those between people and organizations as well as those among organizations.

Above specific learning about conspicuous and inconspicuous discriminations, this study shows that everyday life is a gold mine for personal contemplation, social science research, and philosophical reflection. Through contemplation, people come to know and understand life, its width, depth, and meaningfulness. In social science research, everyday life serves as a natural laboratory for anthropologists, economists, political scientists, sociologists, and other disciplinary scholars to observe social phenomena in the making, to test existing theories, and to stimulate imagination for new concepts and models. By way of abstraction, reflection, and exposition, philosophers and other academicians in the humanities can follow thinkers, such as Socrates, Plato, and Wittgenstein, in finding concrete cases or scenarios from everyday life to exemplify or elucidate recondite, profound, or subtle vantage points. At the conclusion of this book, it is hoped that a new interface will begin for everyday life to enrich scholarship and for theory to enlighten day-to-day living by the ordinary.

References

Abbott, Andrew. 1988. *The System of Professions: An Essay on the Division of Expert Labor.* Chicago: University of Chicago Press.

Abowitz, Kathleen Knight and Jason Harnish. 2006. "Contemporary Discourses of Citizenship," *Review of Educational Research* 76.4: 653–690.

Adler, Patricia A., Peter Adler, and Andrea Fontana. 1987. "Everyday Life Sociology," *Annual Review of Sociology* 13: 217–235.

Alexander, Jeffrey C. 1998. *Neofunctionalism and After.* Malden, MA: Blackwell.

Alvesson, Mats and Kaj Skoldberg. 2009. *Reflective Methodology: New Vistas for Qualitative Research.* Thousand Oaks, CA: Sage Publications.

Anderson, Jeffrey R. 2012. *The Nature of Things: Navigating Everyday Life with Grace.* Bloomington, IN: Balboa Press.

Arnold, Jeanne E., Enzo Ragazzini, Anthony P. Graesch, and Elinor Ochs. 2012. *Life at Home in the Twenty-First Century: 32 Families Open Their Doors.* Los Angeles, CA: The Cotsen Institute of Archaeology Press.

Auge, Marc. 2009. *Non-Places: An Introduction to Supermodernity*, translated by John Howe. New York: Verso.

Baecker, Dirk. 2011. "What Is Holding Societies Together? On Culture Forms, World Models, and Concepts of Time," *Criticism* 53.1: 1–22.

Bakeman, Roger and Vicenc Quera. 2011. *Sequential Analysis and Observational Methods for the Behavioral Sciences.* Cambridge and New York: Cambridge University Press.

Ballman, Donna. 2012. *Stand Up for Yourself without Getting Fired: Resolve Workplace Crises Before You Quit, Get Axed or Sue the Bastards.* Pompton Plains, NJ: Career Press.

Bartos, Otomar J. and Paul Wehr. 2012. *Using Conflict Theory.* Cambridge and New York: Cambridge University Press.

Beck, Ulrich. 2011. "Cosmopolitanism as Imagined Communities of Global Risk," *American Behavioral Scientist* 55.10: 1346–1361.

Berger, Peter L. and Thomas Luckmann. 1966. *The Social Construction of Reality.* New York: Doubleday.

Blau, Peter M. 1975. *Approaches to the Study of Social Structure.* New York: Free Press.

Block, Peter. 2008. *Community: The Structure of Belonging.* San Francisco, CA: Berrett-Koehler Publishers.

Blumer, Herbert. 1969. *Symbolic Interactionism: Perspective and Method.* Englewood Cliffs, NJ: Prentice Hall.

Boeri, Tito, Herbert Brucker, Frederic Doquier, and Hillel Rapopor. 2012. *Brain Drain and Brain Gain: The Global Competition to Attract High-Skilled Migrants.* Oxford: Oxford University Press.

Bold, Christine. 2012. *Using Narrative in Research*. Thousand Oaks, CA: Sage Publications.

Booth, Alan, Karen Carver, and Douglas A. Granger. 2000. "Biosocial Perspectives on the Family," *Journal of Marriage and Family* 62.4: 1018–1034.

Bosanac, Stephen E. and Merle A. Jacobs, eds. 2010. *Work, Occupations, and Professionalization*. Whitby, ON: De Sitter Publications.

Bourdieu, Pierre. 1987. *Distinction: A Social Critique of the Judgement of Taste*, translated by Richard Nice. Cambridge, MA: Harvard University Press.

Bourdieu, Pierre. 1990. *The Logic of Practice*, translated by Richard Nice. Stanford, CA: Stanford University Press.

Bourdieu, Pierre and Loic J.D. Wacquant. 1992. *An Invitation to Reflexive Sociology*. Chicago: University of Chicago Press.

Brinkmann, Svend. 2012. *Qualitative Inquiry in Everyday Life: Working with Everyday Life Materials*. Thousand Oaks, CA: Sage Publications.

Bruhn, John G. 2005. *The Sociology of Community Connections*. New York: Springer.

Bryson, Bill. 2010. *At Home: A Short Story of Private Life*. New York: Anchor Books.

Bureau, Sylvain and Jean-Baptiste Suquet. 2009. "A Professionalization Framework to Understand the Structuring of Work," *European Management Journal* 27.6: 467–475.

Burke, Peter J. and Jan E. Stets. 2009. *Identity Theory*. Oxford and New York: Oxford University Press.

Callan, Sue and Michael Reed, eds. 2011. *Work-Based Research in the Early Years*. Thousand Oaks, CA: Sage Publications.

Caproni, Paula J. 2004. *Management Skills for Everyday Life: The Practical Coach*. Upper Saddle River, NJ: Prentice Hall.

Certeau, Michel de. 2002. *The Practice of Everyday Life*, translated by Steven Rendall. Berkeley and Los Angeles: University of California Press.

Chang, Chingching. 2011. "Enhancing Self-Referencing to Health Messages," *Journal of Consumer Affairs* 45.1: 147–164.

Charon, Joel M. 2009. *Symbolic Interactionism: An Introduction, an Interpretation, an Integration*. Upper Saddle River, NJ: Prentice Hall.

Chen, Shaohua and Martin Ravallion. 2010. "The Developing World Is Poorer than We Thought, but No Less Successful in the Fight against Poverty," *Quarterly Journal of Economics* 125.4: 1577–1625.

Chesters, Sarah Davey. 2012. *The Socratic Classroom: Reflective Thinking through Collaborative Inquiry*. Rotterdam, NL: Sense Publishers.

Christensen, Clayton M., James Allworth, and Karen Dillon. 2012. *How Will You Measure Your Life?* New York: HarperCollins Publishers.

Chwe, Michael Suk-Young. 1999. "Minority Voting Rights Can Maximize Majority Welfare," *American Political Science Review* 93.1: 85–97.

Collins, Patricia Hill. 2010. "The New Politics of Community," *American Sociological Review* 75.1: 7–30.

Collins, Randall. 1975. *Conflict Sociology: Toward an Explanatory Science*. New York: Academic Press.

Collins, Randall. 2011. "Wiley's Contribution to Symbolic Interactionist Theory," *American Sociologist* 42.2/3: 156–167.

Coltrane, Scott. 2004. "Elite Careers and Family Commitment: Its (Still) about Gender," *Annals of the American Academy of Political and Social Science* 596: 214–220.

Cooley, Charles Horton. 1922. *Human Nature and the Social Order*. New York: Scribner's.

Corey, Gerald, Marianne Schneider Corey, and Patrick Callanan. 2011. *Issues and Ethics in the Helping Professions*. Belmont, CA: Brooks/Cole.

Cornwell, Benjamin. 2011. "Age Trends in Daily Social Contact Patterns," *Research on Aging* 33.5: 598–631.

Coser, Lewis A. 1956. *The Functions of Social Conflict*. Glencoe, IL: Free Press.

Crompton, Rosemary. 2008. *Class and Stratification*. Malden, MA: Polity Press.

Csikszentmihalyi, Mihaly. 1997. *Finding Flow: The Psychology of Engagement with Everyday Life*. New York: Basic Books.

Dahrendorf, Ralf. 1959. *Class and Class Conflict in Industrial Society*. Stanford, CA: Stanford University Press.

Dalai Lama. 2011. *A Profound Mind: Cultivating Wisdom in Everyday Life*, edited by Nicholas Vreeland. New York: Harmony Books.

Day, Graham. 2006. *Community and Everyday Life*. New York: Routledge.

DeBell, Paul. 2009. *Decoding the Spiritual Messages of Everyday Life: How Life Shows Us What We Need to Know*. New York: Sterling Publishing.

Demerath, N.J., III. 1996. "Who Now Debates Functionalism? From 'System, Change and Conflict' to 'Culture, Choice, and Praxis,'" *Sociological Forum* 11.2: 333–345.

Dickman, Joel. 1990. "Two Qualms about Functionalist Marxism," *Philosophy of Science* 57.4: 631–643.

Dixit, Avinash K. and Barry J. Nalebuff. 1991. *Thinking Strategically: The Competitive Edge in Business, Politics, and Everyday Life*. New York: W. W. Norton and Company.

Douglas, Jack D., ed. 2010. *Everyday Life: Reconstruction of Social Knowledge*. New Brunswick, NJ: Transaction Publishers.

Droit, Roger-Pol. 2003. *Astonish Yourself: 101 Experiments in the Philosophy of Everyday Life*. New York: Penguin Books.

Durkheim, Emile. 1964. *The Division of Labor in Society*. Glencoe, IL: Free Press.

Dzienkowski, John S. 2012. *Professional Responsibility, Standards, Rules and Statutes, 2012–2013*. Eagan, MN: WestLaw.

Edensor, Tim. 2002. *National Identity, Popular Culture, and Everyday Life*. New York: Berg.

Edwards, Carolyn Y. 2008. *Not Your Typical Day*. Bloomington, IN: Xlibris.

Edwards, Ryan D. 2011. "Changes in World Inequality in Length of Life: 1970–2000," *Population and Development Review* 37.3: 499–528.

Felson, Marcus and Rachel Boba Santos. 2010. *Crime and Everyday Life*. Thousand Oaks, CA: Sage Publications.

Fong, Eric and Ly-yun Chang. 2011. "Community under Stress: Trust, Reciprocity, and Community Collective Efficacy during SARS Outbreak," *Journal of Community Health* 36.5: 797–810.

Freud, Sigmund. 1965. *New Introductory Lectures on Psychoanalysis*, translated by James Strachey. New York: W. W. Norton and Company.

Freud, Sigmund. 2003. *The Psychopathology of Everyday Life*, translated by Anthea Bell. New York: Penguin Books.

Friberg, Tora. 1993. *Everyday Life: Women's Adaptive Strategies in Time and Space*. Lund, Sweden: Lund University Press.

Friedman, David. 1996. *Hidden Order: The Economics of Everyday Life*. New York: HarperCollins Publishers.

Gagne, Nana Okura. 2011. "Eating Local in a U.S. City: Reconstructing 'Community'—a Third Place—in a Global Neoliberal Economy," *American Ethnologist* 38.2: 281–293.

Gallagher, Winifred. 1994. *The Power of Place: How Our Surroundings Shape Our Thoughts, Emotions, and Actions*. New York: HarperCollins Publishers.

George, Linda K. 1993. "Sociological Perspectives on Life Transitions," *Annual Review of Sociology* 19: 353–373.

Goffman, Erving. 1959. *The Presentation of Self in Everyday Life.* New York: Doubleday.

Gordon, Iris and James W. Tanaka. 2011. "The Role of Name Labels in the Formation of Face Representations in Event-Related Potentials," *British Journal of Psychology* 102.4: 884–898.

Gorski, Philip S. 2013. *Bourdieu and Historical Analysis.* Durham, NC: Duke University Press.

Green, Harvey. 2000. *The Uncertainty of Everyday Life, 1915–1945.* Little Rock: University of Arkansas Press.

Griffiths, Robert, ed. 2011. *Annual Editions: Developing World 11/12.* New York: McGraw-Hill.

Habermas, Jürgen. 1975. *Legitimation Crisis,* translated by Thomas McCarthy. Boston, MA: Beacon Press.

Hamilton, Cheryl. 2011. *Communicating for Results: A Guide for Business and the Professions.* Boston, MA: Wadsworth Publishing.

Hanzel, Igor. 2011. "Beyond Blumer and Symbolic Interactionism: The Qualitative-Quantitative Issues in Social Theory and Methodology," *Philosophy of the Social Sciences* 41.3: 303–326.

Hardie, M.G. 2008. *Everyday Life.* Coral Springs, FL: Llumina Press.

Hatch, Nathan O. 1988. *The Professions in American History.* Notre Dame, IN: University of Notre Dame Press.

Hawke, David Freeman.1988. *Everyday Life in Early America.* New York: Harper and Row.

Heath, Shirley Brice. 2012. *Words at Work and Play: Three Decades in Family and Community.* Cambridge and New York: Cambridge University Press.

Highmore, Ben. 2002a. *Everyday Life and Cultural Theory: An Introduction.* London and New York: Routledge.

Highmore, Ben. 2002b. *The Everyday Life Reader.* London and New York: Routledge.

Highmore, Ben. 2011. *Ordinary Lives: Studies in the Everyday.* New York: Routledge.

Hill, E. Jeffrey, Chongming Yang, Alan J. Hawkins, and Maria Ferris. 2004. "A Cross-Cultural Test of the Work-Family Interface in 48 Countries," *Journal of Marriage and Family* 66.5: 1300–1316.

Hirschl, Thomas A., Joyce Altobelli, and Mark R. Rank. 2003. "Does Marriage Increase the Odds of Affluence? Exploring the Life Course Probabilities," *Journal of Marriage and Family* 65.4: 927–938.

Horkheimer, Max. 1972. *Critical Theory,* translated by Matthew J. O'Connell. New York: Continuum Books.

Hutchinson, Elizabeth D. 2012. *Dimensions of Human Behavior: The Changing Life Course.* Thousand Oaks, CA: Sage Publications.

Inglis, David and Christopher Thorpe. 2012. *An Invitation to Social Theory.* Malden, MA: Polity Press.

Isaac, Joel. 2010. "Theorist at Work: Talcott Parsons and the Carnegie Project on Theory, 1949–1951," *Journal of the History of Ideas* 71.2: 287–311.

Isaacowitz, Derek and Jennifer Stanley. 2011. "Bringing an Ecological Perspective to the Study of Aging and Recognition of Emotional Facial Expressions: Past, Current, and Future Methods," *Journal of Nonverbal Behavior* 35.4: 261–278.

Jakobsen, Flemming, Torben Baek Hansen, and Berit Eika. 2011. "Knowing More about the Other Professions Clarified My Own Profession," *Journal of Interprofessional Care* 25.6: 441–446.

Jones, Anthony. 1991. *Professions and the State: Expertise and Autonomy in the Soviet Union and Eastern Europe*. Philadelphia, PA: Temple University Press.

Judson, Karen and Carlene Harrison. 2012. *Law and Ethics for the Health Professions*. New York: McGraw-Hill.

Keating, Joshua E. 2011. "Rich Country, Poor Country," *Foreign Policy* 188: 1–3.

Kerbo, Harold. 2005. *World Poverty: The Roots of Global Inequality and the Modern World System*. New York: McGraw-Hill.

Kirchmeyer, Catherine. 2002. "Gender Differences in Managerial Careers: Yesterday, Today, and Tomorrow," *Journal of Business Ethics* 37.1: 5–24.

Kliman, Andrew. 2010. "The Disintegration of the Marxian School," *Capital and Class* 34.1: 61–68.

Larkin, Jack. 1988. *The Reshaping of Everyday Life, 1790–1840*. New York: Harper and Row.

Lattimore, Dan, Otis Baskin, Suzette Heiman, and Elizabeth Toth. 2009. *Public Relations: The Profession and the Practice*. New York: McGraw-Hill.

Lefebvre, Henri. 2000. *The Production of Space*, translated by Donald Nicholson-Smith. Malden, MA: Blackwell.

Lefebvre, Henri. 2008. *Critique of Everyday Life*, translated by Gregory Elliott and John Moore. New York: Verso Books.

Lenin, Vladimir. 1992. *The State and Revolution*, translated by Robert Service. London: Penguin Books.

Luhmann, Niklas. 1982. *The Differentiation of Society*. New York: Columbia University Press.

Luhmann, Niklas. 1985. "Society, Meaning, Religion-Based on Self-Reference," *Sociological Analysis* 46: 5–20.

Lynch, Daniel R. 2006. "Conclusion-Professions and the Common Good," *Current Issues in Catholic Higher Education* 25.1: 137–141.

Macdonald, Keith M. 1995. *The Sociology of the Professions*. Thousand Oaks, CA: Sage Publications.

Magleby, David B., Paul C. Light, and Christine L. Nemacheck. 2010. *Government by the People*. New York: Longman.

Maher, Chauncey. 2011. "Action Individuation: A Normative Functionalist Approach," *Philosophical Explorations* 14.1: 99–116.

Marcus, Clare Cooper. 2006. *House as a Mirror of Self: Exploring the Deeper Meaning of Home*. Lake Worth, FL: Nicolas-Hays.

Marsh, Robert. 2010. "Merton's Sociology 215–216 Course," *American Sociologist* 41.2: 99–114.

Marx, Karl. 1990. *Capital: A Critique of Political Economy*. New York: Penguin Classics.

Marx, Karl and Friedrich Engels. 2008. *The Communist Manifesto*. Oxford and New York: Oxford University Press.

Mauk, John and John Metz. 2009. *The Composition of Everyday Life: A Guide to Writing*. Boston, MA: Wadsworth Publishing.

McDonough, Tom, ed. 2002. *Guy Debord and the Situationist International: Texts and Documents*. Boston, MA: MIT Press.

McDonough, Tom, ed. 2009. *The Situationists and the City: A Reader*. New York: Verso.

McGoldrick, Monica, Betty Carter, and Nydia Garcia-Preto. 2010. *The Expanded Family Cycles: Individual, Family, and Social Perspectives*. Upper Saddle River, NJ: Prentice Hall.

McIntosh, Paul. 2010. *Action Research and Reflective Practice: Creative and Visual Methods to Facilitate Reflection and Learning*. New York: Routledge.

McKnight, John and Peter Block. 2010. *The Abundant Community: Awakening the Power of Families and Neighborhoods*. San Francisco, CA: Berrett-Koehler Publishers.

Mead, George Herbert. 1934. *Mind, Self, and Society*. Chicago: University of Chicago Press.

Merton, Robert K. 1968. *Social Theory and Social Structure*. New York: Free Press.

Meyer, Joyce. 2006. *The Everyday Life Bible: The Power of God's Words for Everyday Living*. New York: Faith Words.

Miedaner, Talane. 2010. *Coach Yourself to A New Career: 7 Steps to Reinventing Your Professional Life*. New York: McGraw-Hill.

Mik-Meyer, Nanna and Kaspar Villadsen. 2012. *Power and Welfare: Understanding Citizens' Encounters with State Welfare*. London and New York: Routledge.

Mills, C. Wright. 1956. *The Power Elite*. New York: Oxford University Press.

Moore, Thomas. 1992. *Care of the Soul: A Guide for Cultivating Depth and Sacredness in Everyday Life*. New York: HarperCollins Publishers.

Morgan, Leslie A. and Suzanne R. Kunkel. 2011. *Aging, Society, and the Life Course*. New York: Springer.

Myers, David G. 2011. *Psychology in Everyday Life*. New York: Worth Publishers.

O'Brien, Jodi. 2009. "Sociology as an Epistemology of Contradiction," *Sociological Perspectives* 52.1: 5–22.

O'Connor, John. 2010. "Marxism and the Three Movements of Neoliberalism," *Critical Sociology* 36.5: 691–715.

O'Rand, Angela M. and Margaret L. Krecker. 1990. "Concepts of the Life Cycle: Their History, Meanings, and Uses in the Social Sciences," *Annual Review of Sociology* 16: 241–262.

Parker, David. 2009. *Cities and Everyday Life*. New York: Routledge.

Parsons, Talcott. 1951. *The Social System*. New York: Free Press.

Parsons, Talcott. 1954. *Essays in Sociological Theory*. New York: Free Press.

Perinbanayagam, Robert S. 2012. *Identity's Moments: The Self in Action and Interaction*. Lanham, MD: Lexington Books.

Peterson, Christopher. 2012. *Pursuing the Good Life: 100 Reflections on Positive Psychology*. New York: Oxford University Press.

Pink, Sarah. 2012. *Situating Everyday Life: Practices and Places*. Thousand Oaks, CA: Sage Publications.

Platt, Lucinda. 2011. *Understanding Inequalities: Stratification and Difference*. Malden, MA: Polity Press.

Rauhut, Heiko and Fabian Winter. 2010. "A Sociological Perspective of Measuring Social Norms by Means of Strategy Method Experiments," *Social Science Research* 39.6: 1181–1194.

Ray, Larry. 2007. *Globalization and Everyday Life*. New York: Routledge.

Reich, Robert B. 2008. *Supercapitalism: The Transformation of Business, Democracy, and Everyday Life*. New York: Vintage Books.

Rogers, Mary F. 1984. "Everyday Life as Text," *Sociological Theory* 2: 165–186.

Rubin, Beth A. and Charles J. Brody. 2011. "Operationalizing Management Citizenship Behavior and Testing Its Impact on Employee Commitment, Satisfaction, and Mental Health," *Work and Occupations* 38.4: 465–499.

Saks, Mike. 2010. "Analyzing the Professions: The Case for the Neo-Weberian Approach," *Comparative Sociology* 9.6: 887–915.

Sampson, Robert J. and John H. Laub. 1992. "Crime and Deviance in the Life Course," *Annual Review of Sociology* 18: 63–84.

Sandstrom, Kent L., Daniel D. Martin, and Gary Alan Fine. 2009. *Symbols, Selves, and Social Reality: A Symbolic Interactionist Approach to Social Psychology and Sociology.* Oxford and New York: Oxford University Press.

Schatz, Robert T. and Howard Lavine. 2007. "Waving the Flag: National Symbolism, Social Identity, and Political Engagement," *Political Psychology* 28.3: 329–355.

Schlitz, Marilyn Mandala, Cassandra Vieten, and Tina Amorok. 2007. *Living Deeply: The Art and Science of Transformation in Everyday Life.* Oakland, CA: New Harbinger Publications.

Schultz, T. Paul. 1998. "Inequality in the Distribution of Personal Income in the World: How It Is Changing and Why," *Journal of Population Economics* 11.3: 307–344.

Settles, Barbara H., Xuewen Sheng, and Jia Zhao. 2011. "Family-to-Work Conflict: Gender, Equity, and Workplace Policies," *Journal of Comparative Family Studies* 42.5: 723–738.

Sheringham, Michael. 2006. *Everyday Life: Theories and Practices from Surrealism to the Present.* Oxford and New York: Oxford University Press.

Simon, David. 1997. "Development Reconsidered: New Directions in Development Thinking," *Human Geography* 79.4: 183–201.

Skey, Michael. 2010. *National Belonging and Everyday Life: The Significance of Nationhood in an Uncertain World.* New York: Palgrave Macmillan.

Sklair, Leslie. 1997. "Social Movements for Global Capitalism: The Transnational Capitalist Class in Action," *Review of International Political Economy* 4.3: 514–538.

Smelser, Neil J. 1998. "The Presidential Address: The Rational and the Ambivalent in the Social Sciences," *American Sociological Review* 63.1: 1–15.

Smith, Adam. 2009. *The Wealth of Nations.* New York: Classic House Books.

Smith, Dorothy E. 1987. *The Everyday World as Problematic: A Feminist Sociology.* Boston, MA: Northeastern University Press.

Sommers, Christina Hoff and Fred Sommers. 2013. *Vice and Virtue in Everyday Life.* Boston, MA: Wadsworth Publishing.

Sommers, Sam. 2011. *Situations Matter: Understanding How Context Transforms Your World.* New York: Riverhead Books.

Stryker, Sheldon. 2008. "From Mead to a Structural Symbolic Interactionism and Beyond," *Annual Review of Sociology* 34: 15–31.

Sue, Derald Wing. 2010. *Microaggressions in Everyday Life: Race, Gender, and Sexual Orientation.* Hoboken, NJ: Jon Wiley and Sons.

Sumiala, Johanna. 2012. *Media and Ritual: Death, Community and Everyday Life.* London and New York: Routledge.

Sutherland, Daniel. 2000. *The Expansion of Everyday Life, 1760–1876.* Little Rock: University of Arkansas Press.

Sykes, Charles J. 2012. *A Nation of Moochers: America's Addiction to Getting Something for Nothing.* New York: St. Martin's Press.

Teichova, Alice and Herbert Matis, eds. 2011. *Nation, State and the Economy in History.* Cambridge and New York: Cambridge University Press.

Templar, Richard. 2010. *The Rules of Work: A Definitive Code for Personal Success.* Upper Saddle River, NJ: FT Press.

Templar, Richard. 2011. *The Rules of Life: A Personal Code for Living a Better, Happier, More Successful Life.* Upper Saddle River, NJ: FT Press.

Therborn, Goran, ed. 2006. *Inequalities of the World: New Theoretical Frameworks, Multiple Empirical Approaches.* New York: Verso Books.

Thomas, William I. 1928. *The Child in America: Behavior Problems and Programs.* New York: Alfred A. Knopf.

Tilly, Chris and Charles Tilly. 1998. *Work under Capitalism: New Perspectives in Sociology*. Boulder, CO: Westview Press.

Todaro, Michael P. and Stephen C. Smith. 2011. *Economic Development*. Upper Saddle River, NJ: Prentice Hall.

Tomaskovic-Devey, Donald and Kevin Stainback. 2007. "Discrimination and Desegregation: Equal Opportunity Progress in U.S. Private Sector Workplaces since the Civil Rights Act," *Annals of the American Academy of Political and Social Science* 609: 49–84.

Tuan, Yi-Fu. 2002. "Community, Society, and the Individual," *Geographic Review* 92.3: 307–318.

Turner, Jonathan H. 2012. *Theoretical Sociology: 1830 to the Present*. Thousand Oaks, CA: Sage Publications.

Vallas, Stephen P., William Finlay, and Amy S. Wharton. 2009. *The Sociology of Work: Structures and Inequalities*. New York: Oxford University Press.

Vaneigem, Raoul. 2011. *The Revolution of Everyday Life*, translated by Donald Nicholson-Smith. Oakland, CA: PM Press.

Volti, Rudi. 2011. *An Introduction to the Sociology of Work and Occupations*. Thousand Oaks, CA: Pine Forge Press.

Walby, Kevin and Dale Spencer. 2010. "In Conversation with the American Sociological Association President: Randall Collins on Emotions, Violence, and Interactionist Sociology," *Canadian Review of Sociology* 47.1: 93–101.

Walker, Pamela and Patricia Rogan. 2007. *Making the Day Matter!: Promoting Typical Lifestyles for Adults with Significant Disabilities*. Baltimore, MD: Brookes Publishing.

Wallerstein, Immanuel. 1984. *The Politics of the World-Economy: The States, the Movements, and the Civilizations*. Cambridge and New York: Cambridge University Press.

Wallerstein, Immanuel. 1997. *The Capitalist World Economy*. Cambridge and New York: Cambridge University Press.

Wan, Poe Yu-ze. 2011. "(Re-)Problematizing the Luhmannian Constructivist Systems Approach: A Bungean Intervention," *Current Sociology* 59.6: 696–716.

Weisbord, Marvin R. 2012. *Productive Workplaces: Dignity, Meaning, and Community in the 21st Century*. San Francisco, CA: Jossey-Bass.

White, James M. and David M. Klein. 2008. *Family Theories*. Thousand Oaks, CA: Sage Publications.

Woodard, Collin. 2011. *American Nations: A History of the Eleven Rival Regional Cultures of North America*. New York: Viking Penguin.

World Bank. 2011. *World Development Indicators 2011*. Washington, DC: World Bank.

Yap, O. Fiona, ed. 2012. *Annual Editions: Comparative Politics 12/13*. New York: McGraw-Hill.

Zia, Helena. 2000. *Asian American Dreams: The Emergence of an American People*. New York: Farrar, Straus, and Giroux.

Index